D0122362

The Birth of Christianity

The Birth of Christianity
Reality and Myth

Joel Carmichael

Dorset Press
New York

This edition published by Dorset Press,
a division of Marboro Books Corp.,
by arrangement with Hippocrene Books.

1992 Dorset Press

ISBN 0-88029-738-7

Printed and bound in the United States of America

M 9 8 7 6 5 4

Contents

Foreword   vii

Introduction: Jesus of Nazareth   xi

CHAPTER I **The Immediate Background**   1

CHAPTER II **Pilate and Jesus**   27

CHAPTER III **The Elevation of the Jewish Messiah**   47

CHAPTER IV **The Christ—World Savior**   65

CHAPTER V **The Great Divide: The Temple Destroyed**   103

CHAPTER VI **A New Faith—Articulated and Consolidated**   121

CHAPTER VII **Institutionalization**   151

CRITICAL APPENDIX: *The Lost Continent*   173

Notes   217

Bibliography   221

Index   223

FOREWORD

The birth of a great religion is a secular as well as a religious event. In the case of Christianity, this obvious statement is complicated by a unique fact: the core of the religion is fused with real-life events, or, at least, with events whose validity as history is considered a fundamental element of the religion.

This has proved to be most complicated. In fact, the literature, famously vast, on Christian origins has produced no coherent real-life account.

The hundreds of thousands of volumes—lives of Jesus and of Paul, histories of the early Church—consist of either traditional accounts or scholarly and semischolarly tomes that deploy immense energy in dissecting texts, multiplying footnotes to trivia, fleshing out analysis with citations from the Hebrew Scriptures and the Apocrypha, data from the history of the Roman Empire, observations on Hellenistic civilization, and so forth.

The reason for the absence of a simple, ordinary story is profound.

Though the erudition underlying the literature is staggering, scholars have generally taken for granted what they should have been analyzing. The conceptual basis of the Higher Criticism has been misconceived; the result has been a fundamental begging of the question.

The misconception itself arises from a sort of gullibility with respect to the familiar but, in fact, tantalizingly obscure phrase "the Kingdom of God."

This phrase, which in the first three Gospels introduces Jesus and constitutes, as it would seem, the key to his career, is not actually explained in the Gospels. It was to acquire a theological "explanation" only as part of the theory that later became the foundation of the Church. It was incorporated into that theory in a sense that was totally different from its true meaning during the lifetimes of Jesus, John the Baptist, and Paul.

In two previous books of analysis based on the work of many scholars, I demonstrated that the activities of Jesus reflected a movement of religious Jewish activism against the Roman Empire. That movement is best summed up as the agitation for the "Kingdom of God."

In *The Death of Jesus* I traced the crucifixion of Jesus not to his preaching of some offensive doctrine but to his career as a leader of men. He was executed by the Romans as a pretender to power ("King of the Jews") because in their eyes that was what he was.

In *Saint Paul and the World's End* I described the career of Paul, too, as having arisen out of the Kingdom of God movement, at first under the authority of a brother of Jesus, Upright Jacob, an assiduous worshiper in the Jewish Temple of Jerusalem together with other followers of Jesus, and then, after Paul's death and the destruction of the Temple, as an unwitting founder of what became Christian theology.

The analysis called for in these two books was necessary in order to disentangle from the distortions of tradition the true profiles of two men instrumental, in very different ways, in the emergence of Christianity.

I am now synthesizing the positive results of this analysis and telling a story, a simple story—the story of how a seed of faith germinated in a Jewish milieu, sprouted in a Hellenistic society, and in a few generations blossomed into a world religion.

Because of the dynamic contradictions entailed by the emergence of a new faith in the complex interplay between Jews, Greek-speaking pagans, and Romans, anyone interested in the germination and efflorescence of the most complex religion in history will be thrown back precisely on its mythology, which has been powerful enough to bind together disparate and contradictory phenomena, hints of which can nevertheless be extracted from the bias of our documentation and made intelligible.

This new account, then, is an attempt to bypass the preconceptions embedded in centuries of Christian tradition and unconsciously absorbed even by those who do not share those preconceptions.

An explanation of the procedure involved in extracting a real-life story from the profusion of scholarly literature is given in the Critical Appendix.

I hope this short account will clarify the complex and obscure background of Christian origins and restore that background to the plane of real life.

Joel Carmichael

JESUS OF NAZARETH

Jesus was born in Palestine, no doubt in Galilee. He had four brothers and some sisters; both he and his father might have been carpenters.

Jesus first became known in connection with an older man, John the Baptist. Both of them proclaimed a seemingly clear and simple idea: "The Kingdom of God is at hand—repent!" Going about the countryside, Jesus, like John the Baptist, gathered a following and was known as a healer.

Then Jesus left Galilee and, during the Passover festival celebrated by Jews, went up to Jerusalem where he was acclaimed as Herald of the Kingdom of God. He and his followers occupied the Temple and were overcome by the authorities and captured. Jesus and some followers were crucified by the Romans, who proclaimed that Jesus was being executed as "King of the Jews."

Some of Jesus's followers fled to Galilee, where one of them had a vision of Jesus resurrected and immortal. This vision was believed in by some of the followers, who shortly afterwards returned to Jerusalem to settle down for Jesus to return, very soon, as part of the installation of the Kingdom of God.

Jesus's public career lasted no more than a few months. He left nothing in writing; hardly anything unambiguous can be traced to him directly. Skimpy as the above account is, it represents the sum total of what we know about him; it is also the kernel of the tradition that assigns its own origins to his activities.

At the same time, this bald account, though simple, is far from clear.

What was the Kingdom of God? If it was God's design, why were people impelled to *do* anything about it? Why should Jesus have occupied the Temple, an enterprise inevitably involving force? Above all, why should Jesus have been executed by the state as a political enemy?

The moment even the simplest question is asked about Jesus's brief career, we are thrust back into prior events for an answer that will make the account of Jesus's career, now very bare and simple, understandable as well. We must glance back for a moment at the background of religious and political agitation that will clarify the aims of Jesus and John the Baptist.

CHAPTER I

THE IMMEDIATE BACKGROUND
"Forcing the End"

*T*he concept of the Kingdom of God is the key to the agitation that, until about A.D. 135, had churned up Jewry for two centuries, destroyed the Jewish State in the war against Rome of A.D. 66–70, and launched Christianity.

Today its meaning has been transformed. The evolution of Christianity itself has turned the phrase into either a metaphor for ethical behavior or a recondite aspect of theology.

But in the generation spanning Jesus's activities, the concept was wholly palpable, factual, and dynamic. It meant the transformation by God of the natural world into one in which God's will would conduct human affairs directly and hence restore the fortunes of the Jews, the Chosen People.

The concept of the Kingdom of God was rooted deep in the Jewish past. In sharp contrast with the dense intricacies of paganism, in which a wide variety of natural phenomena enjoyed degrees of divinity explained by complex mythologies, the religion of Israel was anchored in the simple idea that the whole of the universe had been brought into existence by the will of a single Being, himself subject to nothing whatever—neither other beings, nor a preexistent order, nor fate, nor hazard.

This Supreme Being—Yahweh, or Jehovah—had revealed himself first to the Jews, who by virtue of a covenant with him became in their own eyes his people. Thus from the very beginning, Yahweh, though the Creator of the universe, had one people of his own to worship him. The Hebrew Scriptures—the Old Testament of the Bible, composed over a millennium—embody this first phase of the national history of the Jews.

Now though the Jewish alliance with Yahweh had been a stupendous success—the liberation from Egypt, the conquest of Canaan, the great settlement, the conquering dynasties—it had been followed by a steady decline as a result of the increasingly oppressive encroachments of great powers climaxed by the Babylonian Exile in 582 B.C.

These vicissitudes were hard to explain. The escalation of Yahweh, originally a local god, to the status of the all-powerful One God, Creator of the Universe, had created a special conundrum: How could Yahweh's helplessness be understood? If the covenant with Yahweh's own people was eternal, what had gone wrong?

The classical Hebrew prophets had found the answer: Despite the malaise of the world and the disasters that had befallen the Chosen People, the Day of Yahweh would infallibly arrive. After a series of horrible calamities and an appalling upheaval on earth and in heaven, a new world, cleansed and regenerated, would be installed, with all the enemies of the Jews, including the great empires of Assyria and Babylonia, lying trampled into the dust by Yahweh's awful might.

But the prophets were also full of ethical feeling generated by the notion that the Creator's will was being flouted. This was why they castigated their people. There had to be some explanation of Jewish suffering, and since the Creator could hardly be blamed, the Jews had to be.

The Jews were destined, said the prophets, to be severely punished, though without being wiped out. A remnant would survive, and from that remnant a new generation pleasing to Yahweh would arise and enter into a new covenant. This new covenant would be modeled on Yahweh's old covenant with mankind instituted after the Flood and later on with the Jews, through Abraham, Isaac, Jacob, and Moses. Yahweh would pour out his spirit on the newly chosen of the Chosen People, the progeny of the remnant. Jerusalem would become a peerless city, worshiping Yahweh in total purity of heart with unheard-of splendor of ritual. Israelites would be united, old hatreds forgiven, and the new Israel would be installed in matchless prosperity. And though all this basically concerned the Jews alone, the pagans too—en passant, so to speak—would bask in the refulgence of Yahweh and of his "Torah"—the Hebrew Scriptures.

The Torah does not mention the resurrection of the dead, the ending of death, or the termination of ordinary history, with rewards and punishments being allocated in the world beyond. The World's End takes place in the world as men know it. This earthliness characterized the classical phase of the Jews' alienation from "ordinary" history. Though the hopes anchored in the World's End idea all included political and suprapolitical motifs, the World's End as a fact remained limited to this world both before and during the Babylonian Exile, which ended in 520 B.C. Thus the Kingdom of God, whose chief beneficiaries were to be the Jews, did not imply the end of history on earth. In this early, classical period the Kingdom of God was simple; Yahweh was to be king. That was all. From that all else flowed.

Still, though it is obvious that there is a natural tension in the contrast between the notion of Yahweh as the timeless Creator of the Universe and the historical fact that this notion was cherished by only one people—the Jews—this tension had never aroused them to action before.

For centuries the Jews, after their upper classes had been

deported to Babylonia in 582 B.C., had been politically quiescent. And when the Persians, after shattering Babylonia, had restored the Jewish elite to an enclave of some twelve hundred square miles around Jerusalem a half century later and encouraged their religious autonomy for a couple of centuries, the Jews engaged in no political activity of any kind.

It was when Greek culture, after penetrating the Middle East for generations, finally achieved a political focus in the third century B.C. that the Jews once again began to play a political role, which lasted until the establishment of the Roman Empire, around the time Jesus was born.

The Greco-Macedonian conquests spearheaded by Alexander the Great changed the face of the Middle East and of the world. Greek culture became a sort of epidemic. It undid the identities of all the nations the Greeks came across. It wiped out, as nations, Babylonians, Arameans, Egyptians, and the many smaller peoples scattered throughout the vast area. By converting the educated classes of all the conquered peoples, it created a new identity for educated people everywhere. "Hellenism" became a cultural commonwealth that transcended politics, even though it was Hellenistic governments that underlay the cultural expansion. Hellenism wiped out the ancient Egyptians, for instance, in a half generation. As soon as they lost heart for teaching their offspring the ancient written language, the Egyptian people became culturally rudderless fellahin.

Hellenization meant far more than a new government or the cultivation of the Greek language. In the area bounded by Egypt, India, and Central Asia, Hellenistic institutions became the very stuff of meaningful life, both public and private. Not only did Hellenism destroy Egypt as a society, it shattered the Persian State, transformed Persian society (though the Persians were to survive the flood and retain their identity), and gave Rome itself its spiritual mold.

Aside from the Persians, the Jews and Romans were, indeed, the only other peoples to survive intact the epidemic of Hellenization—the Romans by swallowing Greek culture whole while conquering the Greeks militarily; the Jews by resisting

Greek culture for a time spiritually and then by digesting some of its elements and integrating them with their own traditions.

Soon after Alexander the Great's conquests in the third century B.C., the Hebrew Scriptures were translated into Greek—a massive and unprecedented enterprise. The Jewish elite in Palestine as well as Jews in general throughout the Diaspora were steeped in Greek. In addition, the Jewish elite were for a time seduced away from Judaism altogether.

The seeds of future ferment were planted. After the collision with Greek culture, the Kingdom of God began to take on a novel, dynamic urgency. There was an upsurge of visionary emotion that began to formulate the possibility of an actual transition to the Kingdom of God that would hinge on a human agent. Since it was difficult to imagine the vastness of Yahweh's power pinpointing specific changes in the world, people began to think of a human being as personifying the God-willed transition, just as kings, priests, and leaders of all kinds have been indispensable symbols of complex social processes. Just as Yahweh, during his ascension to the status of the One God, had had to be fitted out with earthly agencies—angels, the "Word," the "Presence"—so it was felt that the Kingdom of God, too, required an agent of transformation—a herald.

The "Messiah" was that herald. Originally, to be sure, the word itself had meant no more than "anointed one." Being anointed with oil was part of the ancient ceremony of enthroning a Hebrew monarch. The word was also used for foreign rulers such as Cyrus of Persia. Ultimately it became a metaphor for a human being who, like a true prophet, was doing God's will.

In common usage, accordingly, the Messiah had at first meant a flesh-and-blood descendant of the glorious King David, promised eternal dominion in the Hebrew Scriptures (2 Sam. 7:12f.), and was merely supposed to proclaim the Kingdom of God, a transformation of the present-day physical world.

But with the Greek conquests that churned up the Middle East, including Jewry, earthly ideas came to seem inadequate to many Jews. The Kingdom of God heralded by a flesh-and-blood Messiah yielded to the idea of a supernatural world disclosed to the visionary imagination. An otherworldly Messiah from the heavenly heights was to terminate past history and initiate future history. The simplicity of monotheism was fitted out with a sort of auxiliary theory that included a battle between good and evil—conflicts, horrors, wars between angels and demons, heroes partly or wholly supernatural, the idea of a millennium to be followed by universal resurrection, general retribution, the Last Judgment.

Apocalypse, the visionary perception of all such projections, was produced by the collision of the Jews with the Greeks. It flowered most influentially in the book of Daniel, the final addition to the Hebrew Scriptures. It injected what may be called an element of vertical aspiration to the earthbound views of the Torah. The apocalyptic concept of a stupendous cataclysm signaling the destruction of the wicked workaday world and the installation of the Kingdom of God was to transform the spiritual life of mankind forever.

Specifically, it was the reaction to one of the successors of Alexander the Great (the Seleucid king of Syria-Palestine, Antiochus IV "Epiphanes") that set the stage for Kingdom of God agitation on two levels—this-worldly and other-worldly.

In 166 B.C. Judaism was attacked root and branch for the first time by Antiochus IV in a campaign to systematize the Hellenization of the Jews under his rule. He forbade observance of the Torah, circumcision, the dietary laws, and traditional sacrifices. He was, at first, successful. He had the wholehearted collaboration of the Jewish aristocracy, enthralled by the charms of Greek culture and eager to adapt the stark simplicity of Judaism to the elegant cosmopolitanism of their Greek rulers.

And it was just this combination of pagan oppression and Jewish apostasy that brought about the resurgence of Jewry as a political factor. Antiochus IV and the Jewish Hellenizers were fought by Jews—the "Maccabees"—who rejected Hellenism outright. The armed insurrection of the Hasmonean dynasty they founded produced a new Jewish State. For three generations the Hasmoneans flourished. Territorially the Jewish State they established came to exceed, in fact, the holdings of the Hebrew kings at the height of their power.

Yet it was the military triumph of the Maccabees that was to bring about their undoing.

The Roman Republic, which had been expanding throughout the Mediterranean and far beyond, was inevitably drawn into the byplay of rivalries and intrigues among various Jewish princes and their allies. Rome penetrated the entire area, gradually acquiring hegemony via a variety of client-rulers. In 63 B.C. Pompey forced his way into the Jerusalem Temple. For the first time an unauthorized person, and an idol worshiper to boot, stood in the holy shrine of Judaism. Palestine was under a new regime.

The end of Jewish sovereignty, symbolized by the Roman conquest of Jerusalem in 63 B.C. and the extinction of the male Hasmonean line, turned the idea of the Kingdom of God from a mere vision into a seedbed of action. It became a first-class factor in day-to-day politics—the "prehistory" of Jesus and John the Baptist.

For a time, to be sure, the starkness of Roman rule was camouflaged. During the conflict between Pompey and Julius Caesar, Herod (the Great), a Jewish prince, emerged as a favorite of the victorious faction. Herod, married to a Hasmonean princess, ruled the Jews on behalf of the Romans for thirty-seven years. Thus a semblance of independence, or at least of insulation, was preserved. Local life was more or less normal; foreign affairs were handled by Rome.

Herod the Great lived on a grand scale. Vast sums were lavished on splendid buildings; taxation had to be very heavy. But the religious feelings of the populace were buffered by Herod the Great's regime against the realities of Roman rule. Herod himself could be considered by the outside world and also by the Jews of the Diaspora as a real Jewish king—a faint, somewhat misshapen embodiment of the Hebrew monarchy.

At the same time, the royal style he affected outside Palestine was wholly pagan. Also, he aggravated the mistrust felt for him by pious Jews because of his origins (he came from an Edomite [Idumean] family recently converted to Judaism) and because of his personal indifference to Judaism and his infatuation with the intellectual as well as the elegant aspects of Greek culture. These factors, powerfully buttressed by his public extravagance, which exerted tremendous economic pressure on his subjects, kindled the first sparks of political agitation.

From the very outset of his reign, indeed, the Kingdom of God ferment began to bubble, and not only in the realm of visionary speculation. Activists sprang up throughout Palestine. The reign of Herod the Great, in fact, gave rise to the disaffection that after his death in 4 B.C. just around the time Jesus was born, blossomed in the mood of desperation culminating in the Jewish war against the Romans in A.D. 66.

Until Herod's reign the visionary fermentation associated with Apocalypse had been passive. Individuals were not supposed to *do* anything to help Yahweh. The aim of the Maccabees had been the defense of Judaism against the joint onslaught of the Greeks and the apostate Jews. The Maccabees had not intended, themselves, to install the Kingdom of God. Yahweh alone could transmit sovereignty to the Jewish people (Dan 7:14, 18, 27). But after Herod's death the contrast between Yahweh's omnipotence and the subjugation of the Chosen People became inflammatory to many energetic spirits. The situation demanded action, personal commitment. And it was the agitation linked to the Kingdom of God that, taking root during Herod the Great's reign, injected a factor of violence in relations between Jews and between Jews and Romans.

All theories of the Kingdom of God, both this-worldly and other-worldly, assumed that its installation depended exclusively on the will of God; it was to be a material transformation of the entire world brought about by the will of God at a moment of his choosing.

Not all Jews would benefit by it, to be sure: the appeal made by both Jesus and John the Baptist called for "repentance"— only the righteous and pious, from the past as well as from the current generation, could share in the Kingdom of God. The righteous who had already died would be resurrected to participate in the new order of the world.

This concept was to be given a new relevance, and a sharp

agitational point, toward the end of Herod the Great's reign, and after his death was to become the axis of insurrection against the Romans and their upper-class Jewish supporters.

During the decade following his death Herod the Great's succession was uncertain: the Romans refused to let his oldest son, Archelaus, take office; they kept him on probation. Because he proved unsatisfactory to Romans and Jews alike, he was exiled in A.D. 6. Judea-Samaria was reorganized as an annex of the province of Syria and was in the charge of an imperial procurator with full financial and military powers, including the infliction of the death penalty. This procurator, Coponius, was the first of a line that was to include Pontius Pilate, notorious for the sentencing and execution of Jesus.

When Judea-Samaria was absorbed directly into the Roman administration, it was natural to have a census. Emperor Augustus ordered the legate of Syria to carry it out.

A census of people was considered by all pious Jews to be contrary to Yahweh's will. Even when Moses took a census, it was only because Yahweh had specifically commanded him to. Centuries later, when David took a census Yahweh sent a murderous plague (2 Sam. 24). There were also prophecies, such as Hosea's (1:10), and unambiguous statements in the Torah (Gen. 15:5, 22:17, 32:12) that there would be so many Israelites they would be "like the sands of the sea, which cannot be either measured or counted."

The census, furthermore, was an adjunct of the absorption of Judea-Samaria into the direct administration of a pagan power. Thus Judea-Samaria was, according to Roman law, in essence confiscated. This totally contradicted the theory that Yahweh had promised the land to the Jews alone (Lev. 25:23).

It was this census (the starting point of the Gospel of Luke) that launched the movement of dynamic messianism culminating in the Roman-Jewish War of A.D. 66–70. The census, together with the absorption of Judea-Samaria into the Roman administration, initiated the career of Judah the Galilean, outstanding in the throng of Kingdom of God activists flung up during the decade following Herod the Great's death.

Though a thinker, and for that matter, learned, the Galilean was essentially a man of action. His views were basically no different from those of the large grouping of Jews known as Pharisees, who differed from the aristocratic, priestly Sadducees primarily in their elastic attitude toward the Scriptures.

The Galilean was distinguished only by his determination to implement his views. What he did was to digest, as it were, the First Commandment—"You shall have no other gods before me"—and apply his interpretation of it in action. To him the commandment, in the circumstances of the Jews of his time, had a peremptory simplicity about it: if no other God but Yahweh, God of the Universe, could be accepted, and if Yahweh was also sole ruler of the Jews, then no form of allegiance to anyone else whatever could be endured.

But if no alien government could be endured, and if the Romans were about to rule the country directly, without even the fig-leaf of a Jewish king, there was only one recourse—the rejection of Roman rule; not merely inner resistance to the Romans, but active revolt.

Active no doubt *outside* Galilee—whence his sobriquet—the Galilean modeled his tactics on David and the early Maccabees: he would hide in caves in the eastern Judean mountains, and from these and similar bolthold spring out to pounce on small Roman armed units and traveling functionaries and notables; he would also attack the property of rich Jews and harry non-Jewish territories, while sparing the basic Jewish population whose goodwill was vital for the movement. His fate is unknown: he was no doubt killed and his entourage, for a time, scattered (Acts 5:37).

The Galilean's movement against the Romans was an aspect of the World's End crisis. His struggle against the census, against the Roman occupation of the land, against pagan rule in general, with its complex of afflictions, really marked the outbreak of the "pangs of the Messiah." The census merely tested the faith of the faithful, their readiness for the Kingdom of God. From then on only those Jews who refused to obey the Roman emperor could be thought of as *true* Jews.

Israel's creed is easily summed up: "Hear, O Israel, the Lord is our God, one Lord, and you must love the Lord your God with all your heart and soul and strength." (Deut. 6:4). The Galilean simply sharpened the interpretation of this general exhortation to fit the onset of the Kingdom of God by focusing the meaning of the "Hear, Oh Israel" in a political sense, thus breaking its routine ritualism as a formula repeated daily and forcing on the individual repeating it the awareness of its dynamic implications.

Hence the Galilean's attitude was by no means a matter of mere faith. Though crystallized out of the Hebrew Scriptures, it was, in practical terms, a novelty. (We shall see the implications of this view of the "Hear, O Israel" in the career of Jesus.)

The Galilean's innovation, to be sure, reached far into the ancient past preceding the Hebrew monarchy. Israel's "becoming like the other nations" by having a king had been objected to on the principle that Yahweh's people must be ruled by Yahweh alone (1 Sam. 8:19; 12:12; Judg. 8:23). But applying an ancient attitude to the contemporary situation was to have explosive effects. By agitating the people and denouncing them for paying taxes to the Romans and thus for submitting to the rule of mortals—and pagans—instead of God, he had become a secular as well as a religious rebel. In the Gospels we see echoes of Judah the Galilean in the behavior of John the Baptist (Luke 3:7f.; Matt. 3:7) and in that of Jesus too, who also "stirred up the people" (Luke 23:5).

The eternal nature of God is not, of course, contradicted by his intervention in history; hence his transformation of the world into his Kingdom did not entail a reinterpretation of his will. Thus the admonition "Hear, O Israel, the Lord our God is one Lord" *need* not call for activism on behalf of a temporal movement in order to collaborate with God's decision to install his Kingdom.

The question is one of temperament. Judaism, which requires the performance of certain duties, also obliges the pious to repeat the admonition "Hear, O Israel." This had been done for centuries before Judah the Galilean and was still being done, of course, by pious Jews who did not agree with him, i.e., the "quietists."

But if you had the Galilean's temperament, the admonition

could also be considered a clarion call to action. Thus the Galilean's activism exposed the contrast otherwise only implicit between the timelessness of Yahweh and specific temporal action on his behalf. Abandoning the passivity associated with mere belief, the Galilean incited people to action through the conviction that the Kingdom of God and, hence, the dominion of his people, Israel, would be realized *only* if Israel implemented, in real life, the absolute sovereignty implied in the "Hear, O Israel."

The broad concept underlying this was summed up in the phrase "Forcing the End." The activists' "zeal" for Yahweh implied that they would compel him, as it were, to bring about the consummation of his own handiwork.

Thus it was natural to call such activists "Zealots." The word itself implied the otherworldly dimension inherent in religious ardor. Phinehas, the grandson of Aaron, had been zealous for his God (Num. 25:13); and since Phinehas was thought of as an incarnation of Elijah the prophet, who was meant to return one day as the precursor of the Messiah (Mal. 4:5), the concept of "zeal for Yahweh" in and of itself entailed a messianic thrust.

As the Torah gradually became more and more sacred ever since the Babylonian Exile centuries before, what had been "zeal for Yahweh" was gradually transformed into zeal for Yahweh's word, the Torah. In this, as in many other things, the Galilean's enterprise repeated many of the motifs of the Maccabean revolt.

Whether the Galilean's partisans called themselves Zealots at first or not, they were known as such later on. (The actual word first occurs as a description of one of Jesus's entourage; see Matt. 10:4, the New English Bible).

Around this time the contrast between Israel and its neighbors was exacerbated by the expansion of the imperial cults throughout the eastern Mediterranean, especially in Rome. It was becoming more and more commonplace for emperors to claim divinity—to be worshiped as gods. This imperial cult had itself arisen out of the decay of the ancient pagan gods. The Olympic pantheon had long since become a pale shadow, eliciting no emotion. Thus the emergence of the emperors as objects of worship fused with traditional attitudes toward heroes. After Alexander the Great's incredible military triumphs he himself had been apotheosized, as were his successors. The deification of rulers became endemic throughout the area.

Thus the sharpening of the First Commandment into a political weapon heightened the contrast between Jews and pagans. It made the cleavage between them, in fact, unbridgeable. Against the background of deified local rulers of all kinds, the Galilean's unwavering insistence on the implications of the First Commandment transformed politics. No compromise could be possible between the metaphysics of the Roman imperial cult and the imminent Kingdom of God. The simple insight that the First Commandment was broken by the emperor's demand that he be worshiped as a god entailed a struggle for religious freedom—*for those who chose to act.*

It was, in fact, just this notion of freedom that throughout this period of the early Roman Empire constituted the paramount thrust of the Galilean's activism. But it would be anachronistic to imagine that the freedom sought by the activists was a political ambition of secular rebels. What the activists meant was not *mere* political freedom; it was really the redemption of Israel associated with the World's End. To those involved in the struggle against Rome the concept required no analysis; religion and politics made a seamless web.

Political liberty was merely one aspect of the freedom the religious insurgents were willing to die for. From the Galilean's movement of resistance to the Roman census of A.D. 6 down to the suicide at Masada of the last survivors of the Roman War of A.D. 66–70, the freedom sought for Yahweh's people meant the blanket elimination of all institutions imposed by pagan Rome. In A.D. 73, for instance the leader of the Masada garrison was to repeat a motif of Judah the Galilean: "From the very beginning we were struggling to achieve liberty."[1] For him the dead are the happy ones: "They fell in the struggle for liberty."[2]

Thus the theme embedded in the activists' appeal to the people over two generations was in fact their total freedom—under Yahweh.

The World's End redemption of Israel was patterned on the

miracles performed by God during the Exodus from Egypt—this time, to be sure, on a much grander scale. When God gave "signs of freedom" to those who took to the desert in the Galilean's day, the signs really echo the signs given by God to the Israelites who had forgotten the reason for their leaving Egypt and who had reproached Moses for their distress in the desert. Thus, for the Galilean, Yahweh could be provoked to "Force the End" if the Jews showed their readiness for World's End redemption by collaborating with Yahweh in his grand design.

The Kingdom of God and the World's End redemption of the Jews had further implications. If Yahweh, while rectifying the iniquities of the universe, also restored the fortunes of the Jews, it was only natural for Israel to rule the world on behalf of Yahweh. Thus both Israel and its God would rule the cosmos.

This notion of Israel's world dominion on behalf of Yahweh had come up under Alexander the Great's successors (ca. 165 B.C.) and was ramified later on.[3]

Hence, Kingdom of God activists assumed that the role of Israel implied the Last Judgment on all idol worshipers in general and on the oppressors of Israel in particular. That was, in fact, the substance of the national hope held aloft by the Zealots. It is echoed unmistakably in the Gospels:

> Jesus [said], 'I tell you this: in the world that is to be, when the Son of Man [the Messiah] is seated on his throne in heavenly splendor, you my followers will have thrones of your own, where you will sit as judges of the twelve tribes of Israel.' (Matt. 19:28, NEB; see also Luke 22:28)

> 'But we [the pilgrims of Emmaus, after the execution of Jesus] had been hoping that he was the man to liberate Israel.' (Luke 24:21, NEB)

> They asked [Jesus], 'Lord, is this the time when you are to establish once again the sovereignty of Israel?' (Acts 1:6, NEB)

The Zealots concentrated on the old-fashioned, this-worldly, purely national theory of the World's End, centered in the restoration of Israel. Zealot activism revived the flesh-and-blood Messiah. As Roman oppression grew intolerable, by the time of Jesus and Paul the concept of the Messiah became concrete, *actual*.

Massively anchored in ardor, the Zealot movement naturally permeated the Temple milieu. From the very outset the lower strata of the priesthood seem to have been made up of Zealots. It was they, indeed, who in the generation after Jesus were to trigger the war against the Romans by refusing to offer the daily sacrifices in the Temple, an action that honored the Roman emperor and the people of Rome. The custom was maintained by the upper strata as a public demonstration of loyalty to the empire. The lower priests were in a state of constant effervescence. Individual aristocrats, too, were inflamed by the messianic contagion.

Messiahship was in the nature of things disproved by failure. The posthumous career of Jesus was unique. The specific circumstances of his death launched, ultimately, a totally different type of movement, as we shall see, quite outside the orbit of traditional ideas.

There was a perennial crop of messiahs and prophets, all with an assignment from the One God whose intervention was felt to be "at hand" and all of whom went down successively to defeat and death.

At the same time, the collapse of the innumerable messianic movements that proliferated throughout this period could never shake the pious conviction that no matter how things looked at the moment, all would be set right. Yahweh would prevail and redeem Israel in the wake of the *real* Messiah's appearance.

Throughout the Roman occupation of Palestine down to the war of A.D. 66–70 and afterwards, the expectation of a Messiah aroused the most powerful feelings, with a steady intensification of the fervor attached to the conviction that the Kingdom of God at the World's End called for action.

The emotions linked to this idea were intensified by another belief, rooted in contemporary chronology, that the Kingdom of God was "at hand" because the world was entering the Fifth Millennium. Even before the first century attempts had been made to pinpoint the advent of the World's End.[4] When Jesus said, in the wake of John the Baptist, that the "time was fulfilled" and that the "Kingdom of God is at hand" (Mark 1:14–15), we can hear an echo of a prevalent belief that the year 5000 in the calendar of creation according to the Torah was going to bring with it the Sixth Millennium—that of the Kingdom of God.

No doubt it was this prospect that intensified the aversion to the Romans. There is some evidence that though the rapacities and iniquities of the Roman administration were extensive, they may not have been much worse than before or elsewhere. But now, with the feverishness linked to the Kingdom of God agitation inflamed still further by the calculations indicating the near advent of the Millennium, it must have seemed to many that there was, at last, a way out. Thus it was not the Messiah who by his own action alone was to bring the Millennium, it was the scheduled Millennium that was now escorted, as it were, by the Messiah.

Before the second quarter of the first century the Millennium might have seemed too remote to pin specific hopes to it in terms of action, but the appearance of Jesus (around A.D. 30) might have coincided with the current of millenarian speculation in which the year A.D. 30 was pinpointed as the beginning of the new Millennium and hence of the Kingdom of God.

Judah the Galilean was himself considered a Messiah (as in the speech put in Gamaliel's mouth in Acts 5:36f). During the Roman War his grandson, Menahem, behaved with matter-of-factness as King of the Jews, in this context the World's End Messiah.

The notion of a Messiah stemming from the house of David had deep historical resonance. A war Messiah was bound to be considered a scion of the ancient king, a notion that, even though sophisticates might have embroidered it metaphysically, was understood quite literally by ordinary people.

There were other factors in the Kingdom of God ferment. The Romans, indifferent to the religion of their subjects, had one economic objective—to squeeze taxes out of them not only for the state but, more particularly, especially during the first century or so of the empire, for the benefit of the various proconsuls, prefects, legates, and procurators who represented the Roman State in the provinces.

Oppressive as Herod the Great's taxation had been, it was overshadowed by that of the Roman procuratorial regime. A land tax had to be paid in kind, while a head tax was levied on every male child over fourteen and every female child over twelve. Only the aged were exempt. In addition, revenue, cattle, exports, and imports were all taxed. There were market fees, bridge and harbor tolls, town dues.

A special scourge was the ferocious system of tax farming, abolished long before by Julius Caesar but reinstalled by the Romans when they moved into Palestine. Private contractors would buy concessions from the state authorizing them to collect the taxes. They were allowed to make as much personal profit as they could. Because they were government officials, they could force extravagant amounts out of the helpless populace. Countless partisans of the religious activists came from the various propertied groups who were made destitute by the tax-farming system.

In addition to the devastations of the tax gatherers—the "publicans" of the Gospels—the Jews were subject to plundering by governors and procurators who had also acquired their positions by extensive bribery and had to make up for their losses. This was further aggravated by adventurers of all kinds who flocked to the provinces. When heavy new taxes had to be paid, usury at 50 percent was commonplace; if this was not paid, people would be sold into slavery.

The atrociousness, for the Jews, of having their Holy Land governed by idolaters was, in short, compounded by an entirely mundane factor—rapacious exploitation.

The tide of insurrection was sustained by all those without property or by those who had lost it: unemployed soldiers, slaves, shepherds, dispossessed farmers. An element of social upheaval ran through the religious activist movement from its inception. Just as at the outset the fury of the insurrectionists was aimed at the vast luxurious buildings built in the Greek style and lavishly appointed by Herod the Great, so at the outbreak of the Roman War in A.D. 66 there were similar attacks on the great constructions of the aristocrats and the authorities.

Yet the religious motive was predominant. Even if the economic oppression under Rome was only a trifle worse than the rule of the Hasmoneans or more recently of Herod the Great, the component of religious outrage gave it an entirely different dimension. Even though the upper classes accommodated themselves deftly to foreign rule from which, because of their habits, training, and interests, they suffered far less or indeed not at all, the masses of the people were infuriated on two levels simultaneously.

At the same time, the very generality of its following made it difficult to organize the resistance. A major stumbling block was created by the fact that the religion in and of itself was not threatened and that "quietism," its concomitant, was a real possibility for pietists. It was hard to find a specific goal for would-be insurgents to unite around; it was harder still to establish the legitimacy of any given leader.

Judah the Galilean, after all, had simply put himself forward through his interpretation of the Torah. Any pious Jew could do the same. Leaders had to vie with each other to establish their own legitimacy.

The Galilean emulated a principle laid down by the Maccabees, who claimed personal status as royalty just because of their zeal in behalf of the religion. The Galilean and his descendants also took it for granted that, as champions of Yahweh, they had an inherent right to establish a dynasty—a World's End dynasty, of course—whose aim would be attained by bridging the transition between the workaday world and the Kingdom of God.

In any event, the Galilean founded a party with sharply formulated views and a firm organization, all anchored in a simple religious idea. His dynastic succession was to remain the core of the Jewish independence movement that was ultimately to sweep the bulk of the population into the war against Rome.

There were, of course, deep parallels between the Maccabees and Judah the Galilean in that both fought to preserve Judaism. The founder of the Maccabean movement, Matithyahu the priest, showed the same zeal as the Galilean by killing Jews who in their longing for Hellenization were flouting the Torah.

The Maccabees, however, had fought against the attempt to *obliterate* Judaism; after their success, their religious motivation atrophied and they became conventional politicians.

The Galilean and his activists, on the other hand, had no need to defend their religion against the Romans who, with the exception of the demented Caligula in the generation after Jesus, guaranteed Jews religious freedom. Yet it was just such a compromise that the Galilean could not accept. His extremist stance on the World's End crisis meant that Yahweh's all-power forbade any acceptance of pagan rule, tolerant or not. For his partisans, the acceptance of Roman rule was *ipso facto* an acceptance of idol worship and apostasy. They were incapable of negotiating; the concept was meaningless for them. This in itself made them far more rigorous than the Maccabees.

Moreover, by the time the Romans placed Judea-Samaria under their own direct administration in A.D. 6, the Hellenization, far deeper than mere politics, that had been pervasive throughout the eastern Mediterranean had been digested by the Jewish elite as well as by countless ordinary Jews.

Jewish society, precisely by resisting the political straitjacketing attempted by Antiochus IV and his Jewish allies, was all the readier to absorb Hellenism's cultural content. It managed to do this, without abandoning its own traditions, by tucking various elements of Hellenism—literature, ideas, institutions—into the overarching embrace of monotheism.

A knowledge of Greek was *de rigueur* among the Jewish elite. In Alexandria and other Greek-speaking centers the Greek heritage was systematically adapted to Jewish traditions. Pious Jews, such as Philo, busily demonstrated the essential unity between the Torah, properly understood, and the monuments of Greek culture (Plato, Aristotle, Plotinus, Pythagoras).

Accordingly, by the time the Romans had installed themselves as political overlords without camouflage in A.D. 6, Judaism no longer faced the same threat as it had under Antiochus IV. For Judah the Galilean, it was not the Romans' behavior that was offensive; it was the naked fact of their presence.

This itself was a decisive rupture with a tradition centuries old. From the first destruction of Jerusalem to the appearance of Antiochus IV four hundred years later the Jews had been docile. Even later, when the initial upsurge of Maccabean independence had been eroded and a succession of Jewish princes had been subjugated by foreigners, the mere fact of alien rule had failed to provoke a Jewish resistance.

It cannot be overemphasized that the Galilean's activist movement was wholly religious in character. It encompassed, in principle, all Jewry who, as Yahweh's Chosen People, were obliged to live up to the demands of their election. This had nothing to do, of course, with kinship, though born Jews were by nature identified with their religion. But Jewish backsliders, the quietists willing to live in peace with Rome, had to be cast out or killed, whereas pagans who accepted the Torah were welcome. For the Zealots, the remnant of Israel who were to benefit from the redemption of the Kingdom of God were not only the survivors of the clash of arms with their enemies but also the resurrected individuals from among the "righteous" fallen in battle.

Kingdom of God expectations were naturally accompanied by an intensification of religious feverishness. Even in the older Prophets (Isaiah 32:15, 44:3; Ezekiel 11:19, 36:26), the gift of the "Spirit" had been promised as part of the transition to the paradise projected for the future. Thus, when religious fervor was intensified under the Romans and the World's End was felt to be at hand, all Jews who now believed in it naturally claimed for themselves the possession of the Spirit. That is why in Acts 2:17–21 much is made of Joel's citing God as saying "I will pour out my Spirit upon all flesh" as a prelude to the Great Transition (Joel 2:28–32; also Rom. 5:5; Gal. 3:2). Judea, Samaria, and Galilee were in fact thronging with "prophets" of all kinds, all feeling elected by God for the World's End transition: their role required them to be imbued with the Spirit.

The World's End fever also forced on believers a claim to a grasp of history; they also had to be able to predict real-life events. In Acts, for instance, one of the prophets who came to

Antioch from Jerusalem "stood up and foretold by the Spirit that there would be a great famine over all the world" (11:28).

There was, to be sure, nothing clear and unmistakable in the speculation concerning the events of the transitional period between the smashing of secular pagan dominion and the emergence into the Messianic Kingdom thought to precede the Kingdom of God proper. There was no limitation to the endless combinations of forces involved in Yahweh's direct intervention. They might include angels, different processes of dissolution among the enemies of Yahweh, various nations involved in a concerted attack from the East on the people of Israel, and so on.

Generally speaking, it was understood by Jewish visionaries that before the actual redemption, taken for granted as inherent in the emergence of a herald of the Kingdom of God, there would be a frightful era of trial, the "pangs of the Messiah."

Since there were no clear predictions, the shape and nature of this ordeal varied abundantly. Not only Israel would be affected but all the nations on earth, for that matter the natural order itself. The stars in their courses would be shaken up. On earth justice would vanish; there would be natural convulsions, social upheavals, diseases, famine.

In Judea specifically, the Jewish sanctuary, these various horrors would be brought about by a final onslaught of the pagan power. No doubt the historical model for such speculations was Antiochus IV's attack on Judaism two centuries before. This must have been in the minds of all those who had become inflamed by Pompey's conquest of Jerusalem in 63 B.C., during the riots following Herod's death in 4 B.C. (around the time of Jesus's birth), and also under the Roman procuratorial regime, when religious feelings were exacerbated by the Roman control over the Temple itself. This was to be a continuous inflammation for two generations. Only a few years after Jesus's death, for instance, Caligula ordered a statue of himself to be set up in the Temple to be worshiped as a god. A probable insurrection was forestalled only by his death.

The general idea that the redemption of Israel as the result of the hostility of a superpower that was an enemy of God himself could, of course, be traced to Scripture (Ezekiel, Daniel). With the Roman occupation of Judea and Galilee, that enemy of God was naturally Rome, which came to stand for the "Fourth Kingdom" of the book of Daniel. It was just this plausible, indeed compelling identification, in which Rome gave body to the worst forebodings about the peril Israel found itself in, that set its stamp on the World's End fever of the first century: Rome was the natural current embodiment of the evil thought to have been embodied in the major historic enemies of Israel—Amaleq and Babylon, the destroyer of Jerusalem, symbolized, to boot, by Esau, in the current age Edom. Here the role of Herod the Great facilitated the transfer of the hatred from Edom to the Romans. Thus the cosmic role once ascribed to Antiochus IV could be shifted as it were organically to the Romans, whose emperor assumed the features of the World's End tyrant. The evolving Emperor cult naturally helped focus the hatred.

Since there was considerable variation of emphasis on the periphery of the central themes, different groups laid varying emphases on the identity of the chief culprits in the cosmic drama. Thus the Essenes, for instance, took the depravity of their own people (the corrupt priesthood) as meaning that the bulk of the Jews themselves were the chief enemy to be overcome at the World's End; while the major religious activists (the Zealots), though ferociously hostile to the Jewish aristocracy, concentrated on the Romans as their chief opponent.

This was given real-life plausibility precisely by the behavior of the Roman governors, who were constantly threatening the sanctuary and who as defenders of the state naturally took the lead in tracking down and killing all those who were "Forcing the End." It was very easy and natural to identify Rome with the "Fourth Kingdom" mentioned in Daniel, especially in the discussion of the "Days of Wrath" that were conceived of as testing and purifying God's people through the onset of the redemptive crisis. Some natural external events, too, such as the persistent famine under Emperor Claudius (predicted by the "prophet" in Acts), must have lent plausibility to the notion that the World's End catastrophe had finally erupted.

The activists interpreted these horrors so as to derive from them the lesson they were looking for. If the Jews went on docilely obeying the Roman pagans, the horrors could plainly be considered God's punishment for backsliding. On the other hand, if the Jews saw the light and under the pressure of the steadily growing pagan oppression took to resistance, then the "pangs of the Messiah" would be transformed into a purification. The mere sufferings, afflictions, and so on, of the resistance against Rome would then constitute no more than a test of the remnant to be spared. As long as most Jews accepted the pagan yoke, God's wrath was on them. If that was so, the World's End could not be pinpointed. But if the lead of the activists was followed and the masses of the people, inflamed by zeal for Yahweh, launched a Holy War against Rome, the crisis would be ended. Redemption would break forth.

The Holy War itself was, of course, embedded in the Scriptures. Commanded originally by Yahweh himself, the Hebrew volunteers were also exhorted by a priest or by a charismatic leader. By definition, in fact, the Holy War was a mere continuation of the worship of God. This ancient idea had merely been revived by the Maccabees under the goad of Antiochus IV's attack on Judaism. Matithyahu himself was, of course, a charismatic figure. His son, Judah the Maccabee, would pray after exhorting his troops by references to God's miracles in the past. Mere smallness of numbers would not necessarily mean anything: after all, "power came from Yahweh" (1 Macc. 3:18f.).

Even the Prophets after the Babylonian Exile conceived of Yahweh as personally intervening to help his people in the showdown with their enemies. The idea was to be absorbed into apocalyptic visions where God moved not only against the enemies of Israel on the human plane but also against the demonic powers sponsoring those enemies. Thus when the activists embarked on their long-drawn-out campaign against the Romans, they had ready at hand the well-tried concept of a Holy War that could easily be integrated with the World's End war against the pagan world power.

The concept of a Holy War framed the movement that from

Judah the Galilean on steadily gathered enough force to swing the bulk of the population into the bloodbath of A.D. 66–70. Many details that have come down to us from the conduct of the actual war imply that the army and its functioning were modeled on the Scriptures. In Galilee, for instance, Josephus, while still a commander on the Jewish side before deserting to the Romans, convoked a council of seventy notables that was plainly patterned after the seventy elders of the desert (Exod. 24:1; Num. 11:16).

The "desert" was the classical refuge of all enemies of the state. The partisans of Judah the Galilean left the desert for the settled areas only on guerrilla forays, before their success in swinging the masses of the population into the war against Rome. Except for such forays, the activists might have seemed part of the ordinary population.

The desert, a place for testing and trial where God had revealed himself to his people, was to be retreated to for the purpose of renewing the fight for Yahweh against the pagan powers. The recurrent theme of "going into the desert" must be understood politically. Since the Roman administration could not undertake the difficult task of encompassing the desert regions, withdrawal into the desert was not only a form of social protest but also a first-class political, economic, and military strategy. In an epoch of militant piety, the desert—revered in tradition as a place for asceticism, for being tested (Deut. 8:2), for meeting God (Deut. 32:10)—was the natural ideal.

There was also, of course, a deeply rooted tradition of identifying past and future events. The basic model was the Exodus out of Egypt, conducted by God. It was, after all, the desert where Israel, freed by miracles, had gazed for the first time on Yahweh. In a later period, accordingly, under renewed oppression by pagans, the desert, inevitably, had come to mean the World's End redemption of the Jews. Thus, Matithyahu, leader of the Maccabees, fleeing with his sons to the desert to prepare an attack on the pagan power, had set an example for all future activists. His basic appeal was for an unconditional readiness to lose one's life for God (1 Macc. 2:27).

John the Baptist appears, indeed, with a key quotation from the prophet Isaiah:

A voice of one crying out in the desert: "Prepare a way of the Lord, make straight his paths." (Mark 1:3, NAB, from Isaiah 40:3)

Jesus, too, repeatedly illustrates this theme:

At once the Spirit drove him out into the desert, and he remained in the desert for forty days. . . . (Mark 1:12–13, NAB, and parallels)

In short, anyone who, like John the Baptist, heeded Judah the Galilean's call and flouted the census had to follow the example of Matithyahu and his sons—abandon his property, flee to the desert, and stake his life on the outcome.

The activists' contempt for death was famous. The Romans, indeed, thought them out of their minds. Their fanaticism, their readiness to sacrifice all in behalf of a theory, prepared them as it were automatically for martyrdom. What was extraordinary was the number of people prepared to do likewise.

That readiness for death was summed up in a celebrated formula—"carrying the cross." Against the background of the resistance to the Romans, this formula, used in the Gospels repeatedly, has peculiar poignancy, though very soon after the life of Jesus, as we shall see, it came to acquire a vastly different meaning.

The activists identified their current rebellion against the Romans with the premessianic trial that was to purify Israel and crystallize out the remnant that would survive the World's End. Their provisional task, accordingly, was to move the masses of Jewry into a holy war against the pagan power. From the activists' point of view, the docile, peace-loving Jewish aristocrats and priests were their most dangerous enemies. Apostates all, such quietists were standing in the way of the divine plan.

But the pro-Roman Jewish aristocrats in their turn were incapable of controlling the Roman machine of extortion.

Though it took a couple of generations of constant agitation, eventually the activists did succeed, in the generation after Jesus, in launching a national uprising, after holding out in a guerrilla-war against repeated attempts of the Romans to extinguish the countless foci of revolt throughout the country.

To sum up: two generations of religious activists made a potent fusion of two simple ideas—the "national" and the "transcendental" hope for the Kingdom of God.

Jews were not divided in the interpretation of this phrase. The religious activists were no different from other devout Jews, as far as their world-view was concerned: they differed only in the degree of personal activity. It was taken for granted that the outcome of all action was in any case wholly dependent on God's will.

At the same time, of course, this implied a complete fusion between politics and religion. In those days, among monotheists, a distinction between the two would have been senseless. The religious activists were distinguished by one quality alone—the total commitment of the individual based on "zeal for God," with the concomitant assurance of victory and, in case of death, a reward in the World to Come—the Kingdom of God.

CHAPTER II

PILATE AND JESUS

*T*hough the freedom movement launched by Judah the Galilean was ultimately to shatter the Jewish State in A.D. 66–70, his initial operations in A.D. 6 were not to bear fruit for a generation. For a couple of decades his movement was restricted to guerrilla activities in the hill country and the desert. The Roman authorities, evidently unable to stamp the movement out, were not, on the other hand, directly threatened for some time.

Coponius, the first procurator, had only a short period in office (A.D. 6–9). His two successors, Marcus Ambibulous and Amnius Rufus, left nothing considered noteworthy by our sources. The fourth procurator, Valerius Gratus (A.D. 15–26), deposed no fewer than four high priests (the last of these, Caiaphas, was to become notorious for the role attributed to him in the Gospels).

The erosion of the high priesthood into being a pawn of Roman politics made the Jewish aristocracy still more dependent on Roman favor, while at the same time heightening the element of social protest that ran through the Kingdom of God ferment from its origins and provided a matrix for the activities of Jesus and his partisans—all of them "people of the land."

It was under Pontius Pilate, the next procurator, who stayed in office for a decade (A.D. 26–36), that the Kingdom of God agitation began swelling to tidal wave proportions. With the appearance of Jesus following on the heels of John the Baptist, the activist movement began steadily increasing in volume and intensity.

Pilate had a reputation, generally speaking, for a peculiar combination of cruelty, stubbornness, and guile. He is described as having been "naturally inflexible and stubbornly relentless" and was held guilty of "corruption, insults, rapine, outrages on the people, arrogance, repeated murders of innocent victims, and constant . . . savagery."[1]

For some reason, perhaps the political tension, Pilate seemed to have had a particular loathing for Jews and also for Samaritans, a sect whose Judaism was limited to the Five Books of Moses and who were similarly affected by the Kingdom of God agitation.

His term of office began inauspiciously.

After his arrival in Caesarea, the Roman seat of government on the northern coast, Pilate moved the armed forces from there to winter quarters in Jerusalem. Surreptitiously, at night, he brought to the Temple area the busts or medallions with exchangeable portrait heads of the emperors attached to the standards of the Roman legions. This may have been with the express purpose of "destroying the laws of the Jews,"[2] that is, of bringing the Jews into line with other subject peoples who had no reason not to accept such medallions.

But Jewish law absolutely banned such images from the Temple area. Pilate's action was just what Jews had been afraid of for decades. They reacted violently: the city population fell into a fury exacerbated by the indignation of farmers and shepherds who had thronged into the city.

On his way back to Caesarea Pilate was pursued by a crowd of Jews imploring him to remove the standards from the Temple area and to maintain Jewish laws in accordance with Roman as well as Jewish tradition. He refused. Thereupon the crowd fell prostrate around his house, holding this posture for five whole days.[3] On the sixth day Pilate seemed to give in. He went out to the great stadium that served as tribunal, sat down on it, and called in the crowd, apparently in order to answer their request. At the same time he signaled his troups to encircle, three deep, the multitude. Pilate then threatened to have them slaughtered on the spot if they refused to accept the images of Caesar in Jerusalem. The soldiers drew their swords.

At this point the Jews flung themselves on the ground "in a body," stretched out their necks, and declared themselves ready to die. Pilate, astounded, ordered the removal of the images.

Later he inflamed the populace once again by using a sacred fund, intended for ritual purposes only, to build an aqueduct. The city populace, once again furious, ringed round Pilate's tribunal en route to Jerusalem and clamored at him. This time Pilate was ready. He had an armed soldiers' unit dressed as civilians intermingle with the crowd. He ordered the unit upon a signal from him not to use their swords but to beat the rioters with clubs. A great many Jews were killed this time, both by the clubs of the soldiers dressed as civilians and from the crush of the mob itself.[4]

It may well be this incident that is referred to in Luke 13:1, where Jesus is told of "the Galileans whose blood Pilate had mingled with their sacrifices." "Galileans" was a synonym for the Zealots, the Kingdom of God activists inspired by Judah the Galilean and others.

Toward the end of his decade in office Pilate once again tried to bring into Jerusalem—again for the express purpose of exasperating the Jews—some votive shields without images, with a mere inscription featuring the name of the emperor. Some pro-Roman Jewish notables (including four of Herod the Great's sons) who were in Jerusalem at the time attending a feast asked Pilate to remove the shields. They then appealed over his head to Emperor Tiberius himself, who ordered Pilate, in stern language, to remove the shields from Jerusalem immediately and take them to the temple of Augustus in Caesarea.

Since the offensiveness of the votive shields had nothing to do with images, it must have lain in the very inscription itself; the only inscription that would have seemed inevitably offensive was a reference to the divinity of the Roman emperor, which to any of the Kingdom of God activists would, of course, have seemed inherently infuriating on the soil of Israel and especially in the vicinity of the Temple.

During Pilate's term of office Jesus emerged, linked at first to John the Baptist.

Both John the Baptist and Jesus appeared as heralds of the Kingdom of God, by which they meant the material transformation of the world it was necessary to prepare for by "repenting"—by conforming with the Torah in its integrity.

Before Jesus, John appeared as the organizer of a movement of armed dissidence whose rationale consisted of a systematic secession from the orbit of Roman authority. This was accomplished by creating an army sworn to overthrow the Romans and by vowing to live in accordance with the Torah while awaiting the Kingdom of God at the imminent World's End.

This is no doubt the inner meaning of the opening words about John in the Gospels: "John the Baptist appeared in the wilderness. . . . and they flocked to him from the whole Judaean country-side" (Mark 1:4–5, NEB).

Accordingly, from the point of view of the authorities, John the Baptist was a dangerous seditionist, a leader of the "men of violence [who] take [the Kingdom of God] by force" (Matt. 11:12). A man of action like Judah the Galilean and unlike a mere prophet, John was prepared to act:

"The law and the prophets were until John; since then the good news of the kingdom of God is preached, and every one enters it violently." (Luke 16:16)

John's rite of baptism had only an indirect relationship to personal ethics. He called upon his followers "to be united by baptism," but the phrase itself, in Greek *baptismo synienai*, meant a rite of initiation into an association of some kind; in this case, into the Elect of the New Israel. Thus, all those Jews who were quietists in the given circumstances of Roman occupation were tacitly backsliding from the First Commandment and Deuteronomy, and thus were excluded from the imminent Kingdom of God. They were now no better than pagans themselves, since they had endorsed by their quietism the rule of idol worshipers. John's baptism was supposed to cleanse them of this paramount transgression and establish them in the New Israel.

What "baptism in the name of the Lord" meant, in the mouth of John, was recognition of Yahweh as the sole ruler and the abjuration of idols, divine emperors, and the like. Like Judah the Galilean before him, John the Baptist said Jews could be governed only by the Almighty.

John's message was brief, simple, and unmistakable. It was the message of action inherent in the First Commandment. It was, in effect, an oath of allegiance to the One God and to his Herald. Like Judah the Galilean, John the Baptist, too, preached the "way of the Torah."

The New Israel, foreshadowed both by Judah the Galilean's partisans and by the Baptist, was to consist of the purified remnant now constituting the New Elect of Israel. Any Jews who did not take John's baptism as an initiation into the army of the Messiah were to be regarded as hostile pagans.

John's rite of baptism, in short, was an application of the old baptism prescribed for converts to Judaism. The unregenerate Jews who accepted and thus served the Roman idol worshipers were, because of that, apostates who had to be put on the same level as pagans seeking conversion to Judaism.

Thus John's baptism was no more than the first outward sign of the freedom he was accused of inciting the people to seize for themselves. As I have indicated, this notion of freedom had a merely tangential relationship to political liberty. It was the freedom created by the Kingdom of God against the bondage of heathenism, idolatry, and the ensemble of this world's iniquities. It sealed the bestowal of freedom in this Kingdom of God sense—by being a way of escape from the "wrath to come," the Last Judgment. It was a "washing for salvation" as was meant in the pre-Christian, entirely concrete sense of rescue from the destruction about to be visited on this world.

In a word, John the Baptist and Judah the Galilean were "men of violence," Kingdom of God activists. Living in the desert with crowds flocking out to him, dressing simply, eating locusts and wild honey, exhorting the people to live up to the Torah in its integrity, John was "Forcing the End" by personal action.

John was arrested and executed for sedition by Herod Antipas, one of Herod the Great's sons and ruler of Galilee, which was at that time not under direct Roman administration.

Jesus regarded John as the greatest man ever born of woman (Matt. 11:11). He thought John a paramount leader in the campaign for the Kingdom of God at the World's End. Thus John might have been in Jesus's eyes a rival of Judah the Galilean or, at any rate, a successor (John's dates are obscure).

Jesus was launched on his own career by the Baptist and, after a temporary association with him, carried on in his own way after a falling-out or in any case a divergence with respect to strategy.

Thus, if Jesus did, in fact, begin his own activity initially by baptizing, he had concurred with John on secession from the settled areas and on the initiation into the New Elect of Israel "on the outside," away from the power of the idolaters. Later, he diverged from John on strategy and dropped baptism, the hallmark of John's view of organization (see page 82).

We shall see in a moment what might have impelled Jesus to change strategies, but it is clear that while he was associated with John the Baptist he led exactly the same sort of life, abundantly referred to in the Gospels. John's situation is surely echoed in the command to "flee to the mountains" (when the Temple is desecrated, Mark 13:14).

On the natural model of the Maccabees, Jesus, like the Baptist, clung to the desert (Mark 1:12; Matt. 4:1f.; Luke 4:1f., 42, 5:15–16; John 11:54). The parallels between Jesus's early action and those of the Maccabees are striking. In addition to the emphasis laid by Jesus on the abandonment of worldly goods, the founder of the Maccabees, Matithyahu the priest, expressed a summons to action:

'Follow me,' he shouted through the town, 'every one of you who is zealous for the law. . . .' He and his sons took to the hills, leaving all their belongings behind in the town. (1 Macc. 2:27–28, NEB)

This sounds just like Jesus:

> 'Anyone who wishes to be a follower of mine must leave self behind; he must take up his cross, and come with me. Whoever cares for his own safety is lost; but if a man will let himself be lost for my sake . . . that man is safe.' (Mark 8:34–35, NEB)

Also:

> 'No man is worthy of me who cares more for father or mother than for me; . . . no man is worthy of me who does not take up his cross and walk in my footsteps. By gaining his life a man will lose it; by losing his life for my sake, he will gain it.' (Matt. 10:37–39, NEB)

A believer in the Kingdom of God had to be ready, unconditionally, to lose his life.

In the first three Gospels, for instance, the Temple's desecration by pagan rites—the point at which the "pangs of the Messiah" broke out—was to trigger the abandonment of property and the commanded exodus to the desert.

Jesus came to the same end as John. The strategies of both men were merely different approaches to the same crisis—the elimination of Roman power as a prelude to the Kingdom of God at the World's End.

After dropping baptism in his change of strategy, Jesus went back to the settled areas, "stirred up the people," and consorted with tax collectors and sinners. Agitationally speaking, this might have meant that he was recruiting a following from among the Jewish officials of the Roman administration.

It is plain, through the many apologetic layers of the Gospels that the structure of Jesus's enterprise was entirely along the lines laid down by other Kingdom of God activists.

As in the case of Judah the Galilean and his followers, all flowed from living up to the implications of the First Commandment and, in particular, of the "Hear, O Israel."

When Jesus, for instance, is asked by someone what the greatest commandment is, he answers simply:

> "Hear, O Israel, the Lord our God, the Lord is one; and you shall love the Lord your God with all your heart, with all your soul, and with all your mind, and with all your strength. (Mark 12:29– 30, Deut. 6:4)

This cannot be a mere repetition of the cardinal prayer of Judaism, which in public would have sounded banal. In a situation in which Jesus is proclaiming the Kingdom of God as a matter of *urgency,* the meaning of the prayer has been sharpened to the current World's End crisis. Against the background of religiously motivated insurrection against the secular power and its Jewish puppets, the combination of the two concepts—Hear, O *Israel*" and "the Lord is *One*"—can mean only one thing: *Because* the Lord is One and *because* Israel must obey him, all true Jews must, on the eve of the transition to the Kingdom of God, resist the pagan power, doomed now to destruction as part of the divine plan for the World's End.

Jesus's emphasis on the primordial prayer, supreme above all others in Judaism, was really just another way of demonstrating that, since the eternal rule of God was taken for granted and since the Kingdom of God was now expected at the World's End, the believer had to take on himself the yoke of the Kingdom of God *then and there.* He had to repeat the "Hear, O Israel" at that particular time, on the threshold of the Kingdom of God, and by proclaiming his belief in the One God, indicate his readiness to act. Thus repeating the "Hear, O Israel" at that moment was tantamount, in and of itself, to sedition.

Jesus's celebrated saying "Pay Caesar what is due to Caesar, and pay God what is due to God" (Mark 12:17, NEB) had just the same seditious content as the "Hear, O Israel." All Jews took it for granted that the Holy Land did *not* belong to Caesar; hence giving God the things that are God's meant, quite simply, not giving *Caesar* what belonged to God. Jesus was merely repeating what Judah the Galilean before him had meant by rebuking the Jews as "cowards for consenting to pay tribute to Rome."

I have already quoted one of Jesus's most celebrated remarks: "If any man would come after me, let him deny himself and take up his cross and follow me." (Mark 8:34; also Matt. 10:38, 16:24; Luke 9:23, 14:27).

Long after Jesus's lifetime, this remark was to become a metaphor for the essence of the religion that sprang up in his name. For most people its meaning is wrenched out of its historical context; yet this was the traditional formula of all the Kingdom of God activists executed by Rome, of whom there were countless thousands.

The Romans thought the Kingdom of God activists madmen, yet were impressed by their devotion. Here is a description of the sufferings of some of the activists who, in the generation after Jesus, were caught after their retreat to Egypt when Jerusalem had fallen in A.D. 70:

> Six hundred of them were caught on the spot; and all who escaped into Egypt . . . were arrested and brought back. Nor was there a person who was not amazed on the endurance and—call it what you will—desperation or strength of purpose displayed by these victims. For under every torture and laceration of body, devised for the sole object of making them acknowledge Caesar as lord, no one submitted nor was brought to the verge of utterance; but all kept their resolve, triumphant over constraint, meeting the tortures . . . with bodies that seemed insensible of pain and souls that well-nigh exulted in it. But most of all were the spectators struck by the children of tender age, not one of whom could be prevailed upon to call Caesar lord. So far did the strength of courage rise superior to the weakness of their frames.[5]

Crucifixion was the standard Roman punishment of the time, both for the vilest crimes and for sedition.

Armed rebels against the state had to be ready at any time to "carry their cross," that is, to sacrifice their lives in the struggle against the pagan power in the Kingdom of God agitation at the World's End.

Thus the elements of the Gospel that reflect not a later tendency but the situation as it was in Jesus's own lifetime are quite clear. When the authorities "found this man perverting our nation, and forbidding [Jews] to give tribute to Caesar, and claiming to be *Messiah*, a king" (Luke 23:2), and when they said, "He stirs up the people" (v. 5), they make plain statements of fact. (I shall discuss in the Critical Appendix the attempts to camouflage the historical state of affairs in the service of later theologically and politically tinctured views.)

Jesus's movement, accordingly, was characteristic of the Kingdom of God agitation that kept Palestine, and Jewry in general, churned up for well-nigh two centuries spanning his life.

In taking the imminence of the Kingdom of God, now "at hand," as his starting point, in "stirring up the people," forbidding Jews to pay tribute to Caesar, and in putting himself forward as a pretender to power, he was exemplifying in his way the political agitation thought to be entailed by Pharisee religiosity.

In those days nothing was needed to become an agitator for the Kingdom of God but the resolution to stand forth. Personal talent, to be sure, must have been indispensable—self-assurance, magnetism, charisma, authority, and, no doubt, ecstatic gifts.

But it is perfectly possible, indeed likely, that Jesus had a further claim—that the inscription "King of the Jews," noted in all four Gospels as having been put on the cross, was not Roman irony but a simple statement of fact.

There is no reason a priori to dismiss the royal status of Jesus on the basis of his descent from King David. In our present documents, to be sure, such a claim is necessarily subordinated to the larger view of Jesus entailed by his magnification (see page 195).

In any case, Jesus spoke, as it seems, with authority; that is, "not as the scribes" (Mark 1:12), those whose authority had to come from the text of the Scriptures. Practically speaking, this meant that while he accepted the Scriptures, Jesus interpreted them in such a way as to promote his own ideas and thus make himself a leader of men. All those who were stirring up Jewry in behalf of the Kingdom of God perforce behaved in the same way, basing themselves on the common ground of the Torah and the Prophets. All leaders would impose their will via specific interpretations of general views and within that framework achieve and maintain their status.

All Kingdom of God activists were supposed to demonstrate their ability to perform miracles, not like those of ordinary magicians, but miracles of the World's End that would arise out of the movement of national redemption as part of the divine timetable. World's End miracles necessarily included the charismatic ability to interfere with the natural order by healing the lame, the insane, the hysterical, the epileptic, and so forth.

Jesus, too, had countless miracles attributed to him, all of them World's End miracles performed by those heralding the Kingdom: casting out unclean spirits from the possessed, healing the lame and the sick in general, and raising up those who had just died. These miracles were not ascribed to the leader's magical powers but to his divine inspiration. Thus, when Jesus heals sick people before a crowd, they do not praise Jesus but the "God of Israel" (Matt. 15:31).

We shall see in a moment whether Jesus regarded himself as a messiah. Whether he did or not, however, he was bound to exercise the charisma of a messianic leader in the current crisis. The mere enterprise of "Forcing the End" in and of itself gave a messianic or quasi-messianic status to a Kingdom of God activist, even though a messianic claim was not indispensable and not all Kingdom of God activists claimed to be messiahs personally.

The transition from self-conscious leadership, from an awareness, let us say, of one's own charisma, to the awareness of leading a movement inspired by charismatic prophecy is inherently fluid. A prophet who demonstrated his charisma in deeds was bound to become, in the feverish atmosphere of the time, a messianic pretender, that is, a would-be messiah, self-avowed or not, whose claims would be tested by the criterion of success.

This comes out clearly in the plainly charismatic selection of his immediate entourage, most of whom have the aspect of Kingdom of God activists and/or Zealots. Four of Jesus's closest circle are described unmistakably as Kingdom of God extremists: Simon the "Rock," Simon "the Zealot," John and Jacob ben-Zavdi (the "Sons of Rage", see page 196).

Thus the core of Jesus's immediate entourage was explicitly identified with the movement of militant disaffection, beginning with Judah the Galilean, that took shape against the Romans.

After his separation from John, Jesus moved back to the settled areas of Judea and Galilee and proclaimed the imminent advent of the Kingdom of God.

Yet that period of haranguing and, perhaps, recruiting, did not last long. He very soon, perhaps in a few weeks, changed his tactics once again and moved on to Jerusalem, to the fatal denouement of his career.

It is impossible to pinpoint with assurance the reason for his tactical switch. He must have felt an increase in the urgency of the current World's End crisis that made him think God was about to act: Jerusalem was the only place in the world, from the point of view of the Kingdom of God activists, for the World's End to erupt.

All Kingdom of God activists thought the Kingdom was about to break forth; we know that from their behavior. But there is something inevitably elastic, no doubt unknowable, about the lapse of time involved.

In the case of Jesus, curiously enough, the historical documentation, skimpy in all respects, allows us a glimpse into a progressive change in the estimates of just this lapse of time. It may help explain, though there can be no details, why Jesus abruptly ceased "stirring up the people" in the settled areas and went on up to Jerusalem.

Estimates were, of course, bound to vary in the overwrought atmosphere of the World's End fever. Emotions that were roused to action by a sense of urgency or that, contrariwise, had created a sense of urgency in the first place, differed sharply because of temperament.

In the case of John the Baptist and especially of Jesus, we can see an initial feeling of utter immediacy followed very quickly by a series of disappointments.

Thus, at the outset, both John the Baptist and Jesus announced that the Kingdom of God was "at hand" (Mark 1:15), a phrase so simple it can hardly be analyzed. It must have meant, quite literally, that they expected the Kingdom of God to erupt *then and there,* at the very moment of speaking. In going up to Jerusalem, Jesus tells his entourage a parable "because they supposed that the kingdom of God was to appear immediately" (Luke 19:11).

It is pointless to speculate about how long such a mood of exaltation might last. In any case, it soon yielded to something less urgent. Jesus told his followers, setting out for the countryside: "You will not have gone through all the towns of Israel before the Son of Man will have come" (Matt. 10:23), that is, before the Kingdom appears, i.e. a couple of weeks or so. Then there is a final postponement. Jesus tells his audience that "there are some standing here who will not taste death before they see the Kingdom of God" (Mark 9:1); that is, the Kingdom cannot be further off than the lifespan of, say, the youngest present. (This itself, which sounds like a massive postponement from the immediacy of the "at hand," is thought by some to extend an initial postponement. The "some" is thought to stand for an initial "all those"; that is, it represented a stage in an attempt to compensate for an initial disappointment by lengthening the wait for the Kingdom.)

There is still a further stage of postponement, when Jesus says "this generation" will not pass away "before all these things take place"; that is, before the Kingdom appears. (Mark 13:30)

Thus, within the brief career of Jesus we can trace four postponements, with the last one—"this generation"—inherently so elastic that a much later authority (St. Jerome), writing well after the consolidation of the Church, could say that "this generation" meant, really, all mankind; that is, the denouement was postponed indefinitely.

Still, it is plain that Jesus and his followers must have been carried along on a wave of ardor that made it natural for them to move into action in the expectation of success, to "Force the End" through the favor of God.

The specific occasion might well have been the incident I have already mentioned—the introduction of the exchangeable imperial portrait heads into the Temple area, which is chronicled as having thrown the Jews into a state of dismayed fury. The

setting up of images to serve as objects of worship was itself
thought to be the fulfillment of a prophecy in Daniel 11:31:

> "When you see the desolating sacrilege set up where it ought not
> to be . . . let those who are in Judea flee to the mountains; let him
> who is on the housetop not go down, nor enter his house to take
> anything away; and let him who is in the field not turn back to
> take his mantle. And alas for those who are with child and for
> those who give suck in those days! (Mark 13:14–17; also Matt.
> 24:15–19)

This desecration of the sanctuary was to bring about the
World's End (Dan. 12:11); that is, the Messianic Kingdom pre-
ceding the Kingdom of God, which was to end (after 3½ years)
with the full-fledged installation of the eternal Kingdom of
God, including the annihilation of the Prince of This World,
Yahweh's adversary, and of the godless in general through an-
other flood like that which had wiped out nearly all mankind in
Noah's time.

It may well be, accordingly, that it was this or some other
similar action on the part of Pilate that brought Jesus around to
a fateful decision to cease his merely preparatory harangues,
now that the crisis of the World's End had begun with the
"pangs of the Messiah," and to go up to Jerusalem for the
denouement.

The point of going to Jerusalem was to trigger the penultimate phase of the crisis—to "cleanse the Temple" (Mark 11:15)
and enter the city as the Messiah, the king of the Messianic
Kingdom preceding the Kingdom of God.

Jesus may well have intended to make his triumphal entry in
fulfillment of a classical prophecy (Zach. 9:9) of the entry of a
messianic king, or—if Jesus personally did *not* regard himself as
a Messiah—the earliest chroniclers themselves, long after Jesus's
death, intended to give that impression. In any case, the first
three Gospels take pains to demonstrate that Jesus's entry into
Jerusalem was that of a messianic king (Matt. 21:1–7; Mark
11:1–7; Luke 19:29–35).

After his triumphal entry, Jesus went on to "cleanse the
Temple." He "drove out all who sold and bought in the temple,

and he overturned the tables of the money-changers and the seats of those who sold pigeons" (Matt. 21:12).

This was far from simple. The Jewish Temple was enormous. Destroyed in 586 B.C. by Nebuchadnezzar, it had been rebuilt some seventy years later when the Jews returned from their first exile. It was a formidable obstacle to Pompey and his Roman legions in 63 B.C.

Herod the Great had restored it on a magnificent scale. Its rebuilding was begun in 20–19 B.C., and it took so long that almost half a century later—by the time Jesus occupied it—it was not yet finished (John 2:20). Indeed, the work on the outer buildings and the courts was to go on for some eighty years. It was completed a few years before the Roman-Jewish War of A.D. 66–70 and burned to the ground during the siege of Jerusalem in A.D. 70.

The Temple was not merely a house of worship; it embraced a complex of all sorts of administrative buildings, houses for attendants, offices, stables, and a number of great courtyards. It covered an area more than two hundred yards wide and four hundred fifty yards long; it also had a gigantic staff of attendants, numbering some twenty thousand, who performed a wide variety of functions.

It was a public marketplace and also a great treasury. Like other shrines of the Hellenistic world of the time, it amounted to a national bank.

There was an immense accumulation of precious metal as well as great sums of coins and vast deposits made by individual creditors—by widows and orphans as well as by the very rich. Nor were these deposits merely hoarded; the money was constantly being invested. Together with the rest of the Hellenistic world, the Jews had inherited from Babylon the whole system of bills of exchange, bonds, and personal checks. The vast wealth of the Temple was constantly being deployed in money transfers all over the known world. Though Jews could not profit from interest arising out of transactions between Jews, they could and did benefit from the profits of commercial enterprises. The prohibition of interest did not extend to dealings between Jews and non-Jews. For that matter, since the business relations prevailing throughout the Roman Empire were complex, there were no doubt methods of evading the prohibition of interest even between Jews.

The Temple was naturally protected in a manner befitting the most important and most massive institution of the country. Its chief protection was the Roman garrison. This consisted of a cohort of between five and six hundred men, with the usual auxiliaries in camp followers and troops. There was also a Temple police guard that had to be big enough to handle the throngs of people who even in ordinary times would constantly be passing through. The crush reached a tremendous pitch of concentration during the great annual festival of the Passover in the spring, when a vast concourse of pilgrims would come not only from all parts of Palestine but from all over the far-flung Jewish Diaspora.

Passover was notoriously an occasion for agitation. The Romans would routinely have reinforced their standard cohort, no doubt also augmenting an additional force they maintained in Fort Antonia, at the edge of the Temple area. There was one there when Paul was arrested in the next generation (Acts 21); it seems reasonable to suppose it was there before, when Jesus came to Jerusalem.

The very nature of the Passover festival, with throngs of unknown and uncheckable pilgrims streaming through the vast sanctuary, was ideal for guerrilla tactics: rebels could hide weapons under their flowing robes.

Thus the seizure of the Temple had to be accomplished by armed force. If Jesus held it "day after day" (Mark 14:49) he must have been able to withstand at least for a short time the Roman and the Jewish security forces.

The "cleansing" of the Temple, stronghold of the priestly aristocracy, was intended to replace the current priesthood with a pure and holy priesthood that would carry out the prescriptions of the Torah and hence abjure the Roman power. Thus the charge that, like the Zealots in the Roman War of A.D. 66–70, Jesus intended to "destroy" the Temple (Mark 14:56–58) meant simply that he was replacing the major corrupt institution of his society on the threshold of the Kingdom of God.

Jesus never challenged the institution of the Temple as such; he attacked the Temple aristocracy because of its corruption at this particular time. The money changers, pigeon dealers, traders, and so on, were, of course, licensed by the priesthood; hence the overturning of the money-changers' tables and the pigeon-dealers' seats struck at the very heart of the business activities carried on under the Temple's aegis.

The "cleansing" of the Temple took place immediately after Jesus's triumphal entry into the city. It was the seizure of the Temple that precipitated Jesus's execution; it was in its nature a supreme act of sedition, aimed at the Roman power and Jewish priesthood alike.

Since the upper priesthood was itself an outgrowth of the Jewish aristocracy, any attack on the upper priesthood involved the element of social protest I have already mentioned. Hence the call for repentance on the part of all the Kingdom of God activists, including the Zealots, the Daggermen, John the Baptist, and Jesus's following, was not a mere exhortation to the reform of individual ethics. Bondage to the pagan powers—in the current age, Rome—reflected a radical betrayal of the Torah; hence its converse was peremptory. The Torah must be observed, vile paganism rejected, and no taxes paid the Romans who controlled the high priesthood. If this were done, deliverance—freedom—would infallibly come from Yahweh.

The Jewish upper classes, because of either their quietism or their active collaboration with the Roman regime, were a barrier to the redemption of the people as a whole. The priesthood, living in luxurious houses in Jerusalem, reflected a corrupt society growing fat by cooperating with the Romans in enslaving Yahweh's people. Hence Jesus was hostile to the aristocracy not for mere ethical reasons but because the upper classes were actually preventing the eruption of the Kingdom of God.

Thus Jesus anticipated by a generation the Zealot attack on the priestly aristocracy in the Roman War of A.D. 66–70. A decade or two after Jesus's execution, indeed, Daggermen assassinated the high priest (Jonathan), under the Procurator Antonius Felix (A.D. 52–60), an assassination that intensified Zealot activity against the Jewish collaborators of the Romans. In A.D.

66 the Daggermen not only destroyed the house of the high priest (Hananiah) as well as the palaces of the two grandchildren of Herod the Great, Agrippa II and his sister Berenike; they also burned the public archives. They were "eager to destroy the money-lenders' bonds and to prevent the recovery of debts, in order to win over a host of grateful debtors and cause an uprising of the poor against the rich."[6] This was an element in the seizure of the Temple and the election of a new high priest in that year.

The hostility surely felt for Jesus and his partisans by the upper priesthood (Mark 11:18) had a natural logic. It was based on his militant antagonism to their collaboration with the Romans.

Hence, though the indictment, sentence, and punishment of Jesus were all Roman—ordered by Pilate, the Roman procurator, and executed by the Roman State—the sentence no doubt pleased the Romans' Jewish collaborators.

Some Kingdom of God activists claimed no special status; others regarded themselves as messiahs in their own person. Though Jesus immediately after his death was regarded, as we shall see, as having *been* the Messiah, the question of whether *he* thought so is by no means clear.

The question is of special importance, to be sure, for theology. There the subject is a spacious enclave within the vast labyrinth of speculative reflection. For history the self-consciousness of Jesus would seem to be less important.

Historically, in any case, it seems simple. Jesus never claimed to be the Messiah. The key passage is clear. Simon the Rock, asked by Jesus to say "who" Jesus is, responds: "You are the Messiah," whereupon Jesus "gave them [his disciples] strict orders" to say nothing further about it (Mark 8:29–30, NEB). (In theological discussion this is known as the "messianic secret.")

This would seem to show that while the believers in Jesus *knew* him to have been the Messiah after his resurrection, during his own lifetime Jesus never mentioned it. If he had, it is impossible to see why that would not have been remembered, quite simply, by his followers and referred to explicitly.

It may well be that for both Jesus and John the Baptist the older theme underlying "zealotic" action was crucial—the simple conviction that God would transform the world by direct action, with no human agent at all. This may explain why the Baptist sounds like a mere herald, why Jesus himself did not claim to be the Messiah, and why such emphasis is laid in the first three Gospels on the unpredictable but abrupt installation of the Kingdom of God by divine action alone.

There is no record, of course, of what Jesus might have intended to do after seizing the Temple. Given the inherent optimism of the attempt itself and without knowing his state of mind at the time, we can only speculate on whether he had some plan to fall back on if things did not turn out as he had hoped. An entirely cold-blooded, rational plan would, to be sure, have entailed consideration of failure. But if Jesus had been in an exalted state of mind, he might not have even considered failure. On the other hand, since our accounts have twisted Jesus's plan out of its original context, our ignorance here, as in so many other places, may be due merely to the absence of sources.

There may be a veiled echo of a possible consideration of failure when Jesus talks of the scattering of the sheep after the smiting of the shepherd and of leading his people back to Galilee if their hopes are frustrated (Mark 14:27–28), which is what the Zealots, too, tried to do when overcome in the Roman War.

The details of Jesus's abortive enterprise, as described in the Gospels, can be tersely summed up: Priests and scribes plot; Judas Iscariot betrays (for money); there is the Last Supper; there is the prayerful time at the Mount of Olives; Judas comes with a crowd; Jesus is abandoned. He is bound by the chief priests, the elders, and the scribes, and is taken to Pontius Pilate who, seemingly reluctantly, releases a Zealot named Barabbas captured "in the insurrection." Jesus is crucified between two other Zealots as "King of the Jews." In all four Gospels Jesus is explicitly condemned, finally, for sedition alone.

Ordinarily the collapse of Jesus's enterprise might have been expected to entail oblivion. Countless Kingdom of God activists had ended up on Roman crosses. In the genesis of Christianity, the paramount puzzle is provided by just this strange contradiction—the fact that despite his failure as a religious-political leader, Jesus had such an effect on his associates as to initiate an entirely unforeseeable series of events.

CHAPTER III

THE ELEVATION OF THE JEWISH MESSIAH

*T*he very manner of Jesus's execution constituted a knotty conundrum for his followers. Whether or not he had a plan to fall back on in case of defeat (surely most unlikely, in view of the total unpreparedness implied by their dismay), the humiliation of the crucifixion would in and for itself entail a denial of any messianic status. How, indeed, could a Messiah be tortured to death by pagans?

There was, further, a complete vacuum of ideas after Jesus's death. He had not, after all, established anything—neither a new belief nor a new rite. His entire enterprise had been embedded in the very substance of Judaism.

Hence his humiliating death, part of the failure of his movement, left nothing whatever behind for his followers except, indeed, their ancient religion.

From a humdrum, practical point of view they might have been expected to mourn Jesus for a time and then gradually take up the thread of normal life, which, to be sure, might well have meant resuming their agitation for the Kingdom of God, a rapidly growing current of disaffection and violence.

Yet the grief of Jesus's followers was to take an unexpected turn. They did not, in fact, accept the brute fact of his death. Something did happen—something whose consequences were incalculable.

The Gospels, our only records, have the look of a collection of legends, faded memories warped and confused by distance and by the distortions of tendency, further skewed by plainly fictitious details contrived to enhance drama in the face of scepticism. Yet as we pick our way through them we can see that what happened to transform the grief of Jesus's followers over his horrible death was, in essence, simplicity itself—one of them had a vision.

Such a vision is a purely historical datum: the visionary believes in the "truth" of his vision. If others, too, accept it, a social process has been initiated.

The vision was simple and clear. It was a vision of Jesus, who had in fact died in agony on the Roman cross, alive again, though not alive in the ordinary, mundane sense in which, for instance, Lazarus might have been said to have been raised by Jesus from the dead. Lazarus, resurrected, was not meant to live forever.

In the vision, Jesus was not merely raised from the dead; he was "glorified" at the Right Hand of God. And it was precisely this vision, seen by Simon Peter ("the Rock") on the Sea of Galilee and communicated to and believed in by some others, that gave rise to a new chain of events.

Just at this point there is a fusion between a plain, straightforward, historical fact—a vision that is believed in—and the interpretation of that fact. A slightly younger contemporary of Jesus, Saul of Tarsus—later to be known as Saint Paul—was to give this fusion of fact and interpretation a lapidary formulation: "If Christ has not been raised, your faith is futile" (1 Cor. 15:17).

The transformation of the grief of Jesus's mourners brought about a new situation. Whatever had been believed by Jesus and

his followers beforehand about the Kingdom of God was replaced by a belief about Jesus himself.

This was, as we shall see, the first of three stages in the
magnification of Jesus from Jewish messianist, to Lord of the
Universe, to deity.

A special interpretation of Jesus's execution was indispensable: the ignominiousness of the crucifixion had to be explained
away.

In and of itself, the resurrection was a dramatic explanation.
Anyone raised from the dead and glorified at the Right Hand of
God must have been marked for some grand purpose. After
Jesus's glorification it was clear that he had been singled out by
God as part of a cosmic plan.

Jesus's immediate followers still believed, as far as Judaism in
general was concerned, just what Jesus himself had believed—
that Yahweh was about to intervene in history, smash the pagan
powers, and rectify This World. They now merely added to this
the subsidiary belief that the singling out of Jesus by his resurrection meant that the Kingdom would be accompanied by his
Glorious Return.

All this was well within the confines of the basic simplicity of
Judaism. The stages of this early transposition are easily traced:

"Lord, will you at this time restore the kingdom to Israel?" (Acts
1:6)

This is plainly a mere reaffirmation of the ancient belief,
shared by all Kingdom of God activists, that the Kingdom of
God would restore the fortunes of the Jews.

A little later:

'Jesus of Nazareth, a man singled out by God and made known to
you through miracles, portents, and signs, which God worked
among you through him.' (Acts 2:22, NEB)

This repeats a theme of the same writer:

[Jesus is described by the Emmaus pilgrims as a man] "who was a
prophet mighty in deed and word before God and all the peo-

ple. . . . But we had hoped that he was the one to redeem Israel."
(Luke 24:19, 21)

This was no more than the traditional Jewish idea of a
prophet, enhanced by the conviction that he would be the one
to "redeem Israel."

This old view had to be heightened by Simon the Rock's
vision. It had to be turned into the concept that Jesus, who had
begun as a prophet, had been *made* special by God: 'God has
made this Jesus . . . both Lord and Messiah' (Acts 2:36, NEB).

Thus at first things were not very different; one element had
been transposed. The Kingdom of God was still believed in—
this time, however, linked to the person of Jesus, for whom a
great future had been signalized by the divine decision to elevate
Jesus to the Right Hand of God and thus guarantee the validity
of his role as Messiah. In practical terms this meant, in the
beginning, that the original conviction that the Kingdom of
God was about to be installed was now linked to the person of
Jesus. The Kingdom would be installed *after* Jesus came back
again.

Thus, for the time being, the Kingdom of God was not
abandoned; it was merely linked to another experience. The
early believers in Simon the Rock's vision *knew*, unlike predecessors, who had merely been convinced of an interpretation of
scriptural passages that suited them, that the Kingdom of God
had to come now that it was associated with the overwhelming,
palpable fact of Jesus's having been singled out—in full view, so
to speak, of the believers in the vision—as the manifest Herald
of the Kingdom.

In this way, the proclamation of Jesus's death, intertwined
with his resurrection, instantly presented itself to those who
believed in it as the demonstration of God's ultimate and indeed
imminent triumph.

This conviction was held by a handful of people near the
scene of the Vision in Galilee, perhaps a dozen or so at the most.
They did not stay in Galilee long; they left for Jerusalem. No
doubt it seemed obvious to them that if the Kingdom of God
was about to break forth, that could happen initially only in

Jerusalem—the same reasoning that had impelled Jesus himself
to go there.

This small group must have had acquaintances, perhaps from
other pilgrimages. They took their meals in a modest house.
They would have no difficulty in forming a synagogue of their
own without attracting attention; only ten Jews are needed for a
quorum.

The group was very small. There was Simon the Rock, who
had been especially close to Jesus and was in any case one whose
vision had been accepted by the others. (His very sobriquet "the
Rock" might have been due to this founding vision.) There was
also Jacob (the Major) and John ben-Zavdai, and Jesus's brother
Jacob (the Minor), known as Upright Jacob, who must have
derived some influence from his kinship with Jesus even though
at the outset of Jesus's career he had apparently been against it (as
noted in Mark and Matthew). He had had a vision of his own,
very early on (1 Cor. 15:7).

The group had the appearance of ordinary Jews. They were
particularly assiduous in attending services in the Temple,
where Upright Jacob was soon to be celebrated for his piety. In
principle, nothing distinguished them. Their characteristic belief—that Jesus, executed for sedition by the Romans, had been
resurrected—was in no sense a belief that lay outside Judaism. It
was merely an eccentric, personal quirk; though it was also, to
be sure, an aspect of politics, and especially, as we shall see, of
what was, much later, to become theology.

The believers in Simon the Rock's Vision—from now on I
shall call them "Jesists"—still believe in "The One," Yahweh,
the God of Israel. Their only writings were the Hebrew Scriptures. They shared the general Pharisee belief in the resurrection
of the dead, the Last Judgment, and, of course, the imminent
Kingdom of God. They knew themselves to be, like everyone
else, sinful, in need of God's mercy. They had in their minds a
view of the heavenly world, of hosts of angels, of the under-
world populated by Satan and the Evil Spirits: for them the
earth is the playground of the "powers." They believe, like all
normative Jews, in beings intermediate between God and the
world. God's attributes are more or less personified—

"Wisdom," "Word" (*Hokhma, Memra*, etc.). For them Jesus was the Messiah, who had been the Son of David—i.e., the Jewish Messiah, descended from the great King David, now expected to come back and rule a regenerated world as the Son of Man. For them this Messiah was to come down from Heaven and judge the righteous and the wicked. (Matt. 25:31–32).

The Torah, the core of Judaism, is fundamental. Somewhat later, of course, the question of the primacy of the Torah occasioned the splitting away of a new faith. But for the first coterie of Jesists this did not even arise: the Torah was taken for granted.

This Jesist coterie not only shares the same idea of the World's End as all the Kingdom of God activists, but they have the identical stance of dynamic expectation. Both the Jesists and other Kingdom of God activists believed in the absolute sovereignty of Yahweh, and also in his active help in restoring dominion to Israel; both loathed the Romans as pagans who worshiped men as gods; both cherished the Torah and the Temple as absolute values; both were violently opposed to paying the Roman taxes. Jesus had been executed, after all, just like countless Zealots; both groups detested the priestly aristocracy; both, finally, were followed by the "people of the land" against the rich and powerful. For both, in short, three categories of people were enemies—pagans in the Holy Land, the "publicans" who collected taxes for the Romans, and sinners against the Torah.

For the Jesists in Jerusalem the only problem about Jesus's messiahship was that it seemed to contradict the traditional role of the Messiah. Still, if a scriptural basis could be added to the impact of Simon the Rock's vision, this problem might be circumvented, and a harmonious explanation might be presented both of Jesus's messiahship and its apparent failure.

The Jesists very quickly found a cogent explanation of the contradiction: Jesus, who had come as Messiah to destroy the Romans and save his people, had died as a martyr for Israel and also for Israel's sins—i.e., his people had failed to respond: he had been turned over to the pro-Roman aristocracy and to the Roman procurator; all would be set right when he came again, this time, as guaranteed by the vision of Simon the Rock, at the Right Hand of God.

It is plain that there was no place for pagans in this tight design; the very vindication of Israel implied not only the destruction of Rome, but the punishment of the pagans in general:

> "When the Son of Man comes in his glory and all the angels with him, he will sit in state on his throne, with all the nations (pagans) gathered before him." (Matt. 25:31).

Jesus, as messiah-judge, accordingly, was simply meant to judge all mankind from the point of view of a resurgent Israel.

At the same time the Jerusalem Jesists had moved a little away from the original view of Jesus as a mere man delegated, like the classical prophets, to carry out the will of Yahweh. For the prophets of old such a man might have been a mere human being.

But the very fact of the Vision, of seeing in Jesus no longer a human being they had all known, but a being resurrected by the favor of God and glorified at his Right Hand, was a step in the direction of transcendentalizing Jesus; the initial, rather simple view that Jesus, by being resurrected, had passed instantaneously from the earthbound to the heavenly condition already made Jesus no longer a mere man. Still, this might have been easily assimilated because of the proliferation in contemporary Jewry, alongside the old-fashioned notion of a purely human messiah, of visionary, apocalyptic messiahs playing superhuman roles in the great clash of God with the demon powers.

Thus the figure of Jesus, though remembered by living people as a real human being, was susceptible of the sort of magnification possible for people caught up in the tension of waiting for transcendent events. Jesus began ascending, even in Jerusalem.

But this was not yet apparent; its implications, in any case, were not to be drawn within a purely Jewish milieu. The Jerusalem Jesists remained wholly integrated with the Temple milieu throughout their existence.

Initially the Jerusalem Jesists must have been impressed by the rapid percolation of the news of the Vision to so many different parts of the Jewish Diaspora. The news of the Vision was no doubt accompanied by its explanation that Jesus had been *meant* to die in order to rise again, i.e., just the view Paul had "received" upon joining the Jesists shortly after the crucifixion. When the views of the Jerusalem coterie lapped over into the numerous congregations of pagan converts and semi-converts to Judaism—the "God-fearers" and others—that too would have seemed to be promoted by God's grace. It took a few years before the Jerusalem Jesists felt called upon to react to the success of the hellenizing ideas being mingled with their own in the Diaspora.

It is obvious, indeed, that the Jerusalem Jesists had no intention of evangelizing the pagans. That would have seemed incomprehensible to pious Jews whose ideas still revolved around the destinies of Israel, the Kingdom of God, and a Jewish Messiah. The proselytization that did finally begin was associated with the expulsion of the Greek-speaking Jews after the execution of their leader, Stephen. It was these followers of Stephen who first began "preaching the Lord Jesus" to the pagans in Antioch after first having been active with the Diaspora Jews there (Acts 11:19–21).

The harmonizing chronicler of Acts inserts a special incident to bridge over what must have been the original antipathy of the Jerusalem coterie to the very idea of taking their views to the pagans. The book of Acts, mentioning the conversion of Cornelius, the Roman centurion, introduces this by indicating that God had had to prepare Simon the Rock for this by a special revelation (Acts 10:1 and 11:18).

If the Jesists did, after all, accept the fact that their special view of Jesus might profitably be communicated to pagans, they must have insisted that at least those pagans be converted to Judaism, via circumcision, a primary requirement.

This concession—not a real one, in any case, since conversion simply made a pagan a full Jew—implied no change of views on the part of the Jerusalem Jesists, who remained unwavering in their fundamental view that Israel remained the Chosen People as before. The vital necessity of this notion is indicated by Paul himself, even at the very moment of evolving ideas designed for absorption by pagans (as he shows in the powerful metaphor comparing the pagans to a "wild olive shoot . . . grafted" onto Jewry) and exhorting them to remember that it is not they who sustain the "root" but the root that sustains them (Rom. 11:17, 18).

The metaphor itself, indeed, may be a seductive way of pointing out to his superiors in Jerusalem the profitability and justifiability of carrying their ideas to the pagans—another "gate of faith" (Acts 14:27).

For the rest, what distinguished the Jerusalem Jesists from their surroundings was their feeling that they were somehow the Elect, since they alone perceived the true role of Jesus in bringing the Kingdom expected by countless Jews. It was they alone, they no doubt thought, for whom the Great Day of Yahweh forecast by the classical prophets and being fought for by Zealots, Daggermen, and activists of all kinds, would bring happiness. This idea was not uncommon in the turbulent Israel of those days.

Initially there was no organization at all, nor could there have been since at first there was no reason to think the original group would last. The very idea of enduring was obviously the antithesis of the hope and longing that had brought them to Jerusalem in the first place.

This small, family-like group could not have lasted long. In this stage it consisted of "brothers," "believers," those who were of "one heart and soul" (Acts 4:32). Perhaps their conduct was guided, like that of other Jews, by a few ethical precepts. The Sermon on the Mount, a cluster of rules for ordinary conduct, without speculation, no doubt comes from this early period. It might have suited their self-esteem:

> "You are the salt of the earth. . . . You are the light of the world. . . . Unless your righteousness exceeds that of the . . . Pharisees, you will never enter the kingdom of heaven." (Matt. 5:13–20)

At first there was no interest in the real-life Jesus they had all known. Waiting for the World's End, there was no reason to write down anything about a flesh-and-blood Jesus, about his person or his career, or his relations with friends and enemies, or even the World's End miracles that had been attributed to him.

Within the small coterie the only divisions noticeable even a decade or more after Jesus's death were into "apostles, prophets, and teachers" (1 Cor. 12:28). There was still no bureaucracy and no allocation of offices to monitor or control the ideas of the coterie. There were no sacred persons and no hierarchy. The perspective of the group was simply to wait for Jesus the Risen Messiah to come down from heaven, smash the pagan power, and install the Kingdom. There was no need for organization.

Still, as the group kept growing and as the Second Coming kept being postponed, some need for administration was felt.

The earliest record (very late) mentions only two aspects of organization: (1) holding all things in common and (2) making a general distribution of goods according to individual need (Acts 2:44–45). It was this, no doubt, that planted the seeds of the Church as an institution. The Church arose, in germ, out of the community chest.

The "primitive communism" traditionally attributed to this phase of evolution was, to be sure, a later idealization. Barnabas's gift of his possessions to the community is reported as an exception (Acts 4:36–37). The community chest itself was to give rise to the tradition of the inherent meritoriousness of poverty and of Good Works, which meant doing things for the common good and for the poor.

Since the Glorious Return of the Risen One was expected from one moment to the next, no propaganda was carried on by the first Jesists, though of course they communicated their beliefs. They could not have remained incognito in the Temple milieu, especially since they would have been known to be associated with the abortive enterprise of Jesus, notorious vis-à-vis the authorities. They would have been known even though there is no indication of any further activity that might have made them suspect once they were living a quiet life in Jerusalem. (Later on, to be sure, the little coterie did play a role in the agitation that led to the uprising against the Romans in A.D. 66: see Chapter V.)

In the absence of organizational structure, what was important were personal qualities—charisma, the grace bestowed on certain "saints" by the "Spirit," linked almost at once, no doubt, to the Risen Jesus, who unlike the old-fashioned prophet whose authority was derived from God, possessed the Spirit directly through his glorification.

It was the Spirit, in short, that created the incentive for action—not bureaucracy, hierarchy, or organization. It will be a long time before those inspired by the Spirit will be replaced by an actual organization and even longer before the initially elected functionaries become the masters of the group.

Thus, at the outset, before there is any question of organization, the administration and authority of the first coterie are conceived of as being entirely under the auspices of the Spirit (Acts 9–31).

Basically, the "Spirit" was a way of talking about spontaneous or at least pseudo-spontaneous psychic activity. It was not, in its nature, limited by anything; that is, it could not be bureaucratized. It marked, indeed, just that stage of group life that preceded any form of organization. In and of itself it validated, as the symbol of free-floating decisions, whatever was going on in the life of the early coterie.

The Spirit could show itself in more than one form; but mainly in the form of ecstasy and prophecy in the sense of edifying the listeners by "explaining" the Scriptures, by recalling what Jesus had said or was thought to have said, and by phenomena like "glossolalia"—a type of babbling in public, explained as repeating powerful, mysterious ideas from some "unknown language." To outsiders, of course, this might have looked like plain drunkenness (Acts 2:13).

The rule of the Spirit, no doubt, itself marks both the beginning of propaganda—that is, the articulation and promotion of a self-consciously different point of view—and the rudiments of organization entailed by the postponement of the Second Coming. Merely in order to maintain themselves as a group in the

midst of an environment they were, though with a characteristic difference, part of the earliest coterie had to organize
itself.

The first pivot that was to bring about the germination of a
faith unsuspected by either Jesus or the first Jesists took place
within the Jerusalem coterie.

In a Jewish milieu the mere messiahship of Jesus, however
fitted out with transcendental elements, could not, perhaps,
have prospered for very long. It would seem to have required
realization in a practical sense. Thus the upward ascension of
Jesus was held back by the milieu in which it had begun. Even
though his ascension overshadowed his humanity (such as his
biological descent from King David), it was itself limited to
concepts valid only in Judaism.

It was natural for the Jerusalem Jesists to communicate their
excitement to other Jews, countless numbers of whom were
constantly coming to Jerusalem. The Temple was the goal of
pilgrimage for Jews throughout the world.

Thus the primitive, more or less tightly knit group of Jesists
was soon diluted by Greek-speaking Jews from the Diaspora
whose familiarity with pagan culture no doubt made it easy for
them to believe in personal resurrection. It was they who were
to take the initial ascension of Jesus and amplify it, as we shall
see, endlessly.

It was from the moment that such Diaspora Jews, influenced
by the Jesists, stayed on in Jerusalem, no doubt in a special
synagogue with regional associations, that the gradual formation of a new type of community must be assumed. It would
seem clear that once the contagion of the Vision had affected
them, the reason they stayed on in Jerusalem was again a simple
one. They were waiting for the Risen Jesus to appear for the
second time, this time bringing with him, of a certainty, the
Kingdom of God.

The views of the Jerusalem Jesists did not detach them from
the movement for the Kingdom of God that was beginning to
churn up the country and that was to culminate in the A.D. 66–
70 insurrection. Just as they could pray "assiduously" in the
Jewish Temple, so their view of the Kingdom of God, a mere

variant of the general belief, did not preclude the identification of the Jesists with their fellow activists in the swelling tide of insurrection.

It was the Diaspora Jesists (the "Hellenists" of Acts) who, while accepting the primordial lesson drawn by the original believers in the Vision—that God had singled Jesus out as Messiah-soon-to-return—expanded the idea far beyond its original scope. A ferment began that, by leading to the magnification of the person of Jesus, by stressing what was originally a minor difference between the immediate entourage of the lost leader Jesus and the ordinary mass of Jews living within the framework of traditional Jewish ideas (the Sadducees, Pharisees, and so on) escalated that originally minor difference to a higher level.

At first the original core of Jesists must have influenced only small numbers of Diaspora Jews. Then gradually, as that number increased and as the Diaspora Jews became more numerous relative to the original core, the initial harmony in the fervent expectation of the Second Coming began to be eroded by the mere survival of the original group and by the need to cope with real life while waiting for the Second Coming.

Because the Greek-speaking Jews, who had a wider range of ideas, philosophical background, and interests through their Greek-language background, inevitably began not only to expand the simplicity of the original notion of Jesus's role but to project it beyond the boundaries of Jewish tradition, the break between them and their fellow believers widened into a split.

The initial difference, curiously enough, is recorded on a most mundane plane. There were disagreements about the allocation of food at the tables that in the very beginning were communal. The community must have been small enough to warrant such tables (Acts 6:1–5).

The Jerusalem Jesists were to become symbolized in the early tradition as "The Twelve," counterposed to "The Seven," referring to the Greek-speaking Diaspora Jews. "The Twelve" were later considered to have been the apostolic element, representing the "Word of God," while "The Seven" represented material services, the future diaconate.

Nevertheless, though tradition presents the Greek-speaking Seven in this anodyne way, what exacerbated the falling-out was the predilection of the Greek-speaking Jews for propaganda. The group is epitomized in the figure of Stephen, who was "argued with" by members of some regional synagogues (Acts 6:9, 10) and accused of denouncing both the Temple and the Torah.

Stephen was arraigned before the Jewish authorities (the Sanhedrin). He not only defended his views but expressed them in a particularly violent form, culminating in a savage denunciation of Jews for having failed to accept Jesus the Messiah. He was sentenced to death by stoning for apostasy.[1]

Thus, within little more than a decade after Jesus's execution, the idea had already sprouted in the Jesist milieu that the Torah and the cult—the essence of Judaism—had been superseded, in principle, by the resurrection of Jesus and the consequences it entailed.

The Jesist community was split. The Greek-speaking Jews— Stephen's partisans—were deported from Jerusalem. They scattered, some of them going at first nearby to the provinces of Judea and Samaria, and a little later farther north to Antioch in Syria and to Cyprus.

It was in Antioch in Syria, a great capital, that some unknown Diaspora Jews took the first step outside the Jewish enclosure. It was there, for the first time, that some of the Greek-speaking Jews (natives of Cyprus and Cyrene) "spoke . . . to the Greeks, announcing to them Lord Jesus" (Acts 11:19–21). It was in Antioch, too, that the word *Christian* was coined. At that time, to be sure, it meant no more than "Jesist"—someone who believed in Jesus as Messiah (the word *Christ* was only the Greek translation of the Hebrew-Aramaic word *Messiah*).

The Greek-speaking Jews who had left Jerusalem must have been a mere handful. They were only going home or to places they would feel at home in. Nor could the "Greeks" referred to above have been ordinary Greeks. Normal pagans could not have understood either the Kingdom of God, the concept of "repenting," the point of the resurrection of a Jewish Messiah, or, for that matter, the concept of One Almighty God.

The pagans harangued by the exiles from Jerusalem must have been the numerous "God-fearers" (pagans who worshiped the Jewish God but disregarded circumcision and food laws) who clustered around countless synagogues throughout the Mediterranean. Wherever Jews had settled, the orderly rites and their immemorial antiquity had attracted huge numbers of pagans, who though fascinated by Judaism were loath to take on the burden of circumcision and the dietary laws.

It was, accordingly, just such God-fearers who were the first to hear, in their own language, the "Good News" brought them by the Greek-speaking Jews.

The new, enhanced view of Jesus, the failed nationalist leader and would-be messiah who had been "hanged on wood" by the Romans, spread very rapidly, from Palestine to Syria, to Rome itself, and to Egypt. Wherever there were Jewish communities, and they were scattered all over the eastern Mediterranean area and beyond, it would have been natural for Jews returning from Jerusalem pilgrimages to bring with them the exciting news that a Kingdom of God activist had actually been raised from the dead and been *seen* glorified. The use of the word *Christian,* as a species of Jew, must have spread equally rapidly.

In any case, little groups and assemblies, generally associated in the first generation or two with Jewish synagogues, must have been accessible to the abundant speculation fostered by the idea that Jesus's resurrection was an integral part of a divine plan.

The very existence of such coteries in a society that went on living a normal life entailed the emergence of a cult of some kind. Mere feeling cannot remain very long in the form of feeling alone. It must be given some sort of public, that is, social, expression. The awareness of being distinguished from other Jews, if only by the quirk of a special belief in and of itself created a vehicle for the coagulation of both ideas and rites. In turn, the practice of such a cult reinforced the bond already felt by those sharing the same belief. The cult became the manifestation of togetherness.

This meant, quite simply, that the person of the Messiah Jesus, the raison d'être of the coterie to begin with, soon became the focus for the crystallization of the cult. As a group, the believers—the "saints"—would, in the early period, concentrate on Jesus and the longings they associated with his power. What they longed for now was not only the Kingdom of God, like other Jews whose imaginations were inflamed by the tension of the epoch, but for *him* to return with the Kingdom.

This was soon to abbreviate itself to the simple fact of his coming, longed for with ardor. And to bring that about it was equally natural to invoke *his name,* which in the beginning meant that in praying to God, the Jesists designated, with feeling, Jesus as the guarantee that their prayers would be answered.

Thus, when the small coteries found a recruit, he or she had to signal allegiance to the coterie by demonstrating faith in the *name* of the Risen Jesus. Invoking that name became, accordingly, the emblem of the new association.

This was what became the core of whatever the early ceremonial was. It provided a potent mechanism for taking on the status of a member of the New Elect.

Everyone in that era took it for granted that some form of power was inherent in the very nature and shape of a name. In the recollections of the Jerusalem Jesists, moreover, Jesus had demonstrated through his World's End miracles that some aspect of the divine power was inherent in his very person.

The potency inherent in names as such is illustrated often:

"In my name they will cast out demons." (Mark 16:17)

" 'Did we not . . . cast out demons in your name?' " (Matt. 7:22)

"In the name of Jesus Christ . . . walk!" (Acts 3:6)

"And his name [Jesus] . . . has made this man strong." (Acts 3:16)

The antiquity of this turn of mind is attested by what has been a most ancient formula: "Lord, come!" or "Let the Lord come!" (*Maran atha!* in Aramaic).

Thus the very name of Jesus justified and enhanced its use for cultic purposes. The figure of Jesus became not merely the aim of communion but its very instrument.

This took place, of course, against a background of conventional synagogue practices. All the first coteries were, after all, pious Jews naturally grouped around synagogues. Thus the earliest Jesists, too, read the Scriptures, sang psalms, prayed together.

They tended to select, to be sure, passages from the Scriptures that had a point for *them,* passages that highlighted prophecies that Jesus was thought to have realized. Very soon they began exercising their minds ferreting out passages from the Hebrew Scriptures and putting them together as a body of "testimonies" to the truth of their belief. No doubt they favored psalms full of hope, those that exalted the promise, since this was their primary concern. Their prayers, too, must have concentrated accordingly on the supplication for the Glorious Return of their Messiah—the meaning of "Lord, Come!"

Thus, even though the framework of their prayers and supplications remained Jewish and even though they thought themselves, in the first few generations, to be Jewish, such coteries had already launched a dynamic that in its nature tended to create a split between them and Judaism. The mere fact that the background of their hopes, at this time, was constituted by Jewish tradition had little to do with the true emotional intent of their behavior. That intent, linked as it was to a dynamic innovation expected to take place in the universe, was inherently likely to break with normative Judaism unless—of course, it actually took place.

At the same time, whatever their belief in Jesus's special role was, the Jesists in Jerusalem went on sharing the general Kingdom of God perspective that had become commonplace among the Pharisees and lower strata of the priesthood, in contrast with the pro-Roman, "quietist" attitude of the upper priesthood and Jewish aristocracy. That perspective, of the World's End accompanied by the restoration of Jewish dominion naturally entailed thoroughgoing opposition to the Roman Empire, the chief obstacle to the realization of the Divine Plan.

Since all activist Jews believed this, there was no distinction between the Jerusalem Jesists and the other activists, such as the Zealots, Daggermen, and so on, vis-à-vis the Romans. The crucifixion of Jesus was not embarrassing to Kingdom of God activists from a political point of view; he had, after all, died as a victim of pagan oppression and was thus a national hero.

There was, at first, no natural transmission of the early, national view of the risen Jesus to the pagans: the basic framework of the national idea was wholly Jewish, hence, even though the focal position of the Temple created a network of relations between Palestinian and Diaspora Jewry, there was not as yet a bridge to the pagans, which was formed only with the expulsion of the Greek-speaking Jews from Jerusalem.

There were, accordingly, two stages in the magnification of Jesus—the first involving a small transposition of traditional values, from Jesus as messianic pretender and Herald of the Kingdom of God to Jesus as Messiah-Soon-to-Come-Again and as Bringer of the Kingdom of God.

The first magnification was still well within the human scale; the second created an angle of elevation, as it were, that was later on to bring in its train still another type of magnification.

The third stage in the magnification of Jesus, arising, in a way, out of his magnification in the second stage, revolved around Jesus as a divinity whose significance soared far beyond Jewish history and transcended all history. It is summed up in the theory of the Incarnation; Jesus became the Incarnation of the Spirit of God and thus, in a profound sense, God himself.

For the comprehension of the evolution of this third phase we have a record in the letters of St. Paul, which constitute the core of what was, much later, to become the New Testament, and which can be considered, accordingly, the mainspring of the religion whose formation arose out of his ideas.

CHAPTER IV

THE CHRIST—World Savior

*P*aul's ideas, embodied in his Letters, were to become the core of Christianity, though gripped as he was by the conviction of the infallible imminence of the World's End, the notion of creating a new theology could hardly have crossed his mind.

He had been, as he relates, initially hostile to the views of the Jesists: then he had a Vision of his own, in which the Glorified Jesus chided him from the heavens. From then on he was to spend the rest of his life propagandizing on their behalf, though with profound differences that eventually emerged and brought him to an untimely end.

For Paul, and for all believers in the Kingdom of God who also believed in the Glorification of Jesus and in the Incarnation, the difference between them and believers in the Kingdom of God *tout court* was to prove pivotal. Those who did not go beyond the belief that Jesus had been singled out by God to herald the Kingdom could accept that fact as a guarantee of the Kingdom. Mere faith in the imminence of the Kingdom was

65

buttressed by *proof* that its initial phase, despite its oddity, was palpable evidence of the Divine Intention.

But Paul—and others who came to believe in the Incarnation—had a real problem. In the exhilaration that seemed to survive from his vision outside Damascus to the end of his letter writing, Paul had to cope with a specific historical conundrum—the extrapolation, in action, of what the Resurrection, as harbinger of the Kingdom of God, meant in real life.

Paul was not, to be sure, the initiator of all the ideas associated with him. The Kingdom of God agitation that had spread throughout the Diaspora before and after Jesus had prepared a terrain on which the excitement aroused by Simon the Rock's vision struck root in many Jewish communities. Nevertheless it was Paul's adaptation of the ideas he found waiting for him that changed the course of history.

Paul was a slightly younger contemporary of Jesus; he does not seem to have known Jesus personally; the brevity of Jesus's career makes that most unlikely, though Paul might, conceivably, have seen him.

Paul's native language was Greek; he was born into a well-to-do Jewish family, originally from Gush Halav (Gischala) in northern Palestine, which had established itself in Tarsus in Cilicia (now northern Syria), the hub of many trade routes stretching out to Greece, Italy, Cyprus, Phoenicia and Egypt.

Tarsus was not really a Hellenistic community; it had remained oriental (Aramean) despite attempts to hellenize it, especially by Antiochus IV in 171 B.C. shortly before the Maccabean insurrection. Tarsus did have Greek schools and a sort of university that was famous, especially in philosophy, thoughout the Hellenistic world. It was run by Stoics who had infused a good deal of emotion, designed for mass consumption, into their philosophy.

Thus Paul's background was already a mixture of a traditional Jewish Diaspora education and a variety of Hellenistic influences.

Paul's letters show us in miniature the mechanism by which an altogether Jewish phenomenon, which might seem at first glance to have nothing to say to anyone outside the matrix of Judaism, was transformed in the space of a few years into a religion of universal appeal entirely independent of and indeed contrary to the presuppositions of Judaism.

Through his command of Greek, Paul was naturally familiar with concepts like spirit, savior, reason, soul, conscience. If he did have some rabbinic training, as he emphasizes, it may have been reflected in the polemical style he applied to various passages in the Hebrew Scriptures.

Before embarking on the travels he was to be remembered for he established what he called "his gospel" on a foundation laid by others. This took place, in all probability, in Antioch, a haven for a few Diaspora Jews expelled from Jerusalem around A.D. 44, after the execution of Stephen.

Antioch, the third largest city of the Roman Empire, had a very heterogeneous population. It provided a crossroads for all the beliefs, superstitions, and fads of the East. It had a huge Jewish colony consisting of both full converts to Judaism and "God-fearers." It is, perhaps, conceivable that some pagans, without being even God-fearers, nevertheless knew enough about Judaism to find the special function assigned to Jesus understandable and attractive. This was in spite of the fact that at the very beginning, before the concept of Jesus was amplified to the extent it finally was by Paul and no doubt others, it could have had no effect on the ideas or emotions of anyone outside Judaism.

It was in all probability there that Paul himself succumbed to the contagion that had seized hold of countless Diaspora communities. Thus Paul's "gospel" was developed not through any influence stemming directly from the Jesist coterie in Jerusalem. It came entirely through the ferment already aroused in the Diaspora by Simon the Rock's Vision. Its form, moreover, was far removed from the views of the Jerusalem coterie and all those Diaspora Jews who still believed in the specifically Jewish idea of the Kingdom of God.

Thus the source of Paul's own "conversion," his reversal of feeling about the Jesists after his initial hostility, had nothing to do with his having known Jesus personally or the small group of Jesists that had gone to Jerusalem from Galilee after Jesus's execution.

Nevertheless, Paul was inevitably involved in the Kingdom of God agitation that inflamed the Jews. He fell afoul both of the Roman and the Jewish authorities, bringing about a confrontation that undid him.

Paul had first gone to Jerusalem in the Thirties, some time after joining the Jesists, to consult Simon the Rock. At that time he saw Upright Jacob, Jesus's brother, apparently without conversing with him. But when Paul visited Jerusalem again, around A.D., Upright Jacob was unquestionably, to use Paul's phrase, the chief "pillar" of the coterie. It might well have been Simon the Rock's flight to Egypt around A.D. 43–44 that promoted the rise of Upright Jacob.

Since the Jesists were entirely normal Jews, from a religious point of view, and "assiduous" worshipers in the Temple to boot, there was no way for Upright Jacob to exercise any sort of institutional authority over Paul. This was in spite of the fact that within the loosely knit coterie, Upright Jacob had some sort of superiority derived both from his kinship with Jesus and no doubt from his personal qualities.

Thus Paul's last trip to Jerusalem, which he made full of forebodings (all justified, as we shall see), was undertaken in order to justify his propagandizing in the Diaspora. Having apparently concealed or camouflaged his eccentric views for some time, he had at last been talked about enough for the Jerusalem coterie to intervene in order to assess whether or not Paul was in fact presenting Jesism to semi-Jewish pagans in the right way or not.

As leader of the coterie, Upright Jacob had supervised the observance of decisions made about taking meals together with pagans (Gal. 2:11f.). Thus, on his last trip, when Paul finally arrived in Jerusalem to bring the Jesists the funds he had collected for the "saints," it was to Upright Jacob that he had to demonstrate his basic fidelity to the Torah.

I have indicated in outline the thrust of Paul's ideas, as worked out by him while corresponding with and visiting some of the little coteries of Jews plus full and partial converts to Judaism. The situation was evidently amorphous enough for him to be able to work out his ideas over a period of time without irritating his fellow Jesists in Jerusalem too much, though eventually, as we shall see, his idiosyncratic view eventually got him into hot water. It was a view that carried the future with it but at the time, against the background of the mighty Temple, passed well-nigh unnoticed.

In the beginning, the quirk introduced by Stephen and like-minded Jesists was not seen as being of any lasting consequence. It might not even have attracted much attention, especially since for energetic spirits among the Jews the primary problem of the age was the gathering opposition to the Roman Empire, focused by an extravagant faith in the nearness of the Kingdom of God. Thus, since the new faith transported to the Hellenistic milieu by the Greek-speaking Jews expelled from Jerusalem was still centered in Jesus; and since the community of Jesists in Jerusalem was also still preoccupied, in its own way, with the career of Jesus, the failed Jewish Messiah; and since in view of the shared certainty that the Kingdom of God was soon to erupt, there was no reason to think of anything like *doctrine*. Various shadings of views could exist in the Diaspora side by side with each other. Thus the crisis of Stephen's execution and the expulsion of his partisans might not have seemed very important.

Within a couple of decades of Jesus's execution, a cluster of distinct, perhaps mutually hostile, and, in any case, mutually exclusive "gospels"—interpretations of the *meaning* of Jesus— were contending with each other. Paul refers to opponents who preach "another Jesus" and who lay down a "different gospel" (Gal. 1:6–9; and 2 Cor. 11:4).

Of the two factions working against Paul—Simon the Rock's and one he calls "of the Messiah"—both must have laid emphasis on the Jewish messiahship of Jesus as opposed to Paul's cosmic metaphysics. In this dispute Paul displays not only emotional malaise but indicates at the same time that these opponents had so much prestige that his position was under constant attack.

The earliest point at issue was, of course, a cardinal question: Did one really have to be a devout Jew in order to believe in the special role of Jesus, however that might be meant?

As we have seen, this question had been asked very early on by the Stephen group of Greek-speaking Jews. It really was a sort of logical extension of the consequence of believing that Jesus was special in any sense. If he was, that in and of itself downgraded the Torah. That was why Stephen had been executed and like-minded Jews had fled the country.

The Greek-speaking Jews, who on coming to Jerusalem had heard of Simon the Rock's vision in Galilee, must have spread the "news" very quickly. Only a few years afterwards it had been carried to what is now northern Syria and then westward across Asia Minor and Greece to Rome. There were coteries of Jews and semi-Jews touched by it in Corinth, Galatia, Ephesus, Philippi, Colossae, and Rome. These coteries were mentioned by Paul within the first and second decades after Jesus's execution. There are also indications of a very natural similar movement southwest, toward the large Jewry of Egypt, especially Alexandria.

What actually the "news" consisted of is, to be sure, hard to say in view of the contending interpretations referred to in our sources. Paul was in no sense the only "Apostle to the Gentiles," even if "Gentiles" meant pagan converts or semiconverts to Judaism. The coteries of Rome and Antioch were in existence before Paul became active.

But all these coteries, whatever might have been their specific beliefs about Jesus, naturally regarded themselves as subordinate in the nature of things to the central coterie of Jesists in Jerusalem, just as the countless synagogues throughout the eastern Mediterranean regarded the Jerusalem Temple as the anchor of Judaism.

Paul expresses no doubt, for instance, of the absolute priority of the Jerusalem coterie. Even though he elaborated an ideal of the unity of the church—perhaps his most important concept—that naturally transcended the importance of any particular church, there was for him no question of the authority of the Jerusalem Jesists. For him Jerusalem was the center of the new faith as it was the center of Judaism; and despite Paul's all-encompassing, cosmic mysticism, it was from Jerusalem that the new faith had actually begun (Rom. 15:19; Gal. 1:17ff.; 1 Cor. 16:3).

The rationale of all this is obvious. It was there that Jesus had been executed, and of course, Jerusalem, as the center of Judaism and its axis, had to be the backdrop not merely for the crucial events of Jesus's career on earth but for their interpretation. Though Paul does not say explicitly that Jerusalem is the natural center for all devout Jews, it is the basic premise of his somewhat tortured argumentation, since he assumes that without the approbation of the Jerusalem Jesists he might have been wasting his time (Gal. 2:2, " . . . lest somehow I had run in vain.").

The authority of the Jerusalem coterie is thus taken for granted. We can even divine the existence of a sort of network between the Jerusalem Jesists and some of the provincial synagogues, since in Antioch the authority of Upright Jacob is simply invoked and assumed in a dispute recorded by Paul about the cardinal question I have mentioned above; that is, could pagans eat together with Jews? (Gal. 2:9, 11, 12). Nor does Paul question the authority among his own followers of the emissaries from Jerusalem, even though he is preoccupied with resisting their ideas (2 Cor. 11:1ff.).

The cardinal point was demonstrated by something very down-to-earth—his fund-raising for the saints in Jerusalem, which activity he accepted with enthusiasm and which in fact led to his undoing (Gal. 2:10).

The ideological point of Paul's fund-raising was to show that Jesism had made some headway outside the Jewish community. The collection represented several years' activity on Paul's part; it had to be handed over in Jerusalem in a dramatic way, its sensational effect heightened through the presence of eight companions representing semi-Jewish congregations (Acts 20:4ff).

The world at large was to become aware of the potency of the Risen Jesus's role in the salvation of the human race by the mass conversion of the pagans, that is, mankind. Paul conceived of this as the penultimate state of the cosmic drama whose climax was to be the Glorious Return. The prophets Isaiah and Micah would be vindicated. Then, with the pagans converted, the Jews too would see the light and the divine plan be consummated.

Paul's hopes were frustrated by Upright Jacob. After Paul reported on his work and the whole group "glorified God" (Acts 21:18, 19), Upright Jacob told Paul about the report he had heard to the effect that Paul was telling the "Jews who are among the Gentiles to forsake Moses, telling them not to circumcise their children or observe the customs" (Acts 21:21).

Paul was now obliged to show, in public, that there was no truth in this (Acts 21:24); that he had in fact been living up to the Torah. To prove his good faith, he had to take a special (Nazirite) vow, shave his head and purify himself together with four others, whom he had to pay for. (The vow, an ancient one, was also expensive; it was considered a convincing symbol of piety.)[1] If he had refused to take the test, he might have been killed on the spot as an apostate; by submitting in public, on the other hand, he compromised himself in the eyes of his recruits.

All this led to a riot on the Temple premises. Despite the test Paul was recognized by some Jews from Ephesus in Asia Minor as indeed an enticer away from Judaism. He was also accused of having brought into the Temple an uncircumcized pagan (a capital offense).

Paul, arrested for his own safety, was ultimately sent to Rome (around A.D. 55). His crime had nothing to do directly with his beliefs (there was no question of his having been arrested as a "Christian," a concept that did not exist at the time), but as having violated a Temple taboo by starting a riot on the sacred premises. It had nothing to do with his being a genuine apostate. It was authorized by a section of the priestly hierarchy represented by Upright Jacob and the other Pharisee priests and elders who made up the Jesist coterie. Eventually he was executed, no doubt in Rome.

His eccentricities vis-à-vis the Torah and the role of Jesus went unnoticed as long as they did because of their relative insignificance within the framework of the hysteria that gripped the most energetic members of Jewry both in Palestine and in the Diaspora. He must at first have been heard of in Jerusalem as a propagandist for Jesism before his ideas had developed in detail. Spreading the word of Simon the Rock's Vision was in and of itself a good thing, part of calling Jews to action in behalf of the Kingdom of God. The material prosperity of some converts to Judaism around the synagogues was no doubt credited to the influence of the "Spirit."

Yet the logic of his activity was obvious. At the end of his life, his activity filled the Jerusalem Jesist coterie with dismay. At the same time, he could hardly have been considered important in any sense, no more than any of the others in the anti-Torah party that had been expelled in the Forties after Stephen's execution. As long as the Temple was in existence together with a Jewish State, even one oppressed by the Romans, it would have seemed inconceivable for such views to prevail against the Temple's authority.

On the eve of the Roman-Jewish War, accordingly, it would seem that the tendency aimed at breaching the wall of Jewish exclusivism among the Jesists—of enabling pagans to become messianists without becoming Jews—had been steadily dwindling. The Jewish Jesists in Jerusalem were simply integrated with the Temple.

Paul was undone by his confrontation with the Jesists, yet it was his independence of the flesh-and-blood Jesus that was to launch him on his posthumous career as a world-shaker.

Paul's "gospel," indeed, had no essential connection with the historic Jesus at all. Though a few facts scattered about his letters indicate that he thought Jesus was born of a normal Jewish woman in a normal way and was a descendant of King David, Paul shows no interest whatever in Jesus's real-life background. Even in referring to the crucial event of his own life, his conversion, Paul extracts Jesus from his natural habitat to such an extent that he says nothing whatever of the historical circumstances of the crucifixion, either its location in time or place; nor does he mention who did what, neither the Roman soldiers obeying Pilate nor the role of the Jewish authorities. He sees the crucifixion merely as the linchpin of the consummation of the divine scheme that made the demon-rulers of the current world-age, unwittingly and ultimately to their own undoing, crucify the "Lord of Glory" (1 Cor. 2:8). Just this absence of all data confirms, in a way, Paul's "gospel": "the gospel you heard me preach is no human invention" (Gal. 1:11, NEB).

Though Paul's ideas were ultimately—long after his death—to be transformed into a theology of a new religion, he himself had conceived or perhaps adapted them as an answer to a question that for him was purely historical. He had to explain, after his blinding flash of illumination on the road to Damascus, how it was that the Messianic Kingdom that was to be the preamble to the Kingdom of God had not *already* come about.

If Jesus had been resurrected and glorified by God and was, therefore, the Messiah ushering in the World's End Kingdom of God, how was it that the world had not, in fact, been transformed? How could the hiatus between Jesus's resurrection and the Kingdom of God at the World's End be explained.

Before Jesus's resurrection, Jews—no doubt including Jesus—who believed the Kingdom of God was at hand thought that the Messiah was simply to herald and accompany it. This was to create a state of bliss, after which there would be one Last Judgment for all the survivors of the Final Generation and for all the resurrected from all mankind. There was thus to be one state of bliss, one Last Judgment, one Kingdom of God, preceded, to be sure, by an interval (variously calculated) of the Messianic Kingdom, a mere prelude to the Kingdom of God.

Before Jesus's resurrection it had been taken for granted that those who were going to participate in the Kingdom of God would have died normally in order to be granted eternal life in the general resurrection together with the rest of the dead. (This situation, to be sure, had remained theoretical.)

But Jesus's resurrection upset all such calculations for those who believed in it. If God had, indeed, intervened by resurrecting and glorifying a Messiah, it could not be an isolated event; it had to mean something stupendous—that is, the World's End itself. Because of this, Paul thought his generation was already integrated with a process ineluctably working itself out, in which Jesus's death and resurrection were no more than the first phase. The final phase, which could not be very far off, was the Kingdom of God.

Thus the hiatus was utterly baffling. How could the Messiah come *without* being accompanied by the Kingdom of God?

If the Kingdom of God had in fact come about fairly soon after the resurrection, even a little later, there would, of course, have been no need for argument. But people kept dying normal deaths as the years went by, and Paul had to explain why believers who had died before the Messianic Kingdom initiated by Jesus's resurrection were nevertheless still entitled to a share in the Messianic Bliss. Paul had to demonstrate that even those who had died beforehand would infallibly be resurrected at the Glorious Return as long as they had proper faith in the redemptive effect of Jesus's crucifixion.

This was the problem Paul was confronted with, as it were, by history. He had to show that redemption was no longer merely "at hand," as Jesus and John the Baptist had proclaimed, but was *already* there.

He did this by creating a mythology anchored in his view of the Kingdom of God at the World's End as set in train by the resurrection of Jesus.

He amplified some basic concepts drawn both from Judaism and from his pagan environment and fused them together in a new system that, though Paul himself considered it to be inherently transient since it was linked to an event that was shortly to take place, proved cohesive and robust enough to sustain the disappointment of all his own hopes.

I shall indicate the steps taken by Paul (and/or some predecessors) that were to depart from the heritage of Judaism. These were the notion of the Son of God and of the Lord, and a number of rites and ceremonies that were expanded and deepened: baptism, the laying on of hands, the Eucharist.

I shall then touch on a vast umbrella concept, the Being-in-Christ, and its institutional embodiment—the Mystic Body of Christ, which long after Paul was to become the Church.[2]

Let us glance at the auxiliary ideas that were to prop up the concept of the mystic Body of Christ.

By the time Jesus was transposed to a pagan milieu, the word *messiah,* in Greek, *Christ,* had already become more or less meaningless. It had become a mere proper name—Jesus Christ or Christ Jesus. The additional epithet, "Lord," extended the usage of the Greek word *Kyrios* (a rough equivalent of the Aramaic *Maran*) so that the expression "Lord and Christ" became simply a name-plus-title of Jesus in which the original (Hebrew) sense of "Messiah" was missing altogether.

As "Christ Jesus" came to focus the emotions of the evolving coteries, the amplification, ultimately to the point of deification, of the original Jewish Messiah had to be fitted out with details, if the ascension was to be coherent. Of these details the most potent was the contrast established between the older, Jewish formula of the Son of Man and the word *Lord.*

The "Son of Man," taken from Daniel, written just before the Maccabean revolt in 165 B.C., was no more than an element in the Jewish pageant of the World's End. It had no meaning except to those who accepted the Jewish view of history to begin with. Thus the Son of Man had a World's End dimension intrinsically. Detached from the World's End, it was functionally, so to speak, senseless.

I have already indicated the expansion of the importance of Jesus's name for the earliest coteries. Paul was to fuse the magnification of the name with the word *Lord* and give the fusion remarkable potency.

"Lord" is a basic idea in all Paul's letters as well as throughout the Hellenistic parts of the New Testament. Paul expresses it with lapidary sharpness:

> God raised [Jesus] to the heights and bestowed on him the name above all names, that at the name of Jesus every knee should bow—in heaven, on earth, and in the depths—and every tongue confess, 'Jesus Christ is Lord,' to the glory of God the Father. (Phil. 2:9–11, NEB)

Now, since the notion of the "name to which everyone should bow" originally designated Yahweh, the all-powerful unique Creator of the Universe (as in Isaiah 45:23), it is plain that merely by using the Greek word *Kyrios* in the sense of "Lord," the entire substance of Yahweh was transferred to Jesus, without

Paul being aware, apparently, of the logical snag involved, since he goes on to say that this is all to the "glory of God the Father."

The word *Kyrios* was a common word used by Greek slaves for their master. Never used for the classical deities of antiquity, it was commonly applied to the salvation deities of Asia Minor, Syria, and Egypt when they were spoken of in Greek. It was also used for kings.

As the word and concept of the "Lord" became rooted in the emotions and imaginations of the new fellowship, the "Lord" acquired a new psychic dimension at the very moment of invocation. It became an actual, present dimension. For the believers gathered together "in his name," the "Lord" was really present *there and then*. It was an emotional fact of the current moment, independent of the historical or conceptual framework in which the Messiah had been linked beforehand to events in the world at large.

In the beginning, the use of the word *Lord* was dependent on the assumption of the Lord's Glorious Return, as in "the Lord is at hand" (Phil. 4:6, cf. Phil. 3:20).

It is the Lord who sits at the right hand of God and dominates the powers, and it is in the Lord's name that people are baptized.

The very power of the Last Supper is encapsulated in the phrase summing up his death and resurrection: "The Lord Jesus, on the night when he was betrayed . . ." (1 Cor. 11:23f.). The kernel of worship is "Jesus is Lord" (1 Cor. 12:3; Phil. 2:11), a formula that in and of itself represents the working of the Spirit (1 Cor. 12:3).

This notion of the Lord was intertwined with a further amplification of Jesus; he was turned by Paul (and/or his predecessors) into the "Son of God." The "Son of God," fused with the notion of the "Crucified One," constituted a new concept—the essence of the Redemptive Crucifixion in which a celestial personage from before the creation, an incarnation of the Spirit of God, comes down to earth to be the new Adam for a new mankind.

The simple-sounding phrase "Son of God" was the bedrock of this pregnant idea.

On the face of it, the notion that Yahweh, the Jewish God—

all-powerful, invisible, bodiless, unattainable, unknowable—
might have a *child,* might seem preposterous, indeed, gro-
tesquely incomprehensible.

To be sure, Jews famously called righteous Jews and even
righteous Gentile princes "sons of God" in a metaphorical
sense. In the Septuagint, moreover, the phrase "servant of
God," specifically someone inspired by God, was referred to in
a Greek phrase *pais tou theou,* in which the Greek word *pais*
means both servant and child. The transition between *pais*-
servant and *hios*-son was smooth: in Paul's writing it is basic.

Thus a trivial pun may have facilitated a transition of ideas.
Yet Paul's approach to this cosmic myth did not depend on such
wordplay. In his assertion that "God did not spare his own Son
but gave him up for us all" (Rom. 8:32), Paul soared beyond
verbalism to a profound conception of the working out of
human destiny.

For Paul, it was out of the question merely to deny Yahweh.
He took pains to distinguish between God and Lord Jesus. For
Paul, the Lord Jesus remained, somehow, dependent on God (1
Cor. 3:23), obeyed him "even unto death" (Phil. 2:8), and was
subject to him in all things (1 Cor. 15:28):

> For us there is one God, the Father, from whom are all things and
> for whom we exist, and one Lord, Jesus Christ, through whom
> are all things and through whom we exist. (1 Cor. 8:6)

At this point it did not, nor could it occur to Paul that the
relationship between Jesus and Yahweh had to be clarified (it
was not, in fact, to be settled for centuries, until the concept of
the Trinity was devised). In Paul's era it was downright insolu-
ble, since there was, at that time, an intellectually absolute
conflict between the swiftly expanding concept of Christ, Lord
of the Universe, and Yahweh, Creator of the Universe, that
could not be got round. The phrase "unto whom every knee
shall bow" was applied in the Hellenistic Jesist coteries to both
Jesus and God.

At the same time there was no need for Paul, despite his acute
mind, to worry too much about this conceptual puzzle. It did

not matter since, as we shall see, his view of current history made such conceptual problems entirely peripheral to the grand design working itself out, as he thought, with ineluctable immediacy.

For Paul, at that time, it was enough to describe Jesus in the threadbare metaphor mentioned above as the Spirit (2 Cor. 3:17). Jesus was somehow brought into line by the word *Spirit* with the One God, and at the same time referred to as the Son of God. For Paul, accordingly, "the Lord" was more or less a category of creation in and of himself—the category nearest God and hence "divine."

In any case, Paul's magnification of Jesus on a titanic scale, by the use of phrases hitherto reserved for Yahweh, and more particularly the transformation of Jesus into an object of cultic worship, brought about the outright apotheosis of Jesus.

In this way the twin notions of Jesus's execution being on the one hand a "stumbling block for the Jews" (how could a Messiah be defeated and hanged on wood to boot?) and on the other hand a folly for the pagans (how could a Jewish national ambition interest them?) were resolved by a far more grandiose scheme.

It is possible to distinguish a clear-cut line of development in this.

At the very outset, the content of the teaching about Jesus was succinct. It consisted of the bald statement "Jesus is the Messiah" (put in the mouth of Simon the Rock in the Gospel of Mark).

The earliest amplification of this was that God had raised Jesus from the dead (Rom. 10:9). This was soon, perhaps almost immediately, expanded that, i.e.,

> Christ died for our sins in accordance with the scriptures; that he was buried; that he was raised to life on the third day, according to the scriptures; and that he appeared to [Simon the Rock,] and afterwards to the Twelve. Then he appeared to over five hundred of our brothers at once, most of whom are still alive, though some have died. Then he appeared to [Upright Jacob], and afterwards to all the apostles. (1 Cor. 15:3–7 NEB)

This was what was "imparted" to Paul very early on in the formation of the Jesist coteries.

Though Mark was written a generation at least after Paul, it is evident that the terse formulation "Jesus is the Messiah" comes from before the later amplification found in Paul, which proved to be the groundwork of the profundification and ascension of meaning we are discussing. Initially, the paramount factor in the wording of the formulae found above was the fact of Jesus's career, interpreted in toto as the key to a new view of salvation. Thus, in the initial stage of the germination of a faith, the authority for its formulation was ascribed to Jesus not because of what he said but because of *what he was said to be*.

Now, though the early members of the pagan–Jewish fellowship established in Antioch in the Forties, and no doubt elsewhere in various Jewish communities around the Mediterranean, were perhaps unaware of the implications in the contrast between the historical, World's End magnitude of the Son of Man idea, and the extrahistorical, currently present, mystically perceived cosmological magnitude of Christ Jesus as Lord of the Universe, the two ideas are plainly in irreconcilable contrast, both intellectually and, more important, emotionally. As we know, the Son of Man idea, an element of World's End theorizing, was doomed; the other concept was to play a seminal role.

Thus the formation of the "christology" attributed to Paul became the unique channel for the implementation of a pregnant idea resting on two seemingly simple emotional-conceptual pillars: "faith in the Lord" and the ritual of his worship.

Without discussing Paul's actual originality, the achievement associated with his name may be summed up as follows.

Jesus became the all-accomplishing executive agency of God, existent before time and before the world, the Incarnation of the Holy Spirit that constitutes the divine principle of his Being. This Eternal Being, the Lord, is charged with the execution of God's great design for the regeneration and salvation of all mankind.

Jesus's strange death is finally made intelligible. Mankind, sagging beneath the weight of its sins and unable, by itself, to rise and face the divine light, is offered the means to accomplish this by the Lord, who has willingly taken the guilt of all mankind on himself and has expiated their sins by means of his ignominious death.

Now all that was necessary was for mankind to bring about a union with Christ the Lord through faith and love.

The "stumbling block" of the cross has been transformed into the Supreme Mystery—the paramount end of the mission of Lord Jesus.

Paul's master statement—that he preached nothing but "Christ crucified"—is merely the barest indication of the endless range of the potentialities ascribed to this cosmic idea. It was his two-pronged concept—the faith in the Risen Jesus, Son of God and Lord of the Universe, and its ritualized worship—that was to become the launching platform of a new faith.

The expansion of the personage of Jesus was, naturally, paralleled by the expansion of various rites inherent in the formation of religious groups in those days—in this case, baptism, the laying on of hands, and, most important, the consuming of the body and the blood of Jesus (the Eucharist).

All these three rites had, to be sure, Jewish roots. They had been taken abroad by the first Jesists, devout Jews, in addition to circumcision and the dietary laws.

The most general of these three rites was, no doubt, baptism, an ancient custom originally symbolizing the acceptance of a convert.

Baptism is a prime example of how a purely symbolic ceremony could be charged with magical potential.

The Kingdom of God, accepted with ardor, could lead naturally to symbolical expressions. One of the elements inherent in the concept of the Kingdom of God, for instance, was the notion of membership in the Elite who would survive into the Kingdom. This notion, felt as redemption, led naturally to symbols (rooted in various prophetic texts) that enhanced emotionally the expectation of something in the future, and thus to sacraments conceived of as helpful in bringing about salvation, by material means, once the Kingdom of God was installed.

Ezekiel may be taken as a model:

"I will sprinkle clean water upon you, and you shall be clean. . . .
A new Spirit I will put within you." (Ezek. 36:25–26; see also Isa.
1:15–16, 4:3–4; Jer. 4:14; Zech. 13:1)

In this stage the sacraments were merely semimagical. Their
symbolism lent emotional enhancement to an expectation in the
future. We shall see how, with the extinction of the Kingdom of
God in the sense of the material transformation of the world,
the semimagical sacraments within the structure of the Church
that was ultimately to replace the Kingdom of God were to
become fully magical.

In the beginning, baptism, practiced by the Jerusalem Jesists
as an anodyne rite signalizing a distinction of no substance
between themselves and other Jews, was to be expanded in the
Greek-speaking Diaspora into the actual seal of adherence to a
self-consciously distinct group.

Baptism did not go back to the authority of Jesus at all. As I
have indicated above, the ancient rite had been taken over by
John the Baptist, who gave it new life by making it the hallmark
of distinction between his own partisans and the unregenerate
Jews who were paying taxes to the pagan Romans.

Thus, though Jesus in the initial phase of his activity had been
a partisan of John's and had accordingly accepted the rite in that
sense, he had abandoned it on his return to the settled areas to
harangue Jews there as part of his own strategy for "Forcing the
End."

At that point, accordingly, Jesus became known for his *avoid-
ance* of baptism. Not only is there not a single instance of a
baptism administered by Jesus recorded in the first three (Synoptic) Gospels, but it is chronicled explicitly that though his
disciples baptized (John 4:2) Jesus himself never did.

We know from this that the merger between the Jesists and
the partisans of John the Baptist took place very early on, so
that baptism became current practice among the Jesist coteries
both in Jerusalem and elsewhere.

Throughout the Gospels, indeed, the impression is painstakingly made that the Baptist was the "greatest man born of woman" because Jesus said so, but at the same time he was no more than the precursor of Jesus. It is because of this, in fact, that it seems sensible to accept the historical fact that Jesus had been a member of John's group at the outset, since it could scarcely have been invented after Jesus's ascension. At the same time it is obviously soft-pedalled in the attempt to keep John in a revered, but secondary, position.

Thus, after praising John as the greatest man ever born, Jesus goes on to say: "Yet he who is least [perhaps "junior"] in the Kingdom of Heaven is greater than he" (Matt. 11:11). And the much later Gospel of John says, without mincing words, that John was "not the light, but came to bear witness to the light" (John 1:8).

In the Greek-speaking Diaspora, in any case, baptism came to play the same role as circumcision. It separated the baptized from the nonbaptized even more than it functioned as a rite of admission.

At some point it came to play a cardinal role for those pagan God-fearers who, while reluctant to take on the burden of circumcision and the dietary laws, nevertheless revered the God of Israel. In the earliest period, of course, such God-fearers could become Jesists only as part of their attachment to Judaism. It was not until much later that it was to be possible for a pagan to become a Jesist directly, after the early coteries had turned into autonomous self-conscious organizations.

The new group, marked out within the body of Jewry by its special belief in Jesus, naturally stressed the *sign* of its allegiance, baptism, which meant precisely the sign of consecration in such a group as well as the more general sign of purification. Pagans, accordingly, would tend to stress the importance of baptism as distinguishing them from the pagan milieu that they were leaving behind. Thus baptism, distinguishing believers from non-believers, also brought to its recipient, together with purification, a basic sanctification. The baptized recruit became, as it were, the slave of the Lord, the property of God, from then on marked for the Kingdom of God by virtue of the name of "Christ Jesus."

Thus, because of the genesis of the new coteries and the preponderance of pagan recruits, baptism overrode all other observances. Those who received baptism became fellows in the same community as the others who had been baptized. Baptism became in and of itself a criterion of communion, downgrading the importance of what would otherwise seem the "impurity" for normative Jews of associating at the table with nonconverted pagans.

Very quickly, accordingly, if not at the very outset, baptism came to mean the bond that made brothers out of those initiated into what was now becoming a revelation about the unique nature of Jesus. It constituted, in fact, the entry into a new "Mystery"—the "Christian Mystery." It was baptism that implemented the communion of the new believers in "The Christ," by now no longer, of course, the Jewish Messiah whose significance derived entirely from his part in the cosmic drama of the installation of the Kingdom of God, but the prototype of a cosmic authority in his own right.

In a coterie like the mixed Jewish–pagan groups in Antioch, where no one would in any case have been personally familiar with the historical Jesus of Nazareth, once the figure of "The Christ" was detached from the Jewish historical matrix in which the concept had been born, it already contained, as it were, in the logic of its singularity, a dynamic impulse toward expansion. The very fact of having to express on the one hand allegiance to a singular group and on the other, to express a fervent faith in an unknown individual of itself created a chain of self-escalation.

Thus, in a milieu remote from the historical milieu of Jesus in Palestine, both the person of the historical Jesus and his role, that is, his *meaning* in his own historical surroundings, were stripped of everything that had connected him with Judaism and, more particularly, the messianism that had arisen against a Jewish background, in favor of a much grander and potentially limitless concept—that of the Lord.

Paul makes this process obvious: "You all being assembled in the name of our Lord Jesus, and I with you in spirit, with the power of our Lord Jesus" (1 Cor. 5:4 NEB).

For people who could articulate this concept with feeling, the person of the Lord, indeed the actual *name* of the Lord, must in and of itself have been transformed into a constituent element of an actual cult. The mere fact of pronouncing it against the background of an emotionally grounded religious fellowship sufficed, in the feelings of the believers, to establish the real presence of the person of Christ Jesus and the power arising out of his name.

Acclimating baptism in a pagan environment was to enhance the merely symbolic value of traditional baptism by a new and magical dimension fundamentally different from the mere symbolism of baptism implied by immersion (Acts 1:5; Mark 1:8). Baptism as escalated in the Diaspora passes on the Spirit to the convert; that is, it brings about a material–spiritual change. Because of this the baptism associated with John the Baptist could be looked down on in the evolving theory of the Jesists, only a couple of generations later, as being no more than meaningless immersion in water, with no relation at all to the Spirit (Acts 19:1–6).

It was only the baptism established much later on that could "bestow the Spirit" (Mark 1:8). The distinction was introduced very early into the very sources recording the adaptation. The new converts to the Jesist coteries in the Diaspora were necessarily baptized "with the Spirit." The new baptism had the effect of forgiveness of sins through the bestowal of the Spirit as part of the installation of the Messianic Kingdom at the World's End. The one being baptized "confessed," that is, he acknowledged his sins and his belief in Jesus Christ. The baptism was "in" or "on the name" of the "Lord Jesus," an unvarying component of a formula.

Baptism in this early period involved immersion, generally with an actual baptizer present, or it took place, at least, in the presence of the community. Paul himself was baptized (Acts 9:18). He already found the custom established very early on, by the time of his conversion a few years after Jesus's crucifixion.

Baptism itself was an adjunct to a perhaps still more ancient practice—the laying on of hands (to this day the form of transmission of the status of rabbi). This aspect of Jewish practice goes back to the actual behavior of Jesus himself (Mark 5:23; Matt. 9:18, 19:13–15; Luke 4:40, 13:13). The laying on of hands might well have preceded baptism as the first rite of admission to the newly formed Jesist coteries.

But once again, as in baptism, the laying on of hands was no longer a merely symbolical, or commemorative, gesture. It transmitted to recruits the essence of the potency inherent in Jesus: the light, the grace, the power, the knowledge.

In the very early days there was no distinction between one group of believers and another; that is, there was still no organization. Holiness was pooled, so to speak, by all believers. The saint who made a convert also had to make that convert a saint.

The last of the three rites that were practiced in the early Diaspora coteries was the Eucharist—the eating of the body and drinking of the blood of Jesus the Christ.

Insofar as the Eucharist constituted a repetition of an actual meal, it goes back to the Last Supper partaken of by Jesus and his followers on the eve of his arrest. Bread breaking in a Jewish milieu was, of course, accompanied by ritual benedictions. The commemoration of the Last Supper by the Jerusalem Jesists was surely accompanied by symbolical repetitions as part of the commemoration of their lost leader.

At the very outset we see a situation that was, basically, an aspect of human fellowship. No particular significance had been given, as yet, to an ordinary, normal, day-to-day activity (Acts 2:42, 46). Meals consisted of ordinary table fellowship, with bread being broken and people praying. In their daily lives the Jesists were merely described as being assiduous in worship at the Temple, the citadel of Judaism; their breaking of bread took place in the home "with glad and generous hearts."

The eating of the meal was normal; it is mentioned with concrete precision. On the other hand, it was a normal routine that was restricted to the members of the group. In principle, they were listening to the authoritative members of the group (the "apostles") discoursing, in the early days, no doubt, in such a manner as to make it clear to the believers what the point of their communion was. In the beginning, accordingly, it was merely a sign, no doubt unconscious, of fraternity.

Paul (and/or his predecessors) gave the simple rite of bread breaking a cosmic dimension, an effect of power. He welded it to the drama of Jesus's Redemptive Crucifixion. By planting in a terrain prepared before him, he turned the originally simple rite of bread breaking and wine drinking into the focal mechanism, indeed the very axis, of the accomplishment of a new Mystery. He transformed it from the mere symbolic memorial of a beloved leader, which it might conceivably have been in the Jerusalem coterie, into the living, functioning, efficacious mechanism of the cosmic process implied by the meaning of the crucifixion.

Thus, the very kernel of the burgeoning faith as formulated by Paul contained a full-fledged pagan concept:

> The Lord Jesus on the night when he was betrayed took bread, . . . he broke it, and said, "This is my body which is for you. Do this in remembrance of me." In the same way also the cup, after supper, saying, "This cup is the new covenant in my blood; drink it, in remembrance of me." For as often as you eat this bread and drink the cup, you proclaim the Lord's death until he comes. (1 Cor. 11:23–26)

The simplicity of the potent transformation is striking.

Merely by linking the homely notion of "remembering" to a magical symbol, by charging the homely symbols of bread and wine with the full energy of the cosmological Mystery and attaching them to the accomplishment entailed by his conception of Jesus's Redemptive Crucifixion, by making the believers "proclaim the Lord's death until he comes," Paul had created the core of a new faith.

I have used the word *mystery;* it was part of Paul's vocabulary. Let us glance at its background.

In the Roman Empire around this time there was a cluster of divinities resembling each other to the point of confusion. The principal ones were Osiris in Egypt, Dionysius in Greece, Tammuz and Marduk in Mesopotamia, Melkart in Phoenicia (northern Palestine and Syria), Adonis in Syria, and Attis in Phrygia. To top it off, a Persian deity, Mithra, was beginning to penetrate the Roman Empire.

There was a constant interchange of ideas, religious forms, rites of worship, and so on, carried out by countless travelers going back and forth throughout the whole of this huge area, now in the grip of sociopolitical turbulence as never before. Thus travelers to different places in Asia Minor and Mesopotamia, Greece, and Egypt would encounter not merely closely similar trends but well-nigh identical expressions of religious concepts in myths that also resembled each other very closely and were consummated in ceremonies that were very much alike. The myths did not necessarily spring from an identical source but were simply given rise to by fundamental longings common to multitudes of people now undergoing experiences of much the same kind because of the vast upheavals throughout the Roman Empire through constant wars, transfers of populations, enslavements, the spread of commerce, and similar basic phenomena.

The very kinship of such beliefs and rites naturally reinforced the attractiveness of exchanges and their consequent intertwining.

If a single cause can be assigned to this medley of pagan mythologies and practices, it lies in the simple desire to offer people a hope of immortality and a means of securing it. It may well be that the uncertainty of life in the hurly-burly of the establishment of the Roman Empire, the collapse of seemingly stable institutions, and the rending of the social fabric made such longings, perhaps a component of human nature, still more poignant.

In any case, this was the cardinal purpose of all the Mysteries and the rationale of their fundamental rites and ideas.

All the various gods mentioned above were supposed to die at a certain season of the year and be restored to life a little later. Thus we may imagine that the emotions of their devotees were alternately depressed and exhilarated: anguish was followed by joy.

On the other hand, these deities, like the extinct gods of the Greek Olympus before them, were not true gods; they were not conceived of as being masters of the universe but were rather like men. Although imbued with special powers, they were nevertheless subject to fate. They did, in fact, die.

Attis, a shepherd, and Adonis, the son of an incestuous union, were conceived of as actual men deified by the will of the gods. Some of the gods had originally been astral divinities; others were agricultural symbols. Mithra was evidently a solar deity born at the winter solstice on December 25; Tammuz was a god of vegetation killed by the heat of the summer and revived by the first breath of spring.

This was true of Adonis too and of most of the gods who died and rose again. Because of their connection with vegetable life on earth, it was easy to believe in them as solar deities.

Most of these gods were connected with a goddess, too, who personified the earth or the fecundity of nature and gave birth to other gods. This was how the Great Mother Cybele treated Attis; Belti-Aphrodite treated Adonis; Ishtar, Tammuz; and Isis, Osiris. This was also why the gods were coupled with goddesses and simultaneously adored. They were imagined as living together in the same temple. There was, to cap all this off, a movement of steady increase in divine power in all these gods. Because of the importance they exercised in human lives, there was a tendency for them all to become more and more divine and ultimately, within their own spheres, sovereign, though none of them ever ascended to the level of the unique and all-powerful Yahweh.

This was relevant to the evolution of the Jesist coteries because of the form of the cult; that is, the practical, physical interpretation of the myth of the gods of death and resurrection.

Their festivals, for instance, consisted of dramas enacting a characteristic form of the death and resurrection of the god. This was duplicated twice annually, in the appropriate season.

It was this myth, well-nigh standard for all the Mysteries, that came to be thought of as the visible, palpable expression of the vast mystery of human existence. Life, after all, was brief, unsatisfactory, perhaps generally disappointing; happiness was rare and fugitive. This lent force to the compensatory idea that the death of the body would be followed for an indefinitely long period by another type of existence, both blessed and endless, to be enjoyed by people's souls, that is, the nonmaterial part of their persons.

But on the face of it, this was out of the question for people by themselves. An intercessor was indispensable, a divine mediator to link the longings of mortal men to their realizations. It was just this role that was performed by the dying god who was restored to life.

A close parallel was established in the drama of the Mysteries. The god suffers, much like man; he dies, too, again like man. The subsequent restoration of the god to life is a powerful symbol of the god's triumph over suffering and death.

At the same time, the god's terrestrial existence is symbolically dramatized and thus renewed in annual ceremonies. The idea is fixed in the mind of the believer that from the very hour of the god's resurrection the believer himself begins to enjoy the bliss of immortality of the god himself.

Thus, for the believers in these dying-and-rising gods, the problem of salvation is simplified. Since they are already linked to the god's sufferings and death precisely by virtue of their very humanity, all they have to do is contrive the final link in the chain of their association with the god they worship in order to ensure their own resurrection and survival in timeless bliss.

In this framework, accordingly, the contrivance of personal salvation is solved by a sort of a ceremonial charade made up of ritual practices imbued with power—magical procedures.

The believer undergoes, by symbolical stages, the various stages of the ordeals through which the god too has passed. These are the outward signs of an identification with the god that in their nature are capable of transforming the believer's very being. Thus they constitute a guarantee that the believer's own future will be just like that of the god. Beyond the sufferings of life in this world and beyond the death of the body, there is a guaranteed prospect of immortality.

In this way a close fusion of two things has come into being in the mind of the believer. A model has been established in which the destiny of the divine savior—the dying and rising god—is both the model and the guarantee of the destiny confronting the believer. In addition, there is the further satisfaction that the mind of the believer is merely recording an objective fact in his natural relationship to the world. His destiny is not only in his mind, after all, but is itself the reflection of something that has taken place objectively.

Though not all details about these various Mysteries are clear, all such rites have an identical purpose—the integration of the believers' destiny with that of all the believers in the given savior.

Two of these ceremonies are of special relevance to the evolution of the belief in Jesus during its transformation from a mere opinion concerning the role of the historical Jesus into a conviction of his meaning as a cosmic savior.

In the Phrygian cult of Cybele and Attis (and in other Asiatic cults as well, including Mithraism) there was something called a "taurobolium" (the sacrifice of a bull) or a "criobolium" (the sacrifice of a he-goat).

A deep pit was excavated near the temple of the god. The initiates descended into it, and the excavation was covered over with a grillwork on which a bull was ceremoniously sacrificed. Its fresh blood gushed out through the grillwork onto the naked body of the novice, who tried to immerse himself in it. After this ceremonial bloodbath was performed, the beast's genital organs were laid away in a sacred vessel as an offering to the goddess and were then buried beneath a memorial altar.

In the very beginnng these rites were not meant to ensure the immortality of the initiate, but were merely meant to secure the cooperation of Cybele and Attis, who were thought of as in control of nature, just as the Dionysaic initiation was supposed to draw orgiasts of both sexes into a fertile partnership through the magical influence of Dionysius.

However, during the early period of the Roman Empire the taurobolium had evolved into an efficacious, magical means of ensuring immortality, based on the following mechanism of symbolic identification.

The pit was thought of as the kingdom of the dead. Descending into it, the initiate was thought of as dying. The bull was Attis himself, and the blood shed by it during its sacrifice was considered the vital principle emanating from the god. The initiate received it and absorbed it through his very skin. On leaving the pit he was said to have been "born again" and was given milk to drink like a child.

But he was not born a mere *man* again; the magical procedure had transmitted to the initiate the very essence of the god. The initiate had become *an Attis;* from then on he was, for a time, saluted as such. It was incumbent on him now to couple with the goddess. This was accomplished via the offering of the bull's genitals, carried out mystically by rites in the nuptial chamber of the Great Mother. (The mutilation of the bull reenacted Attis's self-castration, followed by his death.)

For a certain length of time, accordingly, the initiate was assured that his fate would be just like Attis's—that a happy resurrection and survival among the gods awaited him.

In many of the cults of the savior and intercessor gods— Cybele, Mithra, the Syrian Baals, and so forth—the beneficial union obtained through initiation was renewed, or perhaps revived, through sacred meals partaken of by members of the cult gathered together at the table of the god. Occasionally this ritual banquet merely symbolized the brotherhood of the initiated fellows; sometimes, however, the common repast brought about a union with the god himself. Thus participation in the god's very substance and all his characteristics was brought about via the communion over the actual food.[3]

In Tarsus, where Paul spent his childhood, one of the two divinities—Sandan and Baal-Tarz (the equivalent of the Greek Sandan and Hercules)—was a god of fertility and vegetation; he was also an intercessor. Once a year a festival was held in his honor. He was shown dying on a funeral pyre and going to heaven. He was looked on just like Attis in Phrygia, Adonis in Syria, Osiris in Egypt, and Tammuz in Babylonia.

Thus Paul was surely familiar with the idea of "salvation" secured through the mediation of a god who died and rose again and whose followers shared his destiny by uniting themselves to him in a mystic union that was acted out not merely by the purely psychological features of subjective reactions but above all by rites that were not only symbolic but potent, magical.

All this would have been public in its very nature. There was, to be sure, a secret aspect—for example, the compelling Mystery that in the mind of the believer had altered his or her very being—but the actual belief and hope as well as the publicly performed rites were all open to nonbelievers.

It is hard to avoid being struck by a structural likeness between the baptism and Eucharist of the Jesist coteries and the procedures of the oriental Mysteries. From Paul himself on, indeed, and down through St. Augustine centuries later, the Church Fathers were themselves impressed by these resemblances and had to explain them away, to be sure in their own manner. They said the Devil himself had sought to deceive people by imitating Christian practices, which had themselves been imitated by the pagan Mysteries.

Historically speaking, this would seem to have been a misunderstanding. Both the essential myths, the principal ceremonies, and the symbols for bringing about salvation go back well before the emergence of the Jesists. In Paul's own day, any number of forms of worship for expressing these myths were well known.

It is plain, in fact, that the similarity goes far beyond a mere resemblance between specific rites. The fundamental issue was a certain conception of destiny and salvation as such. A divine Lord was trusted, a being who was in some way an intermediary between human affairs and the Supreme Divinity (a somewhat vague notion that without being identical with the specific omnipotence and uniqueness of the Jewish Yahweh had been acquiring currency in the ancient world). This intermediary had deigned to live and suffer like a man so that it would be possible for men to resemble him enough to unite with him and thus, through identifying themselves with him precisely by such a union, to be saved for immortality.

Paul even gave the expanded form of baptism current in the early coteries a specific application to the Mysteries: "For as many of you as were baptized into Christ have put on Christ" (Gal. 3:27).

This was, plainly, exactly the form of the taurobolium and criobolium. By baptism the believer in Jesus "puts on Christ," just like a sacred garment of salvation. He goes down into death by plunging into a river or the baptismal pool and rises out of it, after three immersions, just as Christ rose from the tomb on the third day. Like Christ, accordingly, the believer is given the assurance that he too will be glorified and given eternal life.

The baptism devised by Paul and his models did not, to be sure, make the believer "a Christ," as in many Mysteries it made the believer *"an* Osiris," *an* Adonis. That was impossible because of the endless magnification of the persona and role of the new Savior of Mankind and Lord of the Universe. But short of that, Paul's baptism functioned emotionally and conceptually, that is, mystically, on the same plane as the cluster of concepts that established the claims of the taurobolium.

Yet all the above was, so to speak, a matter of modality. The rites, ceremonies, and symbols were to achieve their institutional consummation in the umbrella concepts I have referred to: the Being-in-Christ and the Mystic Body of Christ.

I have said that the urgent problem Paul had to solve, the hiatus between the resurrection of Jesus and the onset of the Messianic Kingdom, had led him to the expansion of the rites and symbols discussed above. But the essence of the problem was epitomized by an intractable, very simple fact of nature. Believers in Jesus's resurrection were dying, as it seemed, "normally." Thus, in order to accommodate the normal deaths going on around him while the Messianic Kingdom, preamble to the Kingdom of God, kept failing to expand beyond the single, though stupendous fact of Jesus's resurrection, Paul invented *two resurrections for believers.*

The persistence of natural death implied, for Paul, that the first entrants to the Messianic Kingdom were already in the resurrection "way of life," and also that even those of the Elect who had died *before* the advent of the Messianic Kingdom would share in it, nevertheless, via Jesus's resurrection.

Like some other messianic theorists, Paul distinguished between the transient bliss of the Messianic Kingdom and the Eternal Bliss of the Kingdom of God. The Elect of the Final Generation (his own) naturally had both. For them the Messianic Kingdom and the Kingdom of God had the same effect. Entry into the Messianic Kingdom, and hence into the Kingdom of God that followed it, was the privilege of the Elect of the Final Generation, the reward of their faith in Paul's expanded concept of Jesus.

But Paul thought the Last Judgment on all the resurrected from all mankind throughout history had to wait for the Messianic Kingdom to yield to the Kingdom of God.

Now, if the Messianic Kingdom was transitory, how could its participants be immortal?

Paul contrived a device to make it possible for believers who had died before the Messianic Kingdom not to have to wait for the general resurrection following the end of the Messianic Kingdom. Their faith was to give them a special privilege.

They would be granted an earlier resurrection for themselves alone. This would enable them to share the Messianic Bliss just like those of the Elect of the Final Generation.

For Paul it was not the dead *in general* who were to be resurrected by the Messianic Kingdom, but those who died full of faith in Jesus Christ. These believers, dying before the Messianic Kingdom, would not have to wait at all. They would be resurrected into the Messianic Kingdom at once; while other people, later on, would be given a second resurrection in which all the people who had ever lived would, before the Last Judgment at the end of the Messianic Kingdom, pass before the throne of God to be dealt eternal life or eternal torment.

In this way believers dying full of faith in Jesus Christ would be given eternal life even in the transitory Messianic Kingdom. Even though they would *look* like everyone else in the Messianic Kingdom initiated by Jesus's resurrection, they would, in fact, be wholly different. Even though still in the Messianic Kingdom, they would have taken on the resurrection "way of life" just like the Messiah himself.

It was this device that brought about the projection of a novel idea. As we shall see, it was to have the most sweeping effect on history.

To explain how mortals could live side by side with the

Eternal resurrected in a transitory Messianic Kingdom, Paul had to contrive an institution to implement his new and original idea.

Taking the existence of the Jesists as his starting point, he created an outsize, symbolic dimension for them as a collectivity. He invented a new condition of the universe—the Being-in-Christ, and along with it a metaphysical institution to implement it—the Mystic Body of Christ.

This concept enabled Paul to assure believers that despite their having died before the Glorious Return, they would not just be dead like other people who had died but would be raised up at the Glorious Return in a preliminary resurrection.

To show how the Elect could benefit practically from the fact of their faith, Paul had to show how the community of the Jesists and the Savior, a community established by the faith of the faithful, could come into existence.

To accomplish this, Paul contrived the broader idea that the divine powers already at work within the person of Lord Jesus could somehow permeate all those linked to him by virtue of their faith. The notion of the permeation had to be made intelligible, and for this the material concept of the Body of Christ was the indispensable material underpinning of the condition of the universe constituted by the Being-in-Christ.

By contriving a palpable, institutional supplement to the mere concept of the Being-in-Christ, Paul brought about an innovation that was to create a new institution, a universal Church amplifying the preordained "community of saints" and physically embodying the communion established by the intermingling of divine powers between the Savior and his worshipers.

In and of itself, this idea was an echo of the notion that the Chosen People, the Jews, contaminated by evildoers of one kind of another, had to purge themselves, leaving only the Elect remnant on hand to become the Elect of the Messianic Kingdom. The concept of election was organically bound up with the concept of sifting.

For Paul the faithful were "called" to sainthood (1 Cor. 1:2, Rom. 1:7). He identified a preexistent community of saints with the inhabitants of a preexistent heavenly Jerusalem and linked this community to a Greek word *ekklesia* (congregation), not merely for a specific, real-life congregation but for the spiritual yet tangible collectivity of the Mystic Body of Christ. For Paul, to be sure, the *ekklesia* made up of "saints" and the "Elect" had meaning only as framed by the imminent installation of the Messianic Kingdom at the World's End.

Paul meant the Mystic Body of Christ to constitute a new kind of *bodily* identity between the Elect and the glorified death-less body of the Risen Christ. For him, this bodily identity was a natural fact—full-bodied, concrete, palpable. Believers were supposed to be, and felt themselves to be, "in Christ" bodily.

They were, in fact, a special race of human beings, entirely extricated from the ordinary category of existence of human beings beforehand. Their belief was not a mere opinion—it turned them into mystical participants in another condition of nature: the death and resurrection of a divine being.

Thus they were not natural people like others, but people who had already passed through death and resurrection along with Jesus. Because of this, when the Messianic Kingdom came about they would be capable, intrinsically, of sharing in the resurrection "way of life," while everyone else would simply die.

Similarly, those who had died before the Glorious Return, though apparently dead in a normal way, were not really dead at all. They would be able to rise again before the general resurrection at the end of the Messianic Kingdom, as long as they had died "in Christ."

For Paul, human beings in the current epoch were *not* equal. It was not people as such who could enter into a special relationship of some kind with God, but only the *elected:* "There is neither Jew nor Greek, there is neither slave nor free, there is neither male nor female; for you are all one in Christ Jesus" (Gal. 3:28).

It was the aim of the Being-in-Christ to wipe out just this hierarchy, for according to Paul it was only "in Christ" that the Elect of the human race were to attain a blissful sameness. That was why he insisted that the Being-in-Christ would terminate once and for all the whole present division of mankind. It was *only* in Christ that *all* divisions would vanish. I.e., the world would be another world.

Paul, like Jewish thinkers in general, took it for granted that God and the universe were totally distinct. God, a unique will, had created the universe but stood outside it. For Paul, history consisted of the emanation of the world from the mind and will of God, its alienation from God, then its ultimate return to God. Thus he conceptualized a cosmic drama in which the return to God was brought about in the current epoch by the redemptive function of Lord Jesus. In this view it was merely common sense to say that everything comes from God, or through God, and will go back to God, but can never, in the current epoch, be *in* God. This is precisely the significance of the World's End: people and the world—every pagan, Jew man, woman—will be in God (Rom. 11:36) only at the *end* of the drama.

Further, men are separated from God not merely by being radically distinct but by an insurmountable barrier—the dominion of angels. For Paul it was the angelic powers, in the current epoch, that prevented a direct relationship between God and man. The chief benefit of being one of the Elect-in-Christ was that the angelic dominion was terminated; the love of God was no longer barred from finding its way to the Elect (Rom. 8:38–39).

Christ had to overcome the Angelic Powers throughout the Messianic Age; it was when death, the last enemy, was destroyed that the power bestowed on Christ would no longer be needed. At that time God would be all in all (1 Cor. 15:26–28). When the present workaday world passes away, once and for all, there will then be a Being-in-God, for which the Being-in-Christ will have been the indispensable preliminary phase.

Paul's key concept of the Being-in-Christ was to revolutionize the conventional sense of time. Beforehand it was simple: a *Then* preceded a *Now*. According to this ordinary, banal view, the death and resurrection of Jesus had taken place in the recent past and, by virtue of having taken place, had enabled Lord Jesus to return in glory in the near future, bringing with him the Messianic Kingdom, prelude to the Kingdom of God.

But Paul's idea of Being-in-Christ made it possible to think of successive periods of time as being, in some way, simultaneous. He could proclaim that the titanic event of Jesus's resurrection was merely the initial event of a whole series whose totality would constitute a new world, and that the Messianic Age had already dawned.

Thus Paul's generation was already in the process of messianic resurrection even though the resurrection of others still lay in the future. Even though the world looked the same, Paul could, uniquely, see forces working that were different from those imagined by others. Jesus's resurrection demonstrated for him that the powers of the supernatural world were undermining the seemingly natural world and triggering, in the immediate future, the installation of the supernatural world.

This blurring of the distinction between succcessive periods of time enabled Paul to intermingle two worlds hitherto entirely distinct—the transitory and the eternal world—just as he had intertwined the concepts of Then and Now. For him alone faith was no longer a trusting reliance on something expected to take place, but a state of mind equipped to digest *current certainties of the psyche*.

He had to destroy this vulgar view of sequentiality in order to reap the benefit of the special resurrection he was reserving for the true believers who had died before the Messianic Kingdom. Thus he claimed something special—that even now, with people walking about looking ordinary, the solidarity of the Elect and the Savior was already working itself out. It was the privilege of the Elect to share resurrection with Jesus before the rest of the dead were resurrected. Indeed, this was what the predestination of those called to the Messianic Kingdom consisted of—they were predestined to acquire the resurrection medium of existence in advance of the Messianic Kingdom.

Without perhaps realizing it, Paul had upset all previous theories of the World's End. He had pulverized the conventional view of time as sequential, and created a special dialectic of progression—simultaneity amidst sequence.

Thus the stupendously novel fact of Jesus's resurrection and glorification had this effect: it not only created a special race of human beings but also a special mode of existence in the universe. It gave rise to a community of human beings unlike all others—bound to each other and to Jesus in a unique manner. Because of Jesus's resurrection the entire community of the Elect to the Messianic Kingdom had been permeated through and through by resurrection, as though it were an attribute that could be shared by many. In Albert Schweitzer's words, they were like a "mass of piled up fuel, which the fire kindled there immediately spreads through."

Paul expressed this literal idea unmistakably: "[Jesus] died for us so that whether we wake or sleep we might live with him (1 Thess. 5:10).

This creation of a new category of people as well as a new category of existence enabled Paul to bypass the apparent conundrum of the hiatus between the resurrection and glorification of Jesus and the postponement of the Messianic Kingdom at his Glorious Return. It was now a mere gap bridged by Paul's contrivance of the Being-in-Christ plus the Mystic Body of Christ. A bridge cannot, to be sure, be extended indefinitely.

Paul's idea was both simple and all-encompassing. It created a situation in which the believer's entire being, including his most elemental thoughts, feelings, and actions, could be brought into a highly charged atmosphere of personal mysticism accessible to everyone.

Accordingly, even though Paul's Being-in-Christ was identical in structure with the Hellenistic Mysteries in which daily life simply went on independent of the mystical experience of the believer, it was far more potent and pervasive because of its historicity, its "objectivity," and its dramatic potential.

We shall soon see how it came about that the tailoring of the institution of the Mystic Body of Christ to fit the original notion of the Being-in-Christ was to lay the foundations of an entirely novel institution that Paul, bound as he was to the history of his own era, could never have foreseen, since for him the world was to end very soon. We shall see what happened when his expectations were not realized and when the World's End he confidently expected, not more than forty years from the date of Jesus's resurrection, did not take place.

It should be recalled once again that none of this may actually have originated with Paul personally. The real initiators of the new faith were the founders, all of them unknown, of the Jesist coterie in Antioch. Nevertheless, through what was, unforeseeably, to happen to the Jewish State and subsequently to Jewry at large, the legacy of Paul's handiwork was far ampler and more clearly and potently defined. Because of his intense activity and because of the strange fact that no one else did any writing, we ascribe to Paul the primary role in bringing about the fusion of two elements: the historical element of Jewish messianism and the conceptual, cosmic element immanent in the Mysteries of the Greco-Roman world.

In this sense it seems quite accurate to ascribe to Paul the primary responsibility of creating the central doctrines of what was ultimately to be consolidated as a new religion—Christianity.

CHAPTER V

THE GREAT DIVIDE: The Temple Destroyed

*T*he intellectual ferment that was to produce a new religion took place initially against a starkly mundane background—the growing Kingdom of God agitation aimed at the Roman Empire.

The movement launched by Judah the Galilean in 6 A.D., when Judea-Samaria came directly under Roman administration, preoccupied Palestinian Jewry for a generation after Jesus and still another generation until the crushing of the Bar Kochba revolt in 135 A.D.

From Pontius Pilate's term of office (ca. 26–36) until the Jewish revolt of 66–70, the country was seething with armed rebellions, intrigues, conspiracies, and countless crucifixions: the various forces of the country—religious rebels, priestly aristocrats, Roman officials, the royal Jewish family and the infuriated Jewish peasantry—plunged society in a massive blood-bath.

After Simon the Rock's vision on the Sea of Galilee Jesus's followers hastened to Jerusalem to await the World's End, now identified in their minds with the Glorious Return of Jesus. In the Temple they were indistinguishable, religiously and politically, from other Jews. Their special view of Jesus's significance did not separate them from other Kingdom of God agitators. The feverish anti-Roman agitation that was spreading throughout the countryside gradually took in more and more Jews in Jerusalem, achieving a critical pitch, as we shall see, from about 63 on.

After the reign of Pontius Pilate, tension between the Roman administration and the population in Palestine steadily intensified: the rapacity of the procurators was on a collision course with the mounting turbulence focused by the Kingdom of God activists.

Pilate himself proved to be ineffective and clumsy; despite his aim of curbing the growing agitation against the Romans he kept exasperating the Jews; during his ten-year term of office he made one administrative misjudgment after another; a final blunder undid him. This, too, had to do with the Kingdom of God fever now affecting more and more people in Judea and Samaria.

Under the influence of one of the many messianic agitators "stirring up the people," some Samaritans gathered together to ascend their holy mountain (Mt. Gerizim) to gaze at the sacred utensils buried in their Temple. This was obviously the prelude to some messianic sally. Pilate turned loose on them a heavily armed force. A great many Samaritans were killed. Others were jailed and the rest dispersed. Pilate executed the most eminent prisoners.[1]

Pilate had gone too far. The Samaritans complained to the legate of Syria (Vitellius), who sent Pilate back to Rome to answer charges of malfeasance. (Pilate's end is unknown.)

Vitellius, having sent out a new procurator, Marcellus, tried to placate the population, especially the Jews. He got the emperor's permission to let the Jews retain the high priestly vestments the Romans had sequestered; he also canceled an unpopular market tax. Vitellius then proposed to spare Jewish sensibilities by not bringing troops through Palestine and entered Jerusalem himself to offer sacrifice.

Nevertheless, Vitellius's rule could not change the cardinal fact of the Roman occupation: Palestine remained in a state of turmoil, complicated by a growing civil-war atmosphere between the Jewish aristocracy, including the upper orders of the priesthood, and the plebeian classes, including the lower priests.

Meanwhile, pious Jews were becoming more and more sharply anti-Roman. This hostility was exaggerated by the economic discontent of the plebeians, which struck even at so fundamental an issue as the ownership of land. There was a clamor for a redistribution of the land (justified by reference to Moses's legacy) and for a remission of debts and similar economic measures in favor of the lower classes.

Thus it was natural for the Romans to stand out as sponsors of the upper classes. The loathing felt for the Romans not only by the Kingdom of God agitators, but also by the masses of plebeians was inflamed by the Romans appearing on a national scale as the champions of the rich. The rich were not only not particularly pious, but they showed leanings toward Greco-Roman culture, much as the Jewish aristocracy had welcomed Greek culture under the Seleucid occupiers two centuries before, which brought about the Maccabean revolt.

The Romans' administrative skill was frustrated by their irritation with Jewish religious extremists as well as the social protesters. The procurators themselves did not bother to conceal their antipathy to Jews qua Jews. Their subordinates, drawn from the non-Jewish population of Palestine and generally imbued with longstanding ethnic grudges, made a point of siding against the Jews in the countless frictions of everyday life (business, religion, and so forth).

Vitellius's conciliatory attempt proved to be a mere interlude. In A.D. 39 or 40, nine years or so after the execution of Jesus, the Jews, including the Jesists in Jerusalem, were confronted by the determination of the half-mad Emperor Caligula to set up his own image to be worshiped in the Temple. This would, of course, have been tantamount to total desecration. This was no doubt the "desolating sacrilege set up where it ought not to be," a harbinger of matchless distress to the Jews (Mark 13:14; from Dan. 11:31).

Caligula's extravagance almost provoked a general uprising, obviated only by his murder early in A.D. 41.

Caligula's successor, Claudius, installed Agrippa I as Jewish king of the restored dominion of his father, Herod the Great. It was into this context of tension that Agrippa I took immediate action against the leading members of Jesus's following in Jerusalem, Jacob ben-Zavdai, his brother John, and Simon the Rock.

Agrippa I's short reign (A.D. 41–44), while it mollified to some extent the antipathy of the Jews in general, had no effect on those infuriated by the very presence of the Romans. When Agrippa I died, the Roman administration reverted to the procuratorial regime. A series of procurators, all rapacious, corrupt, and arrogant, proved to be not only incapable of arresting the spread of militant disaffection, but through shortsightedness brought things to a head.

Thus the era immediately preceding the emergence of Jesus had provided a rich seedbed for his agitation.

The excitement aroused among the Jews in the Diaspora as well as Palestine by the news of Simon the Rock's Vision was not merely because of its miraculous nature. As a portent of something still more stupendous—the expected Kingdom of God—it entailed revolutionary consequences.

From a purely political point of view—that is, from the Roman point of view—the Vision had the effect of a seismic wave. Those who believed in the Kingdom of God at the World's End naturally took the Vision to be another sort of call to action. Just as Jesus had been executed by the Roman State as a seditionist, so those inspired by his example, in the early phase, took it on themselves to continue his Kingdom of God activism in their own way.

The Jewish communities of the Diaspora were churned up, in varying degrees of intensity, by the Good News of the Vision.

The Kingdom of God ferment was working both in Palestine and throughout the Diaspora.

Toward the end of the Forties, for instance, Claudius "expelled the Jews from Rome because, incited by Chrestus, they were constantly creating an uproar."[2] In Alexandria, too, at about the same time, Claudius warned the Jews "not to bring in or admit Jews who come down . . . from Syria or Egypt . . . otherwise I will by all means take vengeance on them as fomenters of what is a general plague infecting the whole world."[3]

Since Judaism, as such, was a completely authorized religion, the "general plague" as well as the "constant uproar" must refer not to the religion itself but to the Kingdom of God activism that had begun to achieve tidal proportions in Palestine from the time of Pontius Pilate on.

The very wording of the sentence used by Claudius echoes something about Paul himself, who had also been a "perfect pest, a fomenter of discord among the Jews all over the world" (Acts 24:5 NEB).

It is impossible to avoid linking this with the execution of Jacob ben-Zavdai (Acts 12:2) by Agrippa I. It was natural for Agrippa, trying to calm things down in his own domain, to take action against Jacob ben-Zavdai and his brother as well as against Simon the Rock, energetic men who made up the core of Jesus's following. Jacob ben-Zavdai was killed as an insurrectionist.

If Simon the Rock had to leave Palestine for a while because of Agrippa I's repression, he probably went to Alexandria, the greatest Jewish center outside Palestine. Alexandria was the traditional haven for refugees, as indicated by Claudius's letter. Simon would naturally have promoted the views of the Jerusalem Jesists, that Jesus as the Jewish Messiah was about to come back in glory. This obviously anti-Roman propaganda would have affected other Jewish centers in the Roman Empire.

With the return to the procuratorial regime after Agrippa I's death in A.D. 44, the violence of the Kingdom of God agitation as well as its repression began gathering real momentum. The first procurator to be appointed after Agrippa's death, Cuspius

Fadus (A.D. 44–45), put to death an outstanding agitator, Tholomaios,[4] whose emergence at this time must surely be linked to the Kingdom of God ferment.

Still more significant was the career of Theudas, a "prophet" who was followed by a great throng who took all their goods with them to the Jordan River. He promised to effect a miraculous division of the river to enable them to get to the country on the other side,[5] plainly on the model of the Exodus from Egypt in which Moses divided the Red Sea for the Jews to get to the Promised Land. Theudas and some followers were killed; others were jailed. There was an organic link between the career of Theudas and that of Judah the Galilean. Though chronologically obscure, the connection is referred to with assurance by Gamaliel in a much later chronicle (Acts 5:34–37).

Cuspius Fadus was succeeded by a Jewish apostate, Tiberius Alexander, nephew of the Alexandrian Jewish philosopher Philo. Tiberius Alexander's term of office (ca. A.D. 46–48) was distinguished by his execution of two sons of Judah the Galilean, Jacob and Simon.[6] Their agitation for the Kingdom of God would have been given a special intensity just because of Tiberius Alexander's apostasy. (He was later to play a role as Roman commander during the siege of Jerusalem.)

From the Fifties on, the inherent incompatibility of the Roman administration and its Jewish opponents, with a large admixture of social protest motifs, kept mounting in tension. The Jews knew it was entirely possible for the Temple to be taken over and a pagan cult established there at the whim of any particular emperor, demented or not. A head-on collision was looming up between the growing activist movement and Roman procurators of increasing ferocity and venality.

Jesists were surely involved in the continuing tension, spearheaded by messianic visionaries of all kinds, that escalated into the great war of A.D. 66–70. The bloody outbreaks under Cumanus (A.D. 48–52), the result of Roman insults to the Temple and the Torah, must inevitably have involved the Jesists, if only because of their identification with the Temple.

From the procuratorship of Felix on (A.D. 52–60), the mood of the Jews was visibly growing more and more extremist. The country was full of messianic agitators all performing World's End miracles modeled on the divine intervention during the Exodus from Egypt and the great settlement in Canaan. The Zealot movement was headed by Eleazar ben Dinai, who had been agitating for twenty years.[7] Eleazar had been hiding out in the hills during this period. Felix succeeded in capturing Eleazar, who was sent to Rome, and crucified many of his followers and also many others.[8]

A new variety of Zealot agitator emerged around this time—the "Daggermen," who specialized in assassinating pro-Roman Jews. Their technique was to mingle with the masses at religious festivals, with daggers hidden in their robes.

Still another group of visionary activists appeared who were also intent on leading an exodus, under God's inspiration, into the wilderness. Like Theudas before them, they were determined to witness the "signs of liberation." Felix repressed this movement with a great slaughter.[9]

The next militant visionary was an Egyptian Jew who collected a huge crowd on the Mount of Olives by assuring them that the walls of the city would collapse at his command and that he would lead them all in the slaughter of the Roman garrison. Felix repressed this too, killing or taking prisoner many Jews, though the Egyptian Jew escaped.[10] (This took place a little before Paul's last visit to Jerusalem, between A.D. 53–58, and his arrest. Paul himself was taken to be the leader of the Daggermen, numbering some four thousand, who were supposed to go out to the wilderness (Acts 21:38).

It was around A.D. 59 that a rift between the higher and lower strata of the priesthood began to gape dangerously. The high priests and a combination of the lower priests and the leaders of the city, who were messianic agitators, had become estranged to the point of reciprocal and mounting violence. The high priests resorted, finally, to depriving the lower priests of their only source of income, namely, their tithes.[11] This plainly indicates a state of de facto civil war between the pro-Roman high priests, members of the Jewish aristocracy and wealthy magnates in their own right, and the lower, pro-Zealot strata.

In A.D. 60, Emperor Nero replaced Felix with Porcius Festus,

around the same time settling a long-drawn-out dispute between the Jewish and the pagan inhabitants of Caesarea in favor
of the pagans. (This was the key event in kindling the insurrection that was to take place six years later.)

By this time the Zealots and Daggermen had been harrowing
up life in Judea. The Daggermen, in particular, had become
daring enough to carry out their lethal operations in public.[12]
Festus, too, put down some armed followers of another messianic visionary who promised salvation to all those who
would follow him into the wilderness.[13] During Agrippa II's
short term of office (A.D. 60–62), the Jews also fell out with him
about a palace he had built that looked down on the Temple.
(Agrippa II's project was aborted through the intervention of
the half-convert Empress Poppea Sabina.)

Just around the time that Nero appointed Albinus Lucceius
(A.D. 62–64) to replace Festus, Agrippa II made Ananus high
priest. (This was Annas II, son of the Annas mentioned in the
Gospels in connection with Jesus.) Ananus furtively convoked a
meeting of the Sanhedrin to try Upright Jacob and some others
on a charge of transgressing the Torah. They were found guilty
and stoned to death.

This infuriated some priests and Pharisees, many of whom
were in the ranks of the Zealots and Daggermen and were also
in the Jesist coterie.[14] Some pleaded with Agrippa II to restrain
Ananus; others went to Albinus to report the whole affair.
Agrippa II removed Ananus from the high priesthood after
Albinus had reprimanded him.[15]

The indignation of the "Pharisees who believed" (Acts 15:5)
at the intrigue that undid Upright Jacob seems to imply that the
insurrectionary views of the Jesist coterie had infected other
Pharisees. We must recall that the Pharisees were a large and
somewhat amorphous camp including, of course, the Zealots
themselves, who were distinguished only in having drawn an
extremist, activist conclusion from the premises accepted, in
principle, by all Pharisees and indeed all Jews.

Jacob was called "Upright" precisely because of his piety,
which in the context of the civil-war atmosphere now rising to
fever pitch must have played a positive role. It was just the

Kingdom of God activists among the lower strata of the priest-hood who were to kindle the uprising of A.D. 66. It was these priests, supported by or identical with the insurgents,[16] who brought things to a head by stopping the daily sacrifice in honor of the emperor and of the Roman people—a virtual declaration of war.

Thus the reason Upright Jacob had fallen foul of the High Priest Ananus was linked to the mounting tension between the pro-Roman quietists and anti-Roman activists. The Jerusalem Jesists were embroiled in the widening rift between the quietists and the militant visionaries. The singling out of Upright Jacob, leader of the followers of his brother Jesus who a few decades before had been executed for sedition, would imply that in the sharpening crisis Upright Jacob was victim of the pro-Roman elements. The procuratorial interregnum was simply taken ad-vantage of by Ananus for his own factional purposes, since despite the corruption and rapacity of the procurators it was still Roman policy to keep things as quiet as possible. Thus the removal of Ananus from the priesthood after the new pro-curator's arrival meant a partial victory for those hostile to the high priests; Ananus had overreached himself. Hence the right-eous Torah-people, supposed to have been infuriated by the condemnation of Upright Jacob, were no doubt Zealots.

Another account of Upright Jacob's death (from a much later chronicler) seems curiously relevant.

Upright Jacob's influence over the rebellious Jews was consid-erable. At around this time the Sadducean upper priests seem to have become alarmed at the possibility of great disturbances, because the people en masse seemed to be expecting Jesus to be coming once again as Messiah. Upright Jacob was called on to quiet them, on this occasion, and was interrogated in public about it.

Upright Jacob was asked, "Tell us, what is the gate of Jesus?" whereupon he confounded his interrogators by suddenly pro-claiming his conviction of the imminence of Jesus's Glorious Return, a proclamation hailed by the crowd with the political salutation "Hosanna to the Son of David!" (This was a demon-stration of faith in militant messianism.) His answers inflamed the Jewish leaders, who flung Upright Jacob down from the Temple battlement and had him beaten to death.[17] This was supposed to have taken place, not in A.D. 62, but in A.D. 66, on the very eve of the outbreak of the Roman War.

There is good reason to believe that Upright Jacob was not merely "pious" but was personally involved in the civil war between the rival factions of the priesthood. There is even some indication, from the same later source, that he himself exercised some priestly office in the Temple, since he had the unique privilege of entering the shrine itself[18] and even wore the high priest's mitre.[19]

This incident, though odd, may refer to a situation (obscured by all chroniclers) in which at a given moment it was sensible for the quietist elements to ask for an opponent's help. The oddity, indeed, is that Upright Jacob not only failed to calm the people but inflamed them further by proclaiming his own revolutionary faith in the Glorious Return of his brother, a proclamation pointed up by the slogan "Hosanna to the Son of David.[20]

Thus the denunciation of Upright Jacob by the High Priest Ananus was itself an integral part of the civil war in Jerusalem on the eve of the Roman-Jewish War. It was played out against the background of mounting Zealot activity that had finally penetrated Jerusalem from the countryside and had taken over the city populace, split as usual into two or more camps. One of the camps, which concentrated the hope of the Kingdom of God activists on its personal candidate was defeated. Its leader, Upright Jacob, was eliminated.

Later on, the Jesists were advised against overeagerness in expecting the Glorious Return.

Take care that no one misleads you. Many will come claiming my name, and saying, "I am he"; and many will be misled by them. . . . If anyone says to you, "Look, here is the Messiah", or, "Look, there he is" do not believe it. Impostors will come claiming to be messiahs or prophets, and they will produce signs and wonders. . . . But be on your guard. . . . (Mark 13:5-6, 21-23 NEB)

In many ways the Romans had great respect for the Jews and their institutions. Still, a strong Jewish society in Palestine was ipso facto ominous if only because it was coupled with widespread Jewish proselytization throughout the Roman Empire. The proselytizing movement, though unfocused, had had a profound effect through social osmosis on the pagan masses. It was considered a menace not only because of the Roman ideal of a state religion accepted by society at large but also because of its effect on the highest strata of the realm. Hence, while Judaism was constitutional for born Jews, the movement of conversion seemed to imperil the empire itself, one more serious danger to be added to the many shredding its social fabric.

Judaism had attracted multitudes among the Aramaic-speaking peoples conquered by Rome. Indeed, the remarkable dispersion of Jewish communities throughout the known world, commented on even a century before Jesus,[21] must doubtless be explained by conversion, especially among women, for whom circumcision naturally was no deterrent. It was so attractive around this time, indeed, that it had even penetrated the court at Rome. We have seen, for instance, that the Empress Poppea Sabina was a semi-convert.[22] In Damascus and Antioch apparently all the women practiced Jewish rites.[23]

Around A.D. 46 the whole of the royal house of Adiabene became Jewish, apparently through the royal harem.[24] Some of the Adiabene princes were even to become Zealots.

During the Roman War,[25] a potent factor in the sharpening of the crisis with Rome was the widespread poverty, especially painful in the countryside. Even in the cities, the true focus of Greco-Roman culture, "the splendor . . . was created by and existed for a rather small minority. . . . The large masses of the city population had either a very moderate income or lived in extreme poverty."[26]

The situation on the land was undoubtedly much worse, especially in Palestine, which was far from being the richest part of the empire. There, any crisis at all would tend to ruin a great many peasants, turning them into victims of moneylenders and forcing the loss of their property. Economically and socially deracinated people would of course be particularly susceptible to the economic propaganda that had always accompanied the Kingdom of God agitators. One of the first acts of the rebels in Jerusalem in A.D. 66 was the setting on fire of the public archives, the repository of the moneylenders' bonds, "in order to win over a host of grateful debtors and bring about a rising of the poor against the rich"; the money-lenders were naturally loathed by the moderates.[27]

The slaves, too, of whom there were a great many—generally converts to Judaism—were also inflamed by the socioeconomic objectives of the insurrectionary party. In the war, one of the Zealot leaders, Simon bar Giora, proclaimed the emancipation of all slaves.[28]

The harshness of the taxation seemed to go beyond the actual capacity of the country. Part of the general Roman system of taxation included land tax, a poll tax, a water tax, a city tax, meat taxes on staples (meat and salt), a road tax, a house tax, and so forth.[29] Taxes were in fact practically ubiquitous. Though this was characteristic of the empire as a whole, its effects were most marked in impoverished Palestine, where the economic situation was exacerbated by the political instability.

Tax collectors, generally Jews, had the worst possible reputation, preserved us in the Gospels, in which the word "publican," in the perspective of the Kingdom of God agitation, meant no more than "sinner."[30]

Corruption of this kind also extended to the Jewish aristocracy, who waxed fat on what amounted to economic extortions from the masses. The high priestly families, all very rich, were also venal. Bribery could secure appointment to many lucrative jobs. The secular aristocracy, headed by Agrippa II, was also notorious for violence and oppression.[31]

Bribery extended throughout the regime. Bribery of the procurators themselves was naturally routine, as I have indicated. Paul, for instance, was expected to bribe Felix to be let out of jail (Acts 24:26). The last and worst of the procurators, Florus, "became a partner" of the Kingdom of God activists, whom he then undertook to avoid molesting.[32] The Roman historian, Tacitus, though as a rule hostile toward Jews, singles him out as a prime cause of the war that broke out in A.D. 66: "the Jews' patience lasted until Gessius Florus became procurator."[33] Albinus, too, could be bribed to release Daggermen.[34]

These instances simply demonstrate the power of the Kingdom of God activists. It was so pervasive that for a limited time it could even attenuate the political conflict.

It would surely be an exaggeration to say that the procurators were headstrong, acting against imperial interests as interpreted in Rome. On the contrary, since they could easily be deposed it must be assumed that in broad outline they were considered to be reliably interpreting the decisions of the center.

The procurators, to be sure, had no agreed-on policy on how to handle the explosive situation in Palestine. There were personal rivalries between some of them (Cumanus and Felix). Florus, who seems simply to have detested Jews as such, had no program for dealing with the insurrection his own policies had provoked. Even though he was supposed to have intentionally instigated the insurrection to cover up his own rapacity and corruption[35] he had no plan to put in operation once the insurgents managed to launch the uprising.

An enormous element of social protest can hardly be overestimated in considering the insurrection of A.D. 66–70. The population as a whole was divided into the pro-Roman elements of the upper classes, a vacillating body of people in the middle, and a majority of plebeians who eventually, under the leadership of the Kingdom of God activists, carried the day. The element of social protest explains the entry of plebeians in general into the insurrectionary movement. The burning of the moneylenders' bonds was bound to seem attractive to the poor.

Social protest united even those who otherwise differed widely. The two Zealot leaders in A.D. 66–70, Simon bar Giora and John of Gush Halav (Gischala), though of different social backgrounds, both loathed the pro-Roman Jewish aristocracy. In spite of the fact that John was a prosperous businessman, his men went in for "ransacking the houses of the rich."[36] Later both John and Simon launched a general attack on the upper classes indiscriminately.[37]

The Samaritans, longtime enemies of the Jews and under the

special protection of the Romans, also backed the insurrection.[38] They did so evidently because of socioeconomic motives that made the uprising transcend its own Jewish setting, and especially because they, too, had a Kingdom of God perspective.

There was even a possibility that the economic upheaval presaged by the social protest inherent in the insurrection might have spread to other countries, creating another problem for the Roman administration.[39]

In addition, there was a tremendous influx of young Jews, including upper-class young men, into the Kingdom of God movement. Youth in and of itself, in fact, was a significant cause of the insurrection.[40] One of the leaders of the Daggermen, Ben Batiah, was the nephew of Yohanan ben Zakkai, the mentor of the peace party;[41] while the one who precipitated the revolt, Eleazar, captain of the Temple (an office just below that of high priest), was the son of the High Priest Hananiah (Ananias).[42]

On the other hand, it was just the quality of the Kingdom of God agitation in its most acute form—the essential religious motif of the uprising as a whole—that made it difficult for non-Jews to take part in it. The Shammaites, Jews who believed in an especially strict interpretation of the Scriptures and were generally middle class and upper middle class, were also strong Zealots. This gave a heavy religio-national tincture to the insurrection that isolated the Jews and made it impossible for them to take full advantage of the element of social protest and extend it to those suffering the same afflictions outside Palestine.

At the outset, in fact, the uprising was entirely national in character. It was only later, as the war became more and more bitter, through the perception of its hopelessness, since after all God failed to intervene, that the element of social protest surfaced dynamically and led to the civil war between the various insurgent groups: Daggermen, Zealots, the groups associated with John of Gush Halav, Simon bar Giora, and so forth.

The leaders of the uprising had formed no strategy in case of victory. Their feeling must have arisen exclusively out of a burning religious conviction that all problems of strategy, indeed, would be solved quite simply by the intervention of God. Moreover, the elements that united for the purpose of the insurrection were far from uniform or harmonious in any sense. If not for the loathing inflamed by the Roman administration, especially by the last procurator, Florus, the radical differences between them would surely have come out even earlier.

The Jesists, as well as the other Kingdom of God activists, were immersed in the same movement of armed revolt against the Romans. Since there were a variety of currents flowing along the same anti-Roman course, nothing would have distinguished the Jesists in this respect from the others. They differed only through their conviction that the Kingdom of God would be installed after the Glorious Return of Jesus. Since being a Zealot also implied a feeling or a mood, the broad milieu that was seething with anti-Roman agitation could have contained many sympathizers not necessarily engaged in a specific organizational activity.

For a long time after Judah the Galilean, the activity of the Zealots took place mainly in the countryside outside Jerusalem. It was not until around A.D. 63, some thirty years after the execution of Jesus, that Daggermen began stirring in Jerusalem. It is more than likely that the Zealots in the countryside would have been living more or less normally in villages and on farms, participating in specific operations as they arose and then fading quietly back home. But as the war atmosphere came to fever pitch toward A.D. 66, all currents converged on Jerusalem.

In the autumn of A.D. 66, the rebels, by their very first acts, committed themselves to an all-out attack on Rome. Not only did Eleazar, captain of the Temple, stop the daily sacrifices for the emperor and for the Roman people—a declaration of war—but various Roman garrisons in Palestine were massacred out of hand.

Unaccountably, the Romans reacted sluggishly. It was three months before the governor of Syria (Cestius Gallus), the chief military support of the procurator in Palestine, dispatched an army. During this time a wave of violence flooded the country. The Jews of Caesarea were totally massacred. In reprisal, a dozen pagan cities, including some Syrian villages, were devastated and countless pagans killed. There were anti-Jewish riots and massacres in Tyre, Alexandria, and many other cities.[43]

The war was prolonged by a strange event. The Roman army, a strong force of legionary and auxiliary units, entered Palestine and advanced on Jerusalem without much opposition in Galilee or Samaria and was about to engage in an attack on the very walls of the Temple, when for some unknown reason Gallus ordered it to fall back and retreat northward out of the city. The retreating forces were mercilessly harried and killed.[44]

The morale of the rebels shot up deliriously. The retreat of the Roman army forces was so unexpected, so unlikely, so inexplicable, that it could be grasped only as the finger of God once again intervening in behalf of the fighters for Yahweh. It was surely one of the greatest defeats ever inflicted on the Roman legions and was exacerbated, moreover, by having been inflicted by amateurs in a key area of the empire, between the Egyptian granary and the lush farmlands of Syria, and on the route to Parthia, Rome's chief contemporary enemy.

The peace party's hopes vanished. The euphoria induced by the victory had the fatal effect of sweeping the Jews, as a collectivity, into the war.

In the spring of A.D. 67, Vespasian, a veteran commander conquerer of Britain, whose appointment by Nero indicates the importance of the Jewish uprising, moved into Palestine with three legions and a strong force of auxiliaries.[45] He had to lay siege to a whole string of fortified towns barring the way to Jerusalem. This complicated his campaign because, though the Jews were amateurish as fighters in the field, their ardor and energy were very effective elsewhere.

Vespasian, perhaps with an eye on the contest for the imperial succession that broke out after the death of Nero in A.D. 68, moved very slowly and cautiously through the countryside north of Jerusalem, gradually isolating it. The sluggish pace of the campaign further buttressed the rebels' hopes.

In A.D. 66, at the very beginning of the revolt, Menahem, the grandson of Judah the Galilean, had come to Jerusalem at the head of his own group of Daggermen. Claiming both charismatic and dynastic authority in the holy war, he had presented himself as "king," [46] only to be assassinated by rival Zealots. From then on there was a civil war situation between the insurgents.

The sluggishness of the Roman campaign in A.D. 68–69, following on the inexplicable retreat of Gallus's army at the outset of the war, had strengthened the mood of exaltation among the insurgents. The great festivals were celebrated at the Temple to general attendance. [47]

The final and decisive battle was the siege of Jerusalem, initiated at last by Titus, Vespasian's eldest son, in the spring of A.D. 70, a little before Passover. The Roman army now consisted of four legions and a great force of auxiliaries. Vespasian, now the emperor, with a need for prestige, urgently required a victory in Palestine, where the Roman legions had been held up for four years.

The Jews, hitherto divided in bloody strife between the two chief factions, led by John of Gush Halav and Simon bar Giora respectively, now united in ferocious resistance. Jerusalem was divided by great walls. There were three major strongpoints: the Temple itself, the Antonia Fortress, and the Herodian palace, which had massive towers. Hence a besieging army could not merely breach the outer walls but had to attack the city section by section. This meant fighting in tight quarters, where untrained combatants could excel and hence intensify and prolong the siege.

It was one of the most frightful attacks recorded. The city was wholly hemmed in by a massive Roman walling-up of the entire area. Famine and sickness helped the Romans. All offers of terms were rejected by the Kingdom of God enthusiasts, who until the very last moment seem to have expected God to intervene. Indeed, if, as some think, Revelations 11:1–3 is a fragment of a Zealot document, it reflects an early aspect of the siege in which the outer court of the Temple was "trodden by pagans" but the sanctuary was still untouched. The rebels still thought God would intervene to prevent the desecration of the actual sanctuary.

Despite the ferocious resistance of the insurgents, the Romans stormed the inner sanctuary. Tens of thousands of Jews were massacred or burned to death in the fire that razed the entire Temple, while the victorious Romans sacrificed to their standards and saluted Titus as imperator.

The seizure of the inner Temple paralyzed all Jewish resistance. They were now merely slaughtered by the legionaries. By the time the bloodbath was over, Jerusalem was a vast heap of smoking ruins covered with corpses.[48]

The debacle meant the virtual end of the revolt (other strongholds, including Masada, were captured a little later).

The Jewish State had been destroyed. Pagan soldiers were now encamped on the ancient shrine of the Jews.[49] Though there was another insurrection under Bar Kochba in A.D. 132–135, the national existence of the Jews was suspended until our own day.

Titus brought his booty back to Rome, including the seven-star menorah salvaged from the burning Temple. Simon bar Giora was taken to Rome to be executed at the foot of the capital; John of Gush Halav was imprisoned for life.

The war had inflicted titanic losses on the Jews, estimated by Josephus at well over 1,300,000. The results were summed up, very simply, in a Gospel:

> "They will fall by the edge of the sword, and be led captive
> among all nations; and Jerusalem will be trodden down by the
> Gentiles. . . ." (Luke 21:24)

CHAPTER VI

A NEW FAITH—
Articulated and
Consolidated

*T*he spread of the new religion was rapid, though not, in retrospect, remarkably so. A couple of centuries passed before it became a factor of importance in the state.

The Jewish debacle of A.D. 70 did not bring about a general repression of Jews throughout the Roman Empire; the Romans did not blame Jews as such for the insurrection. There had, after all, been a substantial Jewish peace party headed by a Jewish royal family. Berenike, Agrippa II's sister, had a lengthy relationship with Vespasian's son Titus, the conqueror of Jerusalem. It was Agrippa II and Berenike, indeed, who had financed Vespasian's and Titus's campaign for the Roman throne.

The Temple, to be sure, was never rebuilt. This put an end to the sacrificial cult and to the high priesthood, hence to the influence of the Jewish aristocracy (the Sadducees) linked to both. The only general measure affecting Jews in the empire at large was the *fiscus judaicus,* a Temple tax levied even after the destruction of the Temple.

Still, Judaism survived. In effect this meant the mainstream of Pharisee opinion largely purged of the militancy that had led to the debacle.

A Pharisee scribe, Yohanan ben-Zakkai, had slipped out of Jerusalem during the last seige and reconstituted a new Sanhedrin in Jamnia (a village near what is now Rehoboth). In effect the authority of the Torah was perpetuated; the tradition was ensured; the canon of the Hebrew Scriptures was closed, the "apocrypha" of the Greek canon remained excluded.

From this time on official Judaism consciously protected itself. A principal Jewish prayer, recited to this day, included a section directed against heretics, which came to include the Jesists.

From then on the rabbis who had inherited the legacy of Pharisaism were to be considered the chief enemies from within the evolving Jesist faith. Though the Jews could not use force against the Jesists, they could still expel them from their still enduring socioreligious commonwealth. This is echoed in a number of passages in John (9:22, 12:42, 16:2) and especially perhaps in Matthew, which often sounds as though the author were still engaged in bitter contention against dominant Pharisaism.

Jerusalem retained a small population, which was to be practically wiped out again during the last insurrection of the Jews under Bar Kochba in A.D. 132–135. Some Jesists came back again as the city more or less settled down under Roman dominion.

Vespasian had ordered all descendants of King David tracked down. The search for "Davidides" was continued under Titus and Domitian, Titus's brother and successor, and even under Domitian's successor Trajan.

There was evidently a real fear of pretenders to Jewish sovereignty. Jesus's kin were regarded as potentially dangerous as late as the end of the first century.

There is a revealing record of two grand-nephews of Jesus

(grandsons of his brother Judah), who were denounced to the authorities and brought to a hearing conducted by Domitian himself.

They admitted being descendants of David, whereupon Domitian asked them what they owned. They said they had only a certain sum of money (some nine thousand denarii), half to each one, and only in the form of some ten acres of land they had to till for a living to pay their taxes. They proved this by showing the emperor their calloused hands and bodies.

When questioned about Jesus the Messiah and about when his "kingdom" would appear, they explained it away by saying the "kingdom" was not "of this world" at all but was celestial and would make its appearance at the World's End, when the "Messiah would appear in glory to judge the living and the dead and to reward every man according to his deeds."[1] Seeing that they were simple men, Domitian released them. The two grandnephews of Jesus survived until the time of Trajan.

No doubt the Davidic origin of Judah the Galilean, whose grandsons had played insurrectionary roles down to the war of A.D. 66–70, was a factor in this fear, especially if there is some truth in the report of an "ambiguous oracle," (presumably derived from the Hebrew Scriptures) to the effect that someone from Palestine, in the turmoil preceding the uprising of A.D. 66, was supposed to become ruler of the world. The insurgents were reported as having "interpreted this falsely to mean one of their own people,"[2] while it was taken advantage of by our sole chronicler, Josephus, to hail Vespasian himself as fulfilling the prophecy. Thus an actual prophecy, turned to the advantage of Jewish would-be messiahs and hence another cause of the intractable opposition to the Romans, still retained its force after the war.

Just before the outbreak of the war, Upright Jacob had been succeeded by a cousin;[3] there was evidently some dynastic principle involved. There was also a tradition that a community of Jesists in Jerusalem was headed by an uninterrupted succession of fifteen Jewish "bishops." After the Bar Kochba revolt in A.D. 135, Hadrian attempted to wipe out the name and the recollection of Jerusalem, christening it Aelia Capitolina; the Jesist community there seems abruptly to have become entirely non-Jewish.[4]

In any case, though the original Jesist coterie in Jerusalem vanished in the debacle of A.D. 70, together with the other insurgents, some community of believers in Jesus existed down to the Bar Kochba revolt, in which some kinsmen of Jesus played a role independent of the Jesists themselves (Bar Kochba persecuted them). After the abortive Bar Kochba revolt, the Romans forbade all Jewish settlement in Jerusalem, as well as all Jewish Jesist settlement, for some time. Jews were forbidden even to visit Aelia Capitolina. Hadrian's initiative was, in fact, the first attempt at genocide, in this case arising exclusively out of the long-drawn-out—two centuries—history of Jewish resistance.

For all the Jewish Jesists, of course, Jerusalem had been the object of reverence. They prayed toward it; Upright Jacob had become celebrated for his incessant praying in the Temple, the true place of prayer. This tradition was carried over to the earliest Christians who interpreted the destruction of Jerusalem as a punishment for Upright Jacob's murder by the Sadducee high priest.

In A.D. 66 the Jesists, completely at one with the other anti-Roman Kingdom of God activists, had formed an integral part of the upheaval directed by the rival militant factions. Like the other activists they must have been heartened by Gallus's incomprehensible retreat as well as by the sluggish pace of Vespasian's campaign. Like the other activists they must have thought that with the issue at last engaged, the denouement must now be at hand. For all peoples the World's End would have come about, the Kingdom of God installed, and world dominion bestowed on Israel.

The whole of the Jerusalem population, as we have seen, was submerged in the long-drawn-out, frightful siege and in indescribable sufferings, massacres, disease, and starvation. The carnage, exacerbated by famine and disease, had affected everyone, including women, children, and the aged. Not merely was

Qumran (the Dead Sea Scrolls community) wiped out in A.D. 68, but the Jesist coterie itself vanished two years later when Jerusalem was laid waste and the Temple burned. (The legend of the flight to Pella, on the other side of the Jordan River, is surely a pious fabrication devised to substantiate the continuity claimed by a much later tradition.)

Those Jesists who retained the essential views of the original Jesist coterie in Jerusalem were dealt a deathblow by the Jewish debacle of A.D. 70. In and around Palestine the groups of Jewish Jesists (the two main groups were called "Nazarenes" and "Ebionites") shriveled rapidly. They clung to the Jewish Torah and refused to accept, for instance, the legend of the Virgin Birth and in general the "Son of God" theory. Their faith in Jesus was limited to a belief in a mere Jewish Messiah who was expected to restore sovereignty to Israel. Only a couple of generations later they were vilified as heretics, while at the same time the original Jesist community that such Jewish-oriented groups had descended from became fossilized and mythologized under the entirely misleading name of the "Mother Church," and brought into line with the emergent success of the contrary tendency—that is, "Paulinism"—by the harmonizing efforts of the writers, editors, and compilers of the basic documents of what was to become the Catholic Church.

Though a new group was to take the place of the original Jesist coterie in Jerusalem long after the war, it remained outside the mainstream of the evolution of the Jesist coteries in the Diaspora, now left wholly vulnerable vis-à-vis the ideas proliferating in the Greco-Roman world.

After the debacle, the Jews of the Diaspora remained emotionally linked to Palestine. For a long time they were a seedbed of disaffection vis-à-vis the Roman authorities. (In A.D. 115 they launched a major revolt in North Africa [Cyrenaica].) But with the collapse of the Bar Kochba revolt in A.D. 135 the Diaspora was finally established as a semiautonomous social organism down to our day.

In those days, of course, religion was a communal matter; the place of individuals in society was defined by their religious status. The question of personal belief was not to arise, in a social sense, for many centuries. Thus the coteries of Jesists, scattered throughout the area wherever there were Jewish communities, initially benefited by the privileged position of Jews and were not, in fact, substantively distinguished from Jews for generations after Jesus's execution.

From the point of view of the evolution of Jesism into Christianity, the collapse of the Bar Kochba revolt removed the last barrier to the triumph of all the Greek elements in the evolving faith. The characteristic Jewish elements were submerged; they became encysted, as it were, within the core of the new faith, to be fossilized and overlaid by layer after layer of Greek ideas, focused by "Paulinism."

It was, in fact, the radical, comprehensive transformation of Paul's ideas, their Hellenization, that was to bring into being the new universe.

Essentially the Hellenization of Paul's ideas, including their Jewish components, was an autonomous process, inherent in the assimilation by outsiders of concepts, alien to begin with, and also made obsolete by history, whose vigor nevertheless enabled them to be integrated with the intellectual flux of a vast, multifaceted society.

Paul's ideas, themselves an attempt to insert a Hellenistic core into a Jewish historical framework, were Hellenized overwhelmingly as a result of two factors:

First, Paul's ideas prevailed among the Jesists and God-fearers because an external event—the Jewish debacle of A.D. 70—cleared the way for their propagation in the pagan world.

Second, another event was to encase Paul's views within an entirely different framework and transform them so profoundly that the transformation itself could pass unnoticed and for many centuries scarcely be acknowledged.

The event was, so to speak, negative. The World's End did not take place; the Kingdom of God remained obdurately nonexistent. The ferment that had originally been generated by the Kingdom of God concept came to an end, and the concept itself shriveled.

The shriveling of the Kingdom of God concept eliminated the thrust of Paul's ideas—their function—and the second generation replaced it unwittingly with an entirely different rationale.

Paul's theories, designed for a specific situation that for him was to achieve its climax within the framework of real-life history, became authoritative for the earliest Church Fathers precisely by the time they had become incomprehensible.

The subsidence of the Kingdom of God idea, accompanied by a natural change in people's feeling about the passage of time, made it simply impossible for the second generation, growing up after the destruction of Jerusalem and the Temple, to grasp the point of Paul's obsessive theorizing about the World's End. Yet that very fact cleared the way for the simplification of Paul's cosmic but history-bound views and, more particularly, for their amplification and adaptation to an audience that by now had become not merely the Elect of the Final Generation but, quite simply, all mankind—the target of Church propaganda.

The ardor that had imbued Paul himself, the mysticism rooted in the Kingdom of God fever, was utterly forgotten. From the second and third generation on believers in Jesus turned aside from the original source of their faith and accepted life in the workaday world.

By a little more than a generation after his death, well after the destruction of Jerusalem, Paul's ideas had been warped almost beyond recognition. By A.D. 100 he was already integrated with the category of "theological literature," brittle, artificial, and lifeless—the antithesis of his anguished letters, throbbing with urgency.

Everything Paul had to say about the Torah, his whole intricate, yet clear and logical extrapolation from received ideas, was pulverized. The evolution of early Church dogma smashed his views to smithereens.

The pagan milieu in which Paul's ideas struck root had assimilated in its own way the alien Jewish view of history, accepting that view as the starting point of its own cosmological projections. When the Jewish husk of the original idea about

Jesus and the Kingdom of God shriveled with the disappointment over the nonoccurrence of the World's End and, more
concretely, through the extinction of the Jerusalem Jesist coterie
in A.D. 70, the Hellenistic core of Paul's cosmic scenario could
be explained in ways he could not have foreseen. His
phraseology was retained at the same time that its content and
function were transformed.

It was only Paul's ardor, after all, that had enabled him to
believe, in the teeth of the evidence, that Jesus's resurrection had
already generated the Messianic Kingdom, hence that believers
had already died and risen again with Jesus and were thus
guaranteed participation in the resurrection way of life at the
Glorious Return.

A couple of generations later this ardor had become incomprehensible and, above all, *unfelt*. The lip service given the
notion of the Kingdom of God at the World's End could not
prevent it from dimming below the threshold of true emotion.

Hence, as the awareness of the indefinite postponement of the
Kingdom of God gradually gained ground, the early Church
Fathers unconsciously reworked Paul's theories along lines that
gave them coherence in an intellectual structure independent of
the World's End fever.

The Hellenization that was natural in any case for the think-
ing of Hellenistic Jesists provided the material for just such a
structure. Christian theology as such may have germinated,
indeed, with the systematic, unconscious distortion of Paul's
ideas.

An example or two will prove illuminating.

The writings of Paul that survived his neglect were already
influential in the scattered coteries of the eastern Mediterranean
a couple of generations later. The Church Fathers Ignatius and
Polycarp were steeped in them; they dwell on themes for which
Paul's vocabulary is indispensable.

Yet despite their immersion in his thought there is a vast
omission. The profound phrase they make much of—the
Being-in-Christ—has been given a wholly different content.
Without noticing it, they have really dropped Paul's basic idea

altogether, together with the source of his logic—the key concept that believers, after dying with Lord Jesus, have already been resurrected with him.

Paul had assumed that the resurrection was the handiwork of the Spirit emanating from God and taking the form of Jesus's resurrection as part of the World's End transition. Taking the same word *Spirit* as his starting point, Ignatius used it to refer to the fusion of flesh and spirit supposed to take place within the Church through the fellowship with Christ, itself to become the guarantee of immortality through resurrection.

Thus Ignatius's idea could sound quite like Paul's—a sort of shorthand streamlining of Paul's idea, with the concept of dying and raising again *with* Lord Jesus merely discarded.

The mechanism that effected the shift in content is easily seen.

For Paul there could be no question of any union between spirit and flesh. For him the flesh was simply eliminated through the dying and rising again with Jesus. The Spirit fused with the psyche as part of the integral body, which after the Glorious Return would be transformed into the Glorious Body.

To Paul's mind the death and resurrection of Jesus brought about redemption simply by virtue of the fact that Jesus had died and been resurrected *as* the Messiah who had become Lord of the Universe. That was why his death was an atoning sacrifice for the Elect. And since he was both a pre-existent Being and the future Messiah, his death, merely an apparent one, in and of itself entailed his inevitable resurrection and therewith the triggering of the resurrection era.

But by the lifetime of Ignatius and others, the World's End theory, even though paid lip service to, had been drained of life. Ignatius believed in the resurrection of the actual body, not the Glorious Body, of the believer. In this scheme of ideas the flesh of the actual body was immortalized, not through participation in a new world but through the inward action of the Spirit. Ignatius did not think flesh perishable in and of itself, and because of that unfit for the working out of the resurrection; he regarded the fusion of spirit and flesh as a process to be found in nature, a process that had been, to be sure, exemplified for the first time in history in the case of Jesus. It was for him, accordingly, an unexplained, unmotivated miracle. Beforehand the flesh was not capable of immortalization; afterwards it was.

Thus, for the hellenized pagans of the era, the redemptive activity of Jesus consisted merely of his coming into the world as himself a union of the flesh and the Spirit, and *because of that* the cognate union of flesh and spirit, leading to the resurrection of the Elect, was made possible. In Ignatius's mind the death and resurrection of Jesus merely manifested a process embedded in nature—the category of resurrection derived from the mode of Jesus' own resurrection.

One intellectual mechanism, in short, has been replaced by another. In consequence, Paul's phrase "in Christ"—shorthand for the complex but clear and logical concept of Being-in-Christ—was used as though it were a merely abstract idea.

This in its turn explains why Ignatius magnified the role of the Eucharist, now itself the *goal* of baptism.

Paul's sacraments, while realizing a magical potential unsuspected by the first Jesists, were in a sense ad hoc—semimagical, so to speak—since they were severely restricted in time. Rooted in Jesus's death, that is, in the immediate present, they remained efficacious until the Glorious Return, the immediate future. But when pagans set about explaining salvation as dependent, not on the installation of the Messianic Kingdom in a universe of historical drama but on the *fact* of Jesus Christ himself, Savior of the Universe, the ad hoc magic became eternalized.

Paul's magic had thus been partial, an auxiliary to a historical event. When the Glorious Return failed and the Church flowered in the void of Paul's shattered ideas, the system inspired by his ideas veered round to a total, timeless amplification of magical procedures.

For Paul baptism had been an indispensable preamble to the Lord's Supper. It constituted the initiation of the believer into the fellowship of the New Elect and was consummated by the partaking of the body and blood of Jesus at the Lord's Supper as a way of participating in the Dying and Rising Again with the Lord.

For Ignatius, however, baptism was merely the preliminary stage of a process that was now independent of the Dying and Rising Again with the Lord, but was consummated by the Eucharist in and of itself. The Logos-Christology laid down in the Gospel of John turned that concept into a fundamentally different, though similar-sounding one. The body and blood of Lord Jesus was now his *flesh* and blood, while the effect of the bread and wine was meant to bring about the fusion of spirit and matter, just as the fusion of spirit and flesh brought about the bodily identity of the believers with Jesus.

From this point of view both the bodily identity with Jesus and the fusion of matter and spirit duplicated the existence of the Savior as an absolute magnitude and encapsulated the whole process in the Eucharist—in a form lending itself to transmission to all believers independent of any historical event.

Thus an unconscious transformation of the phrase "body and blood" into the phrase "flesh and blood" was to pivot the whole of Paul's original history-minded, physical view of the world transformation that framed the role of the Mystic Body of Christ into a different nonhistorical, timeless condition of nature. The function of the Church, now indispensable, was to transmit the Spirit to natural men.

Hence the original belief in a redemption brought about by the Messiah as usher of the Kingdom of God gradually took a form inherently alien to monotheism—a personal resurrection not *with* but *through* Jesus Christ.

The simple phrase "in Christ" had proved capable of bearing within it the whole of this turning inside out. It served as springboard for a novel view summed up in the notion of immortality pure and simple, to be acquired through the Christ independently of anything else and thus to serve as the midwife to the Hellenization of the new faith.

With the shriveling of the World's End concept, Paul's ad hoc devices were made absolute and were integrated with a historical concept embodied in an eternal, ahistorical Church. Paul's

ideas, confined to an imminent World's End he passionately
expected to see in his own lifetime, had become integral parts of
a condition of the universe, parts of the world-stuff.

Paul's Eucharist was conservative—in the deep, psychological
sense of reverting to ancient, suppressed, semi-instinctual
modes of feeling revolving around the ingestion of a deity's
being. It was also historically progressive in that it opened up to
undifferentiated mankind the possibility of joining a new type
of universal community. What had been for Paul a real-life,
historical event—the historical real-life dying and resurrection
of Jesus the Messiah—was translated via the expansion of the
magic of the sacraments and via the shriveling of the World's
End idea into the lives of ordinary people as a personal experience they could all share. It was this basic idea, whose force
could survive even its dislocation from the framework of its
original conception, that created the dramatic tension to be
accommodated by a universal church.

This process, institutional as well as intellectual, had natural
social consequences. From a common-sense point of view, for
instance, it is obvious that Paul's idea about freedom from the
Torah was rational only as part of the Kingdom of God at the
World's End. Mere freedom in the absolute, in an ongoing,
ordinary world, would have been meaningless. As the Church
settled down to life in the workaday world, it perforce had to
build up social norms again. In the nature of things, indeed, it
was itself now the source of all social norms.

The misunderstanding of Paul's ideas was remarkably rapid.
Only a couple of generations later his World's End obsession
was utterly indigestible; the entire mechanism he had devised to
explain the working-out of Jesus's death and resurrection was
simply dropped. Its place was taken by a doctrine *about* the
World's End; and finally, with the indefinite postponement of
the fact, even the doctrine was surrendered. The remark made
about Jesus by Alfred Loisy, the celebrated French scholar, is
even truer about Paul: "What Jesus preached was the Kingdom
of God, what happened was the Church."

Paul's ideas were, essentially, fossilized the moment the

World's End was forgotten. They had failed, so to speak, to pass the test of history.

Thus a real problem is set for the historian. Why did the Final Generation, realizing that it was, in fact, the first generation of those who would have to go on living in the workaday world, not turn to some other method of salvation? How could the Church arise on the debris of its initial hopes? If the premises of a deductive chain are shifted, the edifice built on them must crumble. How could Paul's logic withstand its self-destruction?

For the Christian Mystery kept growing, on the whole steadily. The answer must be found in the very generality of the ideas Paul had devised to explain what was, for him, a purely historical puzzle—the hiatus between the resurrection of Jesus and the onset of the Messianic Kingdom.

We have already seen the structural identity between the pagan Mysteries, with their "pure" magic, and Paul's baptism and Eucharist, with their "auxiliary" magic. We have seen how Paul's basic concepts—the Being-in-Christ and the Mystic Body of Christ—swiftly created a cosmic institution whose Jewish core was swathed in Hellenism.

It was precisely Paul's transformation of the sacraments, against the background of the Mystic Body of Christ, that was to fling a bridge from Paul's palpably materialistic, history-oriented ideas to the timelessness of a new institution, the Church.

From our own vantage point we can see that the procedure was essentially simple, though those living in the epoch of transformation were naturally unaware of it. When Paul's conception of the sacraments as mere auxiliary devices guaranteeing a share in the Messianic Glory was misunderstood by the Church leaders a couple of generations later, with the emotional subsidence of the World's End fever, the sacraments thought of as dependent on the World's End were transformed into a guarantee of immortality pure and simple.

Historically, this was what proved to be the cardinal aspect of the magnification of Jesus promoted by Paul as the copingstone of the World's End.

There was an ineluctable progression between the first magnification of Jesus due to the vision of Simon the Rock on the Sea of Galilee, when the conviction spread that Jesus had been made Messiah and would soon return in glory with the Kingdom; to the magnification of the Jewish Messiah to the Lord of the Universe, still expected to return in glory with the Kingdom of God; to the final magnification of Lord Jesus as an Eternal Entity, entirely independent of any change on earth, whose embodiment was henceforth to be the Eternal Church.

It was these selfsame procedures that for the generations who had forgotten the real-life Kingdom of God survived its failure. The procedures proved capable of implementing satisfactorily the emotions of people via a new institution founded on the pulverization of their historical underpinnings. Thus Paul's devices, in his own mind provisionally and transiently magical because of their link to an impending great change in the real world, became fully, autonomously and timelessly magical within the Church engendered by the misunderstanding of his ideas.

The Jesists who had believed they would be saved after the Glorious Return were gradually, with the succession of generations, replaced by those who believed in the salvational effects of the Deity *there and then.*

This underlay the Church. From then on it was a vehicle for dynamic psychic transformations of its believers while it itself remained static. It became, in fact, an institution embedded in a workaday world.

In this way history-oriented monotheism, based on an absolute distinction between God and his handiwork, was replaced by dynamic magic, capable of transforming the world-stuff it was itself a part of. Paul's generalizing formula, originally linked to an event in history, soared beyond history. It was an absolute abstraction that at the same time was bound up with a new condition of the cosmos, a new institution. Paul's formula could attribute a new sort of reality to the natural world. It created a situation in which a believer could tap a reservoir of power that though aimed at God, was in fact quite independent of God.

Paul's ideas, originally devised to contain the ardor of those inflamed by the prospect of imminent bliss in the Messianic Kingdom, were equipped with an algebraic formula that could be expanded at will. By conquering the fear of mortality in the minds of its believers, the formula could express a state of nature. Freed from their historical integument, Paul's ideas soared aloft as a paradigm for the anguish of all mankind. This possibility had been already contained unbeknownst to Paul, in his basic invention.

If the World's End had already begun, even though it was indiscernible, it meant that people could already be part of the Kingdom of God even when that, too, was missing. Indeed, that was the whole point of Paul's formula which, even though Paul himself thought the Kingdom of God an absolute certainty, nevertheless bridged over its temporary failure through hope. By accommodating the "sooner or later" of the advent of the Messianic Kingdom, Paul's formula also encompassed the "not at all"—the eternal postponement of the Messianic Kingdom.

By eternalizing delay, Paul had solved the puzzle that had agitated him before his conversion. Precisely the delay between the resurrection of Jesus and the advent of the Messianic Kingdom had been the puzzle, and it was by solving that puzzle with a solution he thought of as ad hoc, since it would infallibly be superseded by the imminent advent of the Kingdom, that the ad hoc itself became eternal.

After the failure of the Kingdom of God, in short, Paul's formula proved capable of projecting people into a sublimated Kingdom of God that *need never appear.* It showed that for human aspirations the projection of a hope can replace a reality that has never come about and need, in fact, never ever come about. Vulgarly put, "It is better to travel hopefully than to arrive."

It was this insight, writ large, that characterized Paul's handiwork. What had been, for him, a bridge to salvation, was a bridge that was never to be built. It was to hang in the air, so to speak, with its farthermost end eternally overhanging the suggestion of bliss.

Thus the modest, barely perceptible arc of expectation,

peeping only a little beyond the initial disappointment at the failure of the delay of the Messianic Kingdom and aiming at no more than an interlude of a few months or years, proved to contain an angle of elevation that, just because of the powerful abstractions formulated by Paul, could encompass all horizons seen and unseen.

Paul's ideas, transformed as they were, proved capable of sustaining a universal religion.

Budding Christianity offered its potential clientele many advantages. For those who despaired of reason as a path to personal salvation, it offered a divine revelation—the message of the Hebrew Scriptures (however that message was interpreted) plus the titanic fact of the Risen Jesus. For those in need of philosophy it could put itself forward with composure as the finest philosophy in history. Because of the manner in which the early Christian thinkers fused together organically in their own minds all the ideas taken from Judaism, from the presumed history of Jesus, and from their own Hellenistic education, Christianity could plausibly be presented both as the direct chain between Greek philosophic speculations and the Hebrew Scriptures, and as their joint consummation.

This stitching together of the Hebrew Scriptures and Greek ideas had already had the terrain prepared for it by the work of Philo, a devout Alexandrian Jew who had applied a system of allegory and exegesis to the Hebrew Scriptures in order to make them dovetail with the ideas of Plato. By this, Philo had unwittingly facilitated a cleavage in the world of thought between Judaism and Christianity.

In the Gospel of John, for instance, Jesus the Messiah was presented as an earthly incarnation of the Logos, the Word (of God), according to Alexandrian exegetics, an executive agency of Yahweh and of course coeternal with Yahweh. This was really no more than an extension of Philo's own ideas. On the other hand, it was an extension that, unsuspected by Philo, instantly led to the staggering proposition, in Diaspora Jesist circles, that since the Crucified One was identical with the Word of God, he was also a direct manifestation of God and therefore, in fact, God himself.

It is true that the idea of confining God within a human body was, of course, both blasphemous and incomprehensible from the point of view of Philo or any other Jew. But the train of thought based on Paul's flat statement that "the Lord is the Spirit" could easily be linked to the boundless magnification of Jesus and thus ignore the problem of the body.

The concept of Jesus as God flowered mightily in the terrain of Hellenism with the flexibility and abstract potentiality of the Greek language, for it was both natural and seductive to bring together God and Jesus in a union that at the same time permeated and enveloped the universe.

It was this development that was initially to vex and baffle the original Jesists on Palestinian soil. The Jewish privilege of being "heirs of the Kingdom" was, it seemed, being cheapened. But the major consequence of the Jewish debacle of A.D. 70 was just this: it doomed the Jewish Jesists and their ideas and at the same time rooted the new beliefs throughout the Greco-Roman world.

By the end of the first century, the Jesists, in whom we can now see a sort of proto-Christianity slowly coagulating, already formed a distinct entity with the rudiments of an organization that was both cohesive and potent, very nearly to a degree equaled only by the continuing organization of Judaism. Perhaps the cardinal difference at this time was the absence of a Scripture, that is, a canon, in sharp contradistinction to the amplitude and majestic antiquity of the Hebrew Scriptures.

On the other hand, despite its various frictions, internal rivalries, and the absence of an agreed-on body of beliefs, the proto-Church was unique in the Hellenistic world. Perhaps its chief distinction, socially speaking, lay in its embodiment in a relation to the individual over and above the social bonds that linked him to his past. The proto-Church cut across all past tradition and past attachment. It could appeal, therefore, to any individual merely as a human being.

This democratic appeal was sharply at odds with the vogue of current "philosophies," which essentially appealed primarily to an elite. The newly evolving Christian faith cast a broad net for multitudes—all mankind without differentiation.

At the outset, after all, the doctrine, before its definitive formulation in the imposing edifice of "theology" that was to characterize Christianity at its height, was so simple it required no education or training to grasp. At the same time it quickly evolved a sort of philosophy that could be found attractive to an elite too. In effect, what the first generations of Christian thinkers did was to absorb *all* Greek philosophy, especially neo-Platonism. St. Augustine of North Africa (end of the fourth century) was to say that he had discovered in neo-Platonism exactly the same ideas as in Christianity. All he missed were the Incarnation and the humility of Christ.

The earliest Christianity appealed to both sexes equally; the appeal of its rivals, such as Mithraism, was restricted to men. And whereas the Mysteries on which the structure of the evolving faith was so closely modeled generally appealed to the affluent, since initiation fees were high, the Church welcomed rich and poor alike.

At the same time, although Christianity from its very beginnings was modeled on the Mysteries and although salvation was offered its believers in much the same way, the one element inherited from Judaism—the belief in an all-knowing, all-powerful God, creator of the Universe—even though diluted by the necessity of finding a place for the Son of that God, made Christianity entirely intolerant with respect to other Mysteries which were, each within its own boundaries, generally quite willing to live and let live alongside all rivals. Still, despite this exclusive attitude vis-à-vis rival Mysteries, the Christian Mystery was inherently flexible. The simplicity of its basic idea enabled it to adjust to many current beliefs and popular practices in a way that Judaism, linked to its ancient Scriptures, had found it possible to do only to a minor degree.

The prestige attached to Judaism in the ancient world—the prestige of antiquity and of a venerable tradition propped up on incontestably ancient, sacred Scriptures—was of immense value to early Christianity. Thus the extinction of the Bar Kochba revolt, whether or not it was supported by Jewish Jesists (Bar Kochba had been hailed as a Messiah by the celebrated Rabbi Aqiba, himself tortured and executed by the Romans) had a direct effect on Jewish Jesism. The collapse of the revolt definitely extinguished an idea that for generations had galvanized the most energetic minds among the Jews—the idea that history was about to accomplish its own rectification through a cataclysmic overturn manifesting the finger of God on earth once again, i.e., the Kingdom of God at the World's End. After the revolt collapsed, Jews as a body abruptly turned away from apocalyptic visions in general: the evolving Christian community, about the same time, dropped the idea of the Glorious Return.

As hopes faded for a transformation of the natural world, which for the earliest generations of Jesist believers was symbolized by the Glorious Return, Christian speculation was obliged to amplify its treatment of the spiritual–intellectual implications embedded in the primitive "Kerygma," the rather skimpy message about Jesus. Since with the subsidence of emotional conviction about the Glorious Return Jesus himself was distanced from the workaday world, it was natural for speculation to be shifted to another axis—what Jesus Christ meant *here and now* on earth and what that in turn might imply about the hereafter.

It was just this emergence of an anchorage for the new faith that gave it a different locus. By rooting Christianity in the here and now the faith was transformed. It retained its otherworldly thrust; but since it had to accommodate the needs of life in a workaday world whose permanence had come to be accepted, the evolving institutional life of the new religion was given a different cast.

This paralleled, to be sure, the extinction of Jewish influence implicit in the destruction of the Jewish State and Temple. Jewish historicism—the notion that history, actual or fanciful, is what counts—was replaced by timeless theologizing precisely as the proto-Church struck root in the here and now.

Though Christians went on referring to the Glorious Return, it became a concept that was both emotionally and intellectually fossilized. References to it were no more than lip-service. The emotional and intellectual expectation of the Glorious Return was dislocated entirely. Ousted from its focal position, it became a mere traditional ornament, no more than a metaphor. Believers could no longer live in its expectation.

For the Hellenistic world, after all, the World's End had no sense at all. An integral part of Jewish history and historical thought, in spite of all its visionary elements, it could survive in Hellenistic thought only as an aspect of the magnified Lord Jesus. When the expectation of this Glorious Return shriveled, the locus of belief became radically different. The philosophic dualism of the Hellenistic world, fortified by a general leaning toward spiritualism, nullified the idea of a resurrection of the flesh, together with the material aspects of the Messianic Kingdom and the Kingdom of God that Jewish thought had found natural.

By the end of the first century and the beginning of the second, Greco-Romans were no doubt by far the bulk of the recruits to the new faith. This meant that there was an audience for the ideas projected by both Paul and by the Gospel of John, representing an attitude that was to sweep the field. By the end of the so-called "Apostolic Age" the rupture between Jews and Jesists was consummated. Jesists were Christians.

They were now speaking about Jesus in ways that would no doubt have flabbergasted him. Very soon afterwards Jews were to be denied not only the possession of the "Truth" but even a special position of any kind with respect to the tradition of Moses.

Those Jesist congregations made up of former practicing Jews who had looked up to the Jewish followers of Jesus remained small and destitute. By the middle of the second century there were still some in Syria and Egypt, perhaps in Rome, but they were already swamped by the great congregations composed of former pagans. By A.D. 160, St. Justin could say that Christians observing Jewish practices would be saved if they avoided trying to impose their habits on others; he then added that many Christians would not rub shoulders with them.

By the beginning of the second century, Christianity, though it lacked real cohesion and though its rites, dogmas, and institutions were still elementary, was no longer to be confused with Judaism. Remote from the ideas of Jesus and his immediate kinfolk and entourage, it could offer all human beings immortality. It had become an independent religion.

Even after Judaism and Christianity became formally distinct, to be sure, there were countless communities throughout the Mediterranean area where Christians remained fascinated by Judaism. In many places it was quite usual for Christians to "attend the synagogue, keep the Jewish fasts, and even make gifts of oil on taking part in the festivals celebrated in the synagogue. In Spain there were people who persuaded the rabbi to pronounce a blessing over their fields; so, too, Africa seethed with the observance of Jewish customs and festivals."[5]

As late as the end of the fourth century, John Chrysostom, the celebrated Greek Bishop of Antioch, felt obliged to vilify the Jews. People made a point of calling in Jewish doctors whose ceremonial prescriptions were complied with. Important oaths were sworn in the synagogue; everyone believed that oaths sworn before the ark of the Torah were peculiarly potent. People hoped to derive an advantage from joining in Jewish fasts and festivals, especially on New Year, when the blowing of the trumpet impressed many. A great many people thought, said Chrysostom (in a sermon from autumn of A.D. 386), that there was something particularly valuable about Judaism and that Jews worshiped the true God. In a sermon that may be taken as a model for the attitude of the Church for many, many centuries, Chrysostom denounced the Jews root and branch as idol worshipers and their synagogues as the home of the Devil and his demons.[6] The very heat of his sermons attacking the Jews must be taken as an index of the sympathy felt by many ordinary Christians.

Under the Caesars, culture consisted mainly of a form of literature—rhetoric and philosophy. Thus, in spite of the upheavals in the social and political sphere during the first centuries of the empire, there was a basic similarity of education from one end of it to the other; in fact, a general culture exemplifying the same reasoning habits that served as a matrix for religious ideas.

Philosophy consisted of an attempt to strip the world of its appearances in order to ascertain the meaning of life and to lay down ethical principles independent of any form of science, still less than rudimentary. This was complemented by rhetoric, a mere technique for putting together ideas and words. The flowering of the interest in science that had marked the early Greeks had vanished. Countless absurdities could plausibly be presented uncurbed and uncontrolled by common sense.

Without empirical controls, what passed for philosophy might, of course, be eloquent and ingenious. Abounding in ideas but with no grounding in factual enquiry, it would naturally crumble into systems of thought that revolved, essentially, around entirely arbitrary metaphors. These systems were scarcely more than traditional literary themes on which virtuosos would demonstrate their prowess by improvizing variations. After being elaborated in ways that might be entirely divorced from the original architects of the ideas, the themes could be transposed with ease.

Just as, at the very outset of these attempts at harmonizing ideas, Philo had united with the Hebrew Scriptures various themes of Greek philosophy that interested him, so the neo-Platonists could extract from their fund of ideas a kind of revealed religion that could then be combined by the Christian scholars of Alexandria with the basic elements of Christian faith and so produce still another system of dogmatics. And even though the exposition of these ideas could not be defended rationally, it could also dispense with defense, since their basic elements were in fact already taken for granted in the minds of educated men and so were universally accepted by the educated as well as by the ignorant. Unchallenged premises were thus unconsciously the bedrock of all discussion and propaganda. Every interpretation of life, of destiny, every cult and every religion had to start off from what at bottom were no more than conventional prejudices.

Augustus's attempt to restore the old Roman religion had succeeded only in reviving some temple rites and some actual temples; but he also enhanced the *civic* utility of the official rites and made them a part of true patriotism, that is, loyalty to Rome. This religion had hardly any true ceremonies or, for that matter, any real dogma or theology; it was also emotionally arid.

During the transition between the Roman Republic and the Roman Empire, an era that spans precisely the birth and dissemination of Jesism and subsequently primitive Christianity, the official religion of the Greco-Romans was already a melange of ideas and customs, a syncretism that was established after the Roman conquest of the hellenized East and that consisted of a fusion of the gods of the conquerors with those of the conquered.

Though educated people no longer believed in it, this religion was respected in public, no doubt as part of a general feeling that tradition, law and order, and respectability were in and of themselves good things. Organized religion was looked upon as a curb on the appetites of the unruly and rapacious ordinary people. Thus the elite would also participate in religious rites whenever it was expected of them.

Insofar as it had specific Roman features, the official religion was a sort of esprit de corps, a visible bond between Roman citizens. The elite would express their individual tastes by selecting from the views of the various philosophical schools some metaphysical reassurance or intellectual sustenance that in spite of their skepticism they remained in need of. For the elite the main body of belief was generally Stoicism, heavily tinctured with the attitudes of the eastern Mediterranean (and expressed very often by Phoenicians, Arameans, and so on) or Epicureanism. The ordinary people, almost wholly uneducated, clung to sorcerers and local cults.

This intellectual background was influenced further by some negative factors. Society in the middle of the first century was churned up by countless dislocations: upheavals throughout the body politic, multitudes uprooted by wars and conflicts, general social disintegration.

All this no doubt heightened the value of emotion as a response to anguish and catastrophe. Stoicism could protect only a tiny elite against the afflictions of society, while the skepticism of even this tiny elite was eroded by profound longings for a religious life. Ultimately Stoicism yielded to the more malleable and potentially far more emotional aspects of Platonism. Toward the end of the second century Stoicism had dried up completely. The pagan world was engulfed by a flood tide of religiosity.

Christianity, which had struck root in the Hellenistic world before A.D. 100, had established itself in the following century, and had begun to expand from about A.D. 200 on, represented an emotional answer to these social and political disturbances. The emotionally seductive cults from the East found a ready reception. In the third century Christianity could make substantial headway in the Hellenistic world because public opinion, so to speak, was already being transformed to find it equally seductive.

With the advent, at the end of the second century, of Septimus Severus and his family, and the influx of African and Syrian princes at the apex of the Roman State, accompanied by the influence of mystically preoccupied women, the expression of all sorts of fervor was substantially stimulated. Between A.D. 200 and A.D. 300 a wide variety of beliefs was imported from the East, from the most grossly material superstitions to refined creations of philosophic reflection and self-reflection, which throughout this period began leaning toward a preoccupation with the divine.

All creeds and cults had their followers, who adapted them all to the general pervasive longing for a future of eternal bliss in a mysterious hereafter. The given conglomeration of religious material was rich and diverse enough for each cult to combine its credo with rites of the most diverse origins.

The state religion, reduced to a simple religion of the emperor in accordance with a traditional formula, had absorbed not only the nationalities conquered by Rome but also their deities. Thus, from now on the religious upsurge, focused by the concentration of state power and aimed only at the salvation of the individual, formed a natural seedbed for Christianity.

Ordinary people took for granted a distinction between matter and spirit. The spirit represented the good, the aspirations of the soul; matter was bad. Hence salvation to ordinary people meant the emancipation of the soul from the thralldom of matter and the achievement of immortality through a union with God—not, of course, the God of the Jews, but a somewhat nebulous view of the divine that had been evolving for many generations.

It was this aspect of personal salvation, the immortality of the soul disencumbered of its material straitjacket, that was the objective of the Mystery cults, of Gnosticism—a widespread current of thought aiming at the penetration of the secrets of reality through a mystically acquired and privately guaranteed "knowledge" *(gnosis)*—and of neo-Platonism as well.

This longing, very general at the time, was satisfied by evolving Christianity. The redemption of the individual from the fetters of materialism, with its myriad afflictions, was achieved by the resurrection of an Incarnate God in a way structurally similar to the Mysteries and the ancient myths underlying them, but streamlined and democratized. At the same time, the central element of the new cult, the execution of a God, was linked on the one hand to a historical reality—it had happened—and on the other, because of the Incarnation, transcended via the torrent of emotionality released by the profound symbols of the new faith.

Christianity, entering the maelstrom of contending cults in the first and second centuries, was regarded as another oriental religion, strange only, in the beginning, in propping itself up for a short time on the ancient religion of the Jews, but otherwise a mystical and practical procedure for bringing about the salvation of its believers. Resting, on the one hand, on divine revelation and promising eternal salvation through an all-powerful Mediator, on the other, it claimed to establish on earth, too, a new life through love and virtue.

It was also, as I have indicated, relentlessly hostile to all forms of "syncretism"—the fusion of forms, rites, and myths aiming at a common objective. At the same time, its dogma as well as its practice was still very simple, that is, malleable. It could digest, without really being aware of it, the most fundamental of the religious aspirations and ritual practices it encountered when transplanted onto Hellenistic terrain. For that matter they were unavoidable. There was a constant interplay in the great capitals of the Hellenistic world between masses of people, both elite and plebeian, all longing for the same solutions to the same problems.

Thus, during the third century, as Christianity became embedded in Hellenistic society, it could meet and vanquish all forms of pagan syncretism for the simple reason that it had meanwhile itself become a syncretism too. It had absorbed and digested all the essential rites, the fertile ideas, metaphors, and symbols with which pagan religions were themselves pullulating. It was able to harmonize these through its central concept—the seemingly simple fact of the Incarnation and Redemptive Crucifixion—and without being inferior on any point could grapple with and incorporate or overcome all the inchoate beliefs and practices of its adversaries in the campaign to recruit adepts.

The central attraction of Christianity was unique. It was the only belief at the time that could point to a historical fact celebrated throughout the world—the execution of its own god. Thus the metaphysical and transcendental embroidery that was soon to encrust that fact had an unshakable anchorage, far removed, it must have seemed, from the whimsical fiddle-faddle of the cults and rites whose justification could be found in the minds of men alone.

Still, the absorption of Hellenistic culture was not accomplished overnight. The new faith made its way through various strata of pagan society, borrowing from each stratum and laying the foundations of the hierarchy still extant in the Roman Catholic Church. A graph of its ascension would rise from the most primitive faith of the most ignorant classes of the population to the philosophical sophistication of the intellectuals. The backbone of the new faith was strong enough to sustain it all.

The very first steps had been taken among the plebeians, initially those who for many reasons found solace in clustering around Jewish synagogues. On the other hand, not all the "God-fearers" were plebeian. They included many upper-class women and no doubt some men. Still, until the Antonines in the mid-second century, the upper classes could have been only a tiny minority in the church, whose chief recruits were slaves and laborers. Yet just such slaves carried the new idea into the milieu of free women, and accidentally, some learned men. Thus it was through the learned men that the new faith finally penetrated the upper classes and concomitantly the circles of the professional intellectuals—the philosophers—which it succeeded in doing during the second century.

The collision with thinkers close to the upper classes and the integration of their ideas with the simplicities of the new faith and with the explanation of the destiny of its deity Jesus Christ, both real-life and transcendental, was to make the ramifications of the encounter endless.

Thinkers like Justine Tatian and Tertullian, tormented by problems that could not be solved by current metaphysical speculation, became Christians because of the logical outcome of a personal crisis. For them the Christian faith solved all problems and satisfied all aspirations. On the other hand, that psychic fact did not in itself substantiate the somewhat simple postulates clustered around the bedrock of the Incarnation and the Redemptive Crucifixion. Such new converts, just because they had had an extensive philosophical training, inevitably brought it to bear on their new faith.

Their whole style of thought, their intellectual achievements, were put in the service of a new emotional current. Whether or not they expressed this notion explicitly, they were aware that the religion they had adopted lacked something or other, not, to be sure, in its substance—for example, the Incarnation, an idea as unfathomable as infinity—but in its formulation. In propagating their new faith, accordingly, they naturally found themselves fitting it out with the apparatus of ideas and formulations that gave it all the attraction of a philosophy with the additional potent charm of being *revealed*. They buttressed, amplified, and enriched its apologetics and dogmatics with all the interpretations and intellectual configurations derived from the metaphysics they had all been trained in.

Both Paul's ideas and the somewhat dissimilar though cognate views outlined in John (no doubt composed around the turn of the second century) were alike in being general enough to allow for immense elasticity. The guiding ideas of the first period in the formation of the nascent cult were in fact too general to control the movement of Hellenization, which in its very nature tended to become a hotchpotch.

It was natural for early Christians to borrow from the surrounding culture everything that seemed capable of making the initially inchoate religion more "profound" as well as more satisfying aesthetically. It was easy to find a modus vivendi between the basic postulates of the early faith and the major Hellenistic ideas. The Alexandrian school associated with the name of Origen (around the middle of the third century), for instance, turned Christianity into a revealed and flawless philosophy by splicing together all the magnifications borrowed from Hellenistic culture and the axioms of the new faith.

It was no doubt natural, too, for this process, inherently uncontrollable, to go to extremes. What had begun as a simple confession of faith was transformed during the third century into a complex edifice of ideas that looked unique. In the process of intertwining the axioms of the new faith with beliefs and notions taken over from the Hellenistic environment, it absorbed without inhibition practically everything it found. The general process had run riot; everything was taken in indiscriminately—Olympic paganism, Orphism, various oriental religions and philosophical systems—all of this quite independent of either the historical data, skimpy to begin with, or for that matter of the traditions handed down in the preceding few generations within the community of the believers.

This tendency pretended, in fact, to have a special revelation of its own, which itself justified the most extravagant combinations, all of which together made up a syncretistic system in which Jesus Christ was merely an element. Thus Christianity was twisted out of the historical context in which it had, at least, begun, and became, in fact, well-nigh unrecognizable. It had become no more than one part of a complex cosmogony and abstruse system of metaphysics, neither of which was inherently dependent on it at all.

All these "gnoses" had flourished in the second century. Precisely because of their complexity, capriciousness, and essential endlessness, they provoked the feeling of need for some hierarchical organization that during this same period began to take shape. The evolving faith plainly required both a discipline and an authority that would defend that discipline as well as represent it. Thus the power of the as yet somewhat inchoate clergy was focused, that is, enhanced and fortified, by the quasi-monopoly it rapidly acquired in dispensing the magical power inherent in the sacraments and in institutionalizing the theory underlying and the organization embodying them. The shapeless debates of the second century were the most potent factor in establishing a central authority—in organizing the Church.

Christianity also developed its ritual, for the same reasons and through the same processes, in line with the evolution of its dogmatic framework. It was natural for the Hellenistic milieu to channel pagan ritualism into what had been the simple worship of the earliest period, when that worship had been grounded in nothing more than the "Spirit" and "Truth." The whole of pagan ritualism came to be distributed somehow throughout the evolving Christian ceremonies, even though the genetic relationship between a given Christian and pagan rite may be obscure. In the fourth century, to be sure, some of these pagan rites were uprooted, but this merely accelerated the assimilation of the others.

Thus the simple practices inherited from Judaism, familiar to the earliest coteries—baptism, breaking of bread, laying on of hands, prayer, fasting—were now permeated with a more and more profound and above all mysterious meaning. They were amplified, deepened, decked out by rites taken over from the pagan surroundings, charged with the endless projections encompassed by the Greek and oriental Mysteries, and thus infused with all the ancient powers of magic.

Christianity, no doubt the vastest syncretism in history, had integrated a wide variety of rituals, customs, and attitudes with the sustaining framework of cosmic abstractions powered by emotion. And just because it sought to encompass the heavens it required a foundation on earth—an institution.

CHAPTER VII

INSTITUTIONALIZATION

The Jews were a considerable force in the Roman Empire. In numbers they came to about 10 percent of the population, perhaps some seven million. In Egypt every seventh or eighth person was a Jew; a third of Alexandria was Jewish.

Jews were famous as the oldest living people, except, of course, for the Egyptians, whose elite, however, had been obliterated by Hellenism. The Hebrew Scriptures seemed to go back to the very beginning of time.

Jews had some constitutional privileges. They were exempt from army service and did not have to pay tribute to local gods. Famous as mercenary soldiers, they were generally considered vigorous, manly, and stubborn. At that time they had no reputation for cleverness. The Jews seemed to be respected by the Romans even though Palestine itself was a source of constant irritation.

In Jewish doctrine pagans were to be bound by the seven "Noachide" laws (concerning idolatry, blasphemy, unchastity, bloodletting, robbery, eating the flesof of still-living animals, and justice in general). Any pagan actually dwelling on Jewish land was obliged to obey these Noachide laws, though not the Torah.

Countless pagans were attracted to Judaism in the culmination of a movement of missionary activity that had been promoted by the Hasmonean kings. Before the war against Rome, Jews were very friendly to converts. Judaism had even penetrated the topmost strat of the empire, indeed into Nero's court.

Partial converts to Judaism—"God-fearers"—in addition to living up to the Noachide laws, were expected to obey the Ten Commandments, observe the Sabbath, abstain from outrageous behavior, and pay the Temple tax. Though not admitted to sacrifices, they could take part in rituals and ceremonies. They did not have to be circumcised or to obey the dietary laws. The final stage was, of course, actual conversion; a full convert was simply a Jew in all respects.

It took a couple of generations after the execution of Jesus for the Jewish-oriented Jesists to be submerged in the throngs of pagan recruits and a little longer for the ideas associated with Paul to be wrenched out of their historical context to become the theology of a new institution.

For Paul, as we have seen, there was no point in creating an actual institution, either speculative or organizational, since for him the Kingdom of God was at hand. And even after the destruction of the Temple in A.D. 70, all Jesists still felt themselves to be on the threshold of the only-slightly-postponed Kingdom of God and therefore in no need of organization.

Thus at the outset the unity of believers was simple. They formed the One People of God, the Body of Christ: "There is one body and one spirit . . . one Lord, one faith, one baptism, one God and Father of us all" (Eph. 4:4–6).[1]

At first the organization of the Jesist coteries was hesitant, groping. With no rationale, no attempts at systematization were made. But as soon as the initial disappointment in the failure of the Kingdom of God to appear "immediately" began to be felt and as it steadily became clearer and clearer that the Kingdom was not, in fact, arriving from one day, or month, or year to the next, the first attempts at organization were made.

A couple of generations after Paul we can discern the emergence of two offices: the "bishop" (in the singular) and the "elders" (presbyters, in the plural).

By this time, the bishop as the apex of a pyramid might have been established, though it is difficult to generalize. There was no division into clergy and laity, no priestly consecration (only an ordination in the presence of the group), and no idea that the bishop had been empowered by any authority. It is not even sure that the bishop, when there was one, was the sole leader of the group. The difference between the bishop and the elders was not formalized, i.e., not substantive.

By the time of Ignatius, Bishop of Antioch around A.D. 110, bishops, elders, and deacons had emerged. The organizational structure, moreover, was not intertwined with the basic ideas of the nascent Church—the Christology, the doctrine of the Spirit, the sacraments, and the idea of the church, all of which, taken together, constitute the spiritual as well as organizational justification of the hierarchy. By then God was represented within the community by the bishop. To be sure, it is impossible to analyze the progression from a lay leader of a group in which all are equal to the monarchical position of the bishop, the holder of a sacral office (consummated much later on by the papal office in which the first bishop of the Roman See became the first bishop of the Church, and much later the pope).

With hindsight we can, of course, see that the cardinal concepts of the Incarnation and Redemptive Crucifixion entailed a clarification of social relationships that led to the ramified structure of the later Church: Was it necessary to have an intermediary between Christ and the believer? What made a sacrament effective?

Organizationally, what was the function of the bishop in the mediation needed between God (or Christ) and man? How did this mediation function? Was someone special—a priest—needed to dispense a true, effective sacrament? Could a priest in

his turn be consecrated only by a superior, a bishop? Was the
Church as a totality needed to serve as mediator between God
and man? Was the Church itself the agency of salvation? Why
was it, in fact, needed at all?

But at the beginning of the second century these peremptory
questions had not yet been raised, let alone settled.

Meanwhile, how were the Hebrew Scriptures to be dealt
with?

For the earliest Jesists the Hebrew Scriptures were the only
Scriptures. The first coteries were in no sense consciously leaving Judaism. The god they believed in was still the Yahweh of
the Hebrew Scriptures; when they said "scriptures" or "scripture" that was what they meant. The expressions "canon," "Old
Testament," and "New Testament" were not to come about
until much later.

But though Paul refers to the Old and New covenants as new
facts, and though the word he used in Greek was to be translated into Latin as "Testament" and has thus come down to us in
that form, it was long after Paul before anyone would refer to
the books of the Old Covenant, and later of the New Covenant,
and later still before the word "Testament" came to mean a
collection of books of any kind. For Paul himself, who felt
wholly Jewish, though in a new era because of the resurrection
of Jesus, the Hebrew Scriptures remained unconditionally valid.
It was for him only a question of interpretation.

From the very beginning Jesus was necessarily integrated
with the Hebrew Scriptures ipso facto. Since in real life he had
been wholly identified with messianic though normative Judaism, it was only natural for the earliest coteries to cling to that
primal fact.

The belief in Jesus as Messiah was itself, after all, anchored in
the Hebrew Scriptures, since the very concept of the Messiah,
drawn from the ancient past, was an element in the later view of
Judaism as standing on the threshold of a new age.

Thus the naked assertion that the Messiah *has come* in and of
itself entailed a positive acceptance of the Hebrew Scriptures,
which in turn generated a polemic against official Judaism about
their interpretation.

Around the beginning of the second century the idea of there having been "Twelve Apostles" was worked out. By then the believers, feeling themselves to belong to the "third generation," called for a definition of the second, the "apostolic," generation.

By this time the notion of the Glorious Return, containing within it the bedrock notion of the World's End, was well-nigh extinct, though the weight of the earlier ideas was such that individuals could still go on expecting it. Nevertheless, despite instances of a faith that still clung to this formerly explosive idea, it was already, functionally speaking, a fossil. For that matter even the delay in the Glorious Return no longer needed an explanation. Paul's letters, instinct with ardent expectation of an imminent transformation of the world, were by now entirely relocated on earthly terrain. The World's End meant nothing, and the henceforth authoritative reading of Paul's writings simply ignored his fundamental point of view altogether. With the extinction of his real view, the metaphorization of the Kingdom of God may be said to have begun.

To clarify the status of the Scriptures, Justin Martyr (ca. A.D. 150) distinguished between three elements in the Hebrew Scriptures: the moral law, the prophesying of the Christ, and the cultic law. The first two were still valid, but the cult was extinct.

This attempt at differentiation between the various elements in something accepted as divine itself, necessarily implied a radically different approach. When the question is asked about the validity of the Torah as divine, reason must be applied; the "valid" elements have to be separated from the others. This opened the way for the blanket rejection of the Hebrew Scriptures and led to the emergence of what was to become known as the canon of the New Testament, which was meant either to supplement the Old or replace it.

The process naturally involved a further deployment of the authority now being centralized.

The original authority for the Jesist coteries had, of course, been simply the Lord. This in itself implied an absolute supremacy for the words attributed to Jesus, however scanty they were. Even though Paul says practically nothing about the real-life Jesus, the few things he does mention had absolute authority, for example, the Last Supper (1 Cor. 11:23ff.) and one or two direct commandments (prohibiting divorce and defining marriage, as in 1 Cor. 7:10), which Paul attributes directly to Jesus while nevertheless interpreting them, to be sure, in his own way. Paul does not, to be sure, analyze the historical background of what he reports Jesus as having said at the Last Supper. It has already, en route to Paul, been wrenched out of its historical context.

The somewhat tortuous path that led from an original free form of the Lord's extremely uncomplicated authority to the canonization of the books purporting to contain that authority is too obscure to trace. In fact, down to the middle of the second century we have no documents, nor does any book have any authority whatever. At the same time, two foci of crystallization seem gradually to have acquired recognition: (1) Paul's letters, which contained an outline of the faith now coagulating, and (2) the Gospels, which rounded off the relationship of that faith to the world.

Though the Gospels, at any rate the first three, presented themselves as a chronicle of Jesus's life on earth, they consisted, in fact, of material designed to give instruction about the meaning of that life on earth. (It took some eighteen centuries before this simple, though fundamental, distinction was recognized.)

At first the two collections were independent of each other; when they were combined the first Christian canon may be said to have emerged. The common presupposition for both collections was that the current believers of the second century were separated from the very first believers by an epoch. This came to be known as the apostolic epoch, though this very conception was, as I have indicated, itself a construction of the later theory. It was taken for granted, around the middle of the second century, that the two were essentially a unity, even though Paul by this time had become entirely authoritative for the literary or theological collection. Although the details remain unknown, Paul's status gradually rose after his death until his victory toward the beginning of the second century. Since then he has been the paramount theologian of Christianity.

Soon after A.D. 100 the collection of his epistles numbering ten (Paul's present letters without the three to Timothy and Titus, which came later) had already been formed.

The impact of Paul's brainwork on the evolution of Christianity can hardly be overestimated. With very minor exceptions it was Paul's letters that shaped or substantially influenced all early Christian epistolary literature and subsequently all Christian doctrine.

As for the Gospels, their somewhat camouflaged catechetical structure replaced whatever had been the oral tradition about Jesus, assuming one existed. The oldest Gospel was that of Mark, the model for Matthew and Luke, though by the second century it was still far from canonical. Matthew and Luke supplement Mark and while retaining its ground plan give it a new shape. John, no doubt written around the beginning of the second century, represents an entirely different theological tradition. In the absence of authority, to be sure, anyone could handle traditional material as he wished.

There is no way of knowing just how these particular Gospels came to be regarded as authoritative. Each one had been revered in some particular community. One can only assume that in the give-and-take of intracommunal relations as the Church came to be organizationally shaped, the contention and compromise were worked out in the canon that has come down to us.

The tradition was not yet extinguished by the emergence of the Gospels in the second century. Bishop Papias of Hierapolis in Asia Minor, for instance, says stoutly that he esteems the "oral tradition" (we have no way of knowing what it was) far more than the books being put together at that time in what was to become the canon.

Throughout the first half of the second century, in fact, the idea of a canon consisting of the Four Gospels had not yet emerged. What was required for the very concept of a canon, of course, as well as its corollary, the antithetical idea of "apocrypha," was a central authority.

The first attempt to form a canon came about as the result of a determined effort to take an alternative approach to the two already mentioned. An attempt was made to replace the

Hebrew Scriptures entirely. This attempt was made around A.D. 140 by Marcion, the son of a Jesist who came to Rome from Sinope on the Black Sea.

Marcion made a systematic effort to justify discarding the Hebrew Scriptures altogether. The logic of the evolution of a new faith had persuaded him that the Hebrew Scriptures were now simply pointless. The God of the Scriptures was no longer the same as the God of Jesus Christ. Yahweh was no more, he thought, than the creator of the World, the God of mere righteousness. The real God—the good God—dwells outside the world altogether; and it was this good God, who out of compassion for men embroiled in the iniquities arising out of the world created by Yahweh, who has revealed himself in Jesus Christ. For Marcion, therefore, redemption meant redemption from the world and from the Torah, whose meaning was only for the world.

He maintained, further, that this had been the same view as that of Jesus himself and of Paul, but that the teachings of both had been warped.

Accordingly, Marcion put together a canon, his own—the first Christian canon. It consisted of nothing but the ten letters of Paul and the Gospel of Luke. Paul's far-reaching mythology was logically independent of the Hebrew Scriptures despite Paul's personal view of them as indispensable. Paul, it is true, regarded his whole system as justified only by the titanic event of the Kingdom of God, imminently to be installed. When that failed to happen a different logic supervened—the same logic that turned his history-bound explanation of the resurrection into a timeless theology. Marcion was merely drawing different conclusions from premises that had been altered by the collapse of the Kingdom of God theory and the consequent need for the Church to go on living in this world.

Marcion dropped from Luke as a mere forgery whatever clashed with his doctrine. Thus he eliminated the account of Jesus's birth (Luke 1 and 2), designed originally to demonstrate to Jews that Jesus came of the royal line of King David (marred toward the end only by the insertion of the legend of the Virgin Birth). Since, for Marcion, the Redeemer was not born a man at all (he merely appeared from heaven in the fifteenth year of the reign of Emperor Tiberius), Marcion started off his Luke from the opening of chapter 3.

In this way the first Christian canon eliminated the Hebrew Scriptures entirely from the substance of the evolving faith. There was to be a complex clash of views revolving around the very essence of the new faith as such: the very idea of God as manifested in the relationship of God to the world, in the Creation and the Redemption, in the relationship between God and the Christ, in the nature of Christ, and in the validity of the tradition underlying the "truth" of the evolving Church.

For some time, to be sure, this remained totally unorganized. There was still no center for the far-flung coteries professing, with varying emphasis, the cluster of ideas of which a few were soon to emerge as orthodox, that is, official.

Still, toward the end of the second century the idea of a canon pervaded the Christian coteries even without an organizational focus. In any event, the canon became what was now to be considered the Old Testament, that is, the Hebrew Scriptures (themselves canonized a relatively short time before) rounded off by a standard, i.e., agreed-on collection of Christian writings. Though some details remained a subject of debate—and were, indeed, never settled—they were no more than details.

Marcion's single Gospel was replaced by the Four Gospels that are familiar. This number was explained by the Church Father Irenaeus (ca. A.D. 186) as embodying the concept of the four winds, i.e., the four points of the compass. In addition, the number conforms with the number of heavenly beings mentioned in Revelation 4 (cf. Ezekiel 1): man/angel (for Matthew), lion (for Mark), ox (for Luke), and eagle (for John).

Irenaeus, the mentor of Tertullian in Africa, Clement in Alexandria, and Hippolytus in Rome, represented a critical stage in the standardization of beliefs and institutions. His enterprise of orderly centralization was continued by ecumenical councils and much later by the papacy. It culminated, logically, in the papal infallibility decree of 1870.

It was some time before this collection of Four Gospels itself became sacred. For a long time the Syrian Church, for instance, accepted a sort of "harmony" of the Gospels, all four being reworked into one. Also, the Gospel of John, which fits so badly from an integrated point of view with the other Three (Synoptic) Gospels, was occasionally challenged, but without result. On the other hand those who disputed its authenticity, i.e., its aptness, were never accused of heresy.

The apostolic section of the evolving canon took in the ten letters ascribed to Paul and was never challenged; it was augmented by three more letters (two to Timothy and one to Titus). The apostolic canon was expanded to take in the "catholic" epistles, though variously in different places. There was a consensus in favor of recognizing 1 Peter and 1 John, gradually added to by the five others, thereby making up the seven that have since been accepted as official.

The question of the criteria involved in the establishment of a canon was scarcely raised in a self-conscious manner. There was simply a widespread desire for information about the Savior that could be considered reliable. The legacy ascribed to the earliest phase of the faith was thought of as calling for documentation. It had its roots in an era well before the formation of a central authority, when the production of gospels as such was not thought of as a peril to the community. After the first, philosophical campaign of Marcion around A.D. 130–140, the feeling was accentuated that the broader the basis for documents attesting to Jesus's life on earth and its meaning the better. If an individual passing as an "apostle" could produce a "gospel" there was no objection to it. But in the absence of a central authority, the validity of such a gospel was not established by an ecclesiastical office but only by the consensus that the witness was reliable, that is, knowledgeable.

This very fact, to be sure, had to be buttressed, ultimately, by just such an authority. What standard of common sense, for instance, could decide the validity of the varying accounts in the Four Gospels? How could the reliability of the authors, whoever they were, be assessed? The notion that Matthew and John were apostles, for instance, was itself a decision of *some* ecclesiastical authority, even before the emergence of a center.

The reliability of the two non-apostles, Mark and Luke, also had to be laid down from above.

In this period inspiration, too, was irrelevant. It was not until the following generation (under the influence of Origen) that the notion of "inspiration" was transferred from the Old Testament to the New. Beforehand the question of inspiration versus a formal book was meaningless. It was essentially an idea that could prove attractive to people preoccupied with the subject only after the concept of "Scripture" as distinct from "Spirit" had achieved a substantial degree of formalization. In the early period there could be no conflict in principle between "Spirit" and "Book"; the book itself was intertwined with the life of the Church.

The fledgling faith had to contend, of course, with many rivals—not merely the Mysteries themselves, of which it could present itself as the seal and simultaneously the obliterator, and Judaism, which it could claim to have superseded; but others of which we have only hints, such as the cult revolving around one Simon the Magus, a Samaritan who seems to have been a genuine rival. He is, indeed, the only head of a non-Christian sect mentioned in the New Testament (Acts 8:9ff.), where he is treated as a mere self-styled embodiment of the "Great Power" inherent in God. Later on he was to be treated by the Church Fathers (apparently with no historical information) as the father of the "Gnostic heresy."

It was, indeed, Gnosticism in all its forms (asceticism, ritualism, libertinism, docetism) that at one time seemed to be about to become the standard form of the new faith. By taking a radical interpretation of the Christology, that is, by making absolute the Incarnation and thus splitting off from the concept of Jesus any form of humanity at all, Gnosticism split God and the world, as well as salvation and the world. Had this prevailed it would no doubt have transformed Christianity into an unorganized group of individuals with a merely spiritual view of things.

But this was soon swept aside by the tide of secular organization that was to turn Christianity into a world institution. By the beginning of the second century the way was open to the establishment of Christianity both as a new religion and as a new organization.

Two or three generations after Paul, accordingly, the Torah was no longer a "problem." Consummated by the destruction of the Jerusalem Temple, the problem whose solution had been adumbrated early on by Stephen and the Hellenists had been solved; the Torah was dropped. What had been a potential conflict between Jews and full pagans within the new Jesist sect had evaporated.

That alone, however, did not solve the problem of the Scriptures, which had formed an integral element of the day-to-day belief of the early Jesists as well as the bedrock of their religious feelings and worldview. How could the Scriptures be adapted to the changing views of the Jesist community at the very moment their essential elements had been discarded?

From the point of view of the functioning, so to speak, of the evolving faith, a new role had to be devised for the Hebrew Scriptures.

Basically, of course, they were held to prophesy the advent of the Christ (as in Matthew). In addition, they were still regarded as the repository of God's commandments, of which the major ones, in particular the Ten Commandments, were still held to be valid. If a figurative style was in favor, the Old Testament was thought to have prefigured salvation by the demonstration of God's intervention in history. It also contained a sort of prototype of Christian life (as in 1 Clement, which has a substantial admixture of material drawn from the Hebrew Scriptures).

Throughout the formative period of the new Church, indeed, all the major elements were drawn from Jewish precept, even after the structure of belief itself had been transformed by the expanding concept of the Savior.

The ritual itself was drawn from Jewish experience. Scripture reading, preaching, prayer, all reflected the preponderant influence of the synagogue.

Sunday, as a day of reunion, was taken for granted in Paul's day (1 Cor. 16:2. It seems to have been for the purpose of taking up a collection for the "saints" in Jerusalem). There was also a regular custom, around the beginning of the second century, of meeting for morning worship and instruction.

By the middle of the second century the essential elements of a Sunday liturgy, as we are familiar with it today, were established.

In the first part of the service the congregation would hear a reading from the Gospels or the Prophets, over a fixed period of time. Then the officiant would give a sermon of exhortation to the congregation, including catechumens as well as serious non-Christians.

In the second part the congregation would be reduced to the baptized. It would begin with a prayer for the salvation of Christendom and its moral perfecting for achieving eternal salvation. The members would then give each other the kiss of brotherhood as a symbol of Christian unity.

Then the "offertory" would be made. The members of the congregation would bring the officiant bread, wine, and water. He would recite, over the gifts arranged on the table, the prayer of thanksgiving. The congregation would respond with "Amen" and invoke the Logos, which the officiant would pray to descend onto the bread and wine so that it could become the saving body and blood of Jesus.

After this culminating rite, deacons would distribute the consecrated gifts to those present, later taking them to the absent, to the sick, and to prisoners. The service would conclude with the collection of voluntary offerings deposited with the officiant to enable him to succor the sick, widows, orphans, and so forth.[2]

From the earliest times on, Easter was celebrated at the date established for Passover in the Jewish calendar, the day of the full moon of the spring month (14th Nisan). The content, of course, now encompassed the Passion and crucifixion of the Christ.

Accordingly, by the middle of the second century or, more precisely, after the Bar Kochba insurrection against the Romans in A.D. 135 was crushed, the chasm between Judaism and Christianity could no longer be bridged without a special act of conversion; though, as we have seen from the example of Chrysostom, social relations between Jews and Christians were to be relatively intimate for centuries.

These complex developments took place against a turbulent background. The relations of the new sect with the Roman State were of primary political importance.

In modern terms the Roman Empire was not highly organized. There was, for instance, no imperial police force; nor were the provinces, governed by more or less sovereign governors, in any way homogeneous. They were a congeries of allies, free cities, vassal rulers (themselves with variously defined relationships with the central government), and territories under direct rule. Because of all this there was no uniform treatment of the evolving faith.

Before the collapse of the Jewish State and Temple in A.D. 70, the Roman government had acted against the Jews only in special circumstances, since Judaism, a *religio licita,* was constitutionally authorized and institutionally anchored in special privileges. The Jewish rejection of divine images, for instance, was accepted even after the Roman-Jewish War.

Before that the Roman authorities had done nothing to track down the Jesists after the crucifixion of Jesus, though, as we have seen, some special measures were taken against the members of Jesus's family.

Under Claudius in the Forties the expulsion of the Jews from Rome as well as the riots in Alexandria around the same time were probably because of the eruption of some messianically inspired riots our sources shed no light on. Similarly, the action undertaken by Nero in A.D. 64 might have had something to do with that. After a great fire, "death penalties were pronounced on Christians, a sect that had succumbed to a new superstition dangerous to the public." There is some indication that repressive measures remained in effect for some time.[3]

On the other hand, though the Christians were not convicted of arson but only of "hatred of the human race," part of the "absurd and repugnant Jewish way of life,"[4] it would have been only natural for the Roman State to be hostile to the new sect whose founder, after all, had been executed for sedition. This made them ipso facto a criminal sect.

In any case, the destruction of the Zealot movement in the debacle of A.D. 70 inevitably attenuated, after a time, the culpability of the Christians, who were themselves changing very rapidly vis-à-vis the Roman State. From A.D. 70 on, the Roman authorities were affected by the new sect only if it caused riots or other disorders.

Around A.D. 112, for instance, Pliny, governor of Pontus-Bithynia, wrote the Emperor Trajan asking whether the "name itself" of a Christian was punishable—that is, whether the Jesists as such were still a criminal sect—or whether it was necessary to specify particular crimes they had actually committed. Pliny's letter indicates that there may have been social problems, such as damage to business, that on various occasions played a role.

As late as A.D. 112, therefore, it remained a question in law whether the association was itself illegal, in which case a confession would have been the equivalent of condemnation, or whether specific evidence had to be presented to the authorities. As governor, Pliny himself, for instance, had the Christians condemned if they refused to abjure their specific beliefs, a procedure that was approved of by Trajan, who nevertheless laid it down that Christians were not to be hunted down by the authorities, nor were anonymous denunciations to be heeded.

Popular prejudice was, to be sure, widespread. It interpreted the meetings of worship, culminating in the banquet of believers (the Agape), as orgies. The notion was that Christians slaughtered and devoured children (apparently a misinterpretation of the Eucharist).

Trajan's orders to Pliny held good for some time. If valid accusations were laid before the authorities, Christians had to offer sacrifice or die. That is. the question of tolerating Christians was dealt with not judicially but politically. Christian hostility to the state, even though it was not articulated, was regarded as judicially well-established but not punished as such. All Christians were given the opportunity to demonstrate the contrary by sacrificing before a statue of the emperor. It was only when they expressly refused, and hence violated the reverence felt to be due the majesty of the emperor and the tutelary gods, that the death penalty would be incurred.

In any case, however, the state did not persecute Christians as such; even the imperial edicts prohibiting the profession of the religion never led to general persecutions. The edicts themselves were mere repetitions of Trajan's guidelines, and the manner in which they were carried out was left to the political judgment of the provincial authorities.[5]

Despite a widespread impression, the cult of the emperor apparently played no role in state intervention. The notion that Christians had to exchange the formula "Jesus is Lord" for "Caesar is Lord" is legendary.[6]

The Roman governors, to be sure, had extensive powers. They could make their own enquiries into facts, evaluate them, and pronounce judgment. Thus, under Trajan as well as his successors, it was always possible for the situation of a given Christian coterie to deteriorate in some specific province. The result was that in spite of the exaggerations of Christian martyrdom made by the later Church, it seems that under the early Roman Empire "the actual outbreaks of persecution were limited in area and duration."[7]

On the other hand, the new sect never became an enemy of the state. This stemmed, very naturally, from the interpretation given to the crucifixion from the very beginning, perhaps most markedly by Paul, the interpretation that eschewed a violently hostile view of the Roman Empire and that was, in fact, the theme of all the Gospels. From the time of the Jewish debacle on, the Jesists distinguished themselves from the obvious other alternative taken by Jewish apocalypticism and by one Jewish political tendency—the Kingdom of God activists.

Thus it was this strand—the otherworldly theme of the Jewish visionaries—that became an integral part of the triumph of the new sect, especially after the collapse of its this-worldly, violent rival, the Zealots, whom the original Jesist coterie in Jerusalem had been intimately allied or identified with and were, in fact, submerged together with in A.D. 70.

On the level of theology, to be sure, the book of Revelation is, of course, the precise opposite. For the author of Revelation the universe is filled with an out-and-out war in which the Beast, obviously the Roman Empire, has emerged from the abyss demanding worship. Nevertheless the whole scene is mere fantasy. Set in heaven, it does not purport to give any flesh-and-blood people any instructions that would involve the authorities. For this very reason, perhaps, it could ultimately survive to be included in the Christian canon; it could satisfy theory without endangering the believers.

The text of Romans 13:1–7 (as well as related passages in 1 Peter 2:13–14) tells the believers, quite simply, to obey the authorities and be still. In Paul's formulation of the World's End theories that he shared with others, there was no need to involve the new sect in trouble with the authorities of this world when it was about to pass away at any moment.

This theory was bound to prevail. Since all World's End theories put a foreseeable and indeed imminent term to the workaday world, there was no need for the new sectarians to emigrate from this world even in theory. The ones who chose to emigrate from this world and did so, in practice as well as in theory, either perished physically in Palestine after the Jewish debacle in A.D. 70 or else lived out their disappointed lives.

In the passage from Romans cited above Paul avoids mentioning cases in which the state might require a religious confession that would inevitably be repugnant to sincere believers, but the related passage in 1 Peter 2 specifically enjoins the believer to wear a mask on all occasions: "Be subject for the Lord's sake to every human institution, whether it be the emperor as supreme, or to governors" (1 Pet. 2:13–14). It is evident that this prudent advice is given with an eye to possible persecutions. This was part of the advice given to pray for the well-being of the authorities, not, of course, for their conversion (1 Tim. 2:1–2 and 1 Clement 61). In theory, the Church, generally speaking, was not supposed to lay itself open to martyrdom at all but simply to defend itself against false accusations and to propagandize on behalf of the new faith.

In its early formulations this theory, too, was connected with the World's End.

The early Jesists, as they diverged from Judaism, found themselves grappling with a social problem. Life in the Hellenistic environment was universally characterized by religious and cultic practices of all sorts. The Mysteries, of course, could participate in anything, since the adept's commitment to the rites and theory of his particular Mystery did not prevent him or her from participating in any other cult whatever while preserving his Mystery commitment within a special sphere.

Though Judaism was still a *religio licita,* the Jesists were in a peculiar position. Still considered, in a way, an offshoot of Judaism, they were the target of growing hostility from the leaders of the many Jewries scattered throughout the empire. At the same time, they required of their membership an *active* denial of all other religious connections, an echo of the exclusiveness characteristic of monotheism.

If we cast a glance backward at the Church as it took shape around the beginning and until the end of the fourth century, and compare it with the small Jesist coterie of the first generation, we find a dramatic transformation.

Instead of a small group of Kingdom of God activists integrated with Jewry, assiduously praying in the Temple of Jerusalem, distinguished from most Jews only through a hope linked to a specific Jewish hero and playing a role in the Kingdom of God agitation holding the country in its grip, we see, two and a half centuries later, a religious organization encompassing a cross-section of a vast congeries of peoples. All members of the organization have a unique awareness—they are the Church of Christ, the elect of mankind.

This church has by now rejected Israel root and branch; Israel is said to have abandoned the ways of the Lord and to be abjectly straying far from the truth. Moreover, Israel's rejection of the Incarnation has made it a natural ally of Satan. Paul's nuanced relationship to Jewry has been dropped together with his timetable.

For Paul, the failure of the Jews to grasp the implications of the Resurrection, the proof of the Incarnation, had been a "Mystery": as the premier people in the world, the only one with whom God had had a covenant, they would inevitably perceive, very soon, the titanic significance of the Incarnation and be present to usher in the Kingdom of God together with all converts.

But with the forgetting of the Kingdom of God as a palpable reality, and with the institution of an Eternal Church, the role of the Jews as de facto allies of Satan itself became eternalized. This did not, of course, entail their extinction: Jewry was bound to survive, even though in abject circumstances, as Witness to the Triumph of Christianity. (This essentialization of Evil in "the Jews" was to play a persistent role in history.)

Yet, aside from doctrine, though the church has rid itself of all the practices of the Jewish Torah except for some customs that have been charged with an entirely different meaning, it has managed to preserve the Hebrew Scriptures, now the Old Testament, part of a new canon of its own whose rationale is established by the New Testament.

This in itself is surprising, since whether or not one might claim that the Hebrew Scriptures remain valuable because they lead up to the New Testament, the massive texts of the Old Testament, whose origins go back thousands of years and which took well-nigh a millennium for the composition of its various sections, are restricted, after all, to the history and ideas of the Jews, one people among others. One might have thought that Christianity might, perhaps, have gained from discarding the Torah altogether (the aim of Marcion and his school).

Yet the historical origins of the early Jesist coteries, with the primitive habit of relying on the Bible as prophetical for the early purpose of propagandizing among Jews and semi-Jews, had congealed into a veneration for the Hebrew Scriptures despite the logic of the detachment from the tradition they embodied. The veneration of Christians, following the Jesists, for the divine authority of the Bible was thus firmly anchored. The attempts that had been made to get rid of all aspects of Judaism had been unable to overcome its original genetic connection with the new faith.

Thus the Church, for which the faith of Israel had been a mere starting point, has gradually pieced together a new and complex system of dogmatics revolving in its essence around the speculation dealing with the person of Christ—"Christology"—by now, of course, long since expanded to identification with God.

This whole work of inflation and expansion was dependent for its elements on the reflections I have indicated as arising out of the earliest magnifications of Jesus within the framework of Jewish history, buttressed and ramified by the rich material taken from the philosophical and religious doctrines of the Greco-Roman (Hellenistic) milieu.

This whole system of dogmatics, expressed in the rule of faith presumably based on the opinion of the majority, as interpreted, of course, by a central authority, has got to the stage of being presented to the world as a revealed, perfected system of philosophy, an all-embracing, changeless explanation of the world, of life, of destiny.

From the merely organizational point of view, the Christian Church has the aspect of an established institution. Originally organized in private assemblies modeled on the Jewish synagogue or on pagan associations, by the beginning of the third century it has assigned both its administration and its spiritual functions—conceptually speaking, a seamless web—to a body of clergy in a hierarchical order. The chief clergy have adopted the habit of consulting about the ensemble of activities involving morals, faith, and discipline. A majority opinion from among these higher clergy is expressed in concerted public pronouncements.

The clerical authorities preside over rites that have been borrowed, more or less directly, either from Judaism—the handful of rites mentioned above—or from the pagan Mysteries. These all have been integrated with Christian aims. The principal rites have been recharged with the magical power familiar to adepts of the secret cults of Greece and of the Middle East.

By the beginning of the third century Christianity has finally become a real religion, plausibly presented as the most complete of all religions, since it has taken what it can regard as the best from them all. It can also maintain that it is the most comforting, the most compassionate of all. To achieve salvation, an ignoramus need only believe without understanding and obey the authorities, while the philosophically minded can speculate endlessly on the dogmas, which, rooted in the bedrock of the Incarnation and the Redemptive Crucifixion, are themselves endless.

At the same time, though manifestly itself a complex syncretism, Christianity proclaims a comprehensive and indeed fanatical exclusiveness. It cannot share believers with any other religion, nor can it tolerate rivals.

Ramified, articulated, and insulated against other social entities, the Church stands out against the animosity of the state as well as that of the larger society it has not yet won over. Challenging the fabric of that larger society and permeating it steadily, the Church will be ready to assume its leadership in another century when, through the conversion of Constantine the Great in A.D. 325, it will become both a source of state power and an unchallengeable repository of spiritual authority.

CRITICAL APPENDIX

THE LOST CONTINENT

*T*he reader will have observed that the story he has read is not the traditional one. Its background, the real-life roots of what came to be Christianity, is centred in a set of circumstances that are only glancingly and indeed—if we look at the New Testament alone—incomprehensibly referred to in conventional accounts.

The fundamental enigma of the New Testament is the answer to a simple question: Why was a herald of the Kingdom of God executed as a rebel against the State?

No real-life explanation of this seemingly strange fact is given in the documents themselves; the deep meaning extracted by St. Paul from the Crucifixion is, of course, the foundation of the church, but the Kingdom of God itself, which is the starting point, is not explained at all.

That would seem, nevertheless, to be the nub of the matter. How is it, then, that the Kingdom of God has been misperceived for almost 2,000 years?

How is it that the movement of the Kingdom of God activists—Zealots and others—which smashed the Jewish state and launched Christianity, has been disregarded? How is it that the interconnection between Judah the Galilean and the Zealots, and Jesus the Nazarene, John the Baptist and Saul of Tarsus—St. Paul—is not obvious?

To grasp the reasons for this, the organizing principle of the scanty documentation that supports the vast literature on Christian origins must be established. We can start from the plain fact that all those documents were composed after the death of Jesus.

Paul's letters are of course by far the oldest source for the history of the new faith, but Paul was writing in a situation many years after the events described in the first Gospels; his own viewpoint influenced the writers and editors of the Gospels. More particularly, Paul died before the Roman-Jewish War 66–70, which was surely uppermost in the mind of the author of Mark, whose ground-plan was followed by the other two Synoptic Gospels.

Paul's letters, taken together with the Gospels and Acts of the Apostles, disclose a baffling enigma—the dense obscurity overhanging the two decades—roughly A.D. 60–80—between the letters written by Paul, a real individual, and the anonymous compilations in the Gospels that came into being one by one after the destruction of the Jewish State and Temple in A.D. 70.

This enables us to see, graphically displayed, a profound, inexplicable, and of course camouflaged contrast between the official version of Christian origins and the realistic glimpses tantalizingly suggested by Paul's urgent, passionate, real-life struggle and by the random nuggets of historical actuality embedded in the Gospels themselves.

From this point of view the indifference of both church historians and academic scholarship to the fate of the Jesist coterie in Jerusalem, headed, after all, by Jesus's brother, is bewildering. If the "Mother Church" ever existed, its total silence is incomprehensible. If its leaders had ever had anything self-aware to say, it would have been easy and natural for whatever it was to be circulated throughout the far-flung Jewish Diaspora. It is obvious that the very concept of the Mother Church, as well as the phrase itself, is profoundly misleading.

Around the middle of the Fifties—the time of the riot occasioned by Paul on the Temple premises—it is possible to infer a crisis in the history of the Jewish state and hence within the coterie of the Jerusalem Jesists. From then on all remains blank. We are thrown back on the evolution of the Zealot crisis that erupted in the Roman War of 66–70. Then, as the earliest documents of the new sect, starting with Mark, began to be assembled afterwards, we can once again see the beginning of a continuity, in which, however, the first phase in the evolution of the new faith—the lives of Jesus, John the Baptist, Upright Jacob, and Paul himself—is twisted about to conform with the later tradition embodied in Mark, Matthew, Luke, Acts, and John.

For the author of Mark, the problem, as indicated, was simple: Since Mark had to nullify any identification of Jesus with the Zealots whose agitation had launched the war of 66–70, he had to exculpate him from the charge of being an activist in general, and an enemy of Rome in particular. To do this he had to denature the Kingdom of God—to depoliticize it by twisting its undeniable association with Jesus out of its sociopolitical background and by giving it an elusive other-worldly meaning. The corollary of this was to slide past the attack on the Temple and the resulting execution of Jesus for sedition.

Thus it was the convergence of two concerns that led to the apologetic distortion of the historical account in the Synoptic Gospels.

One concern was to stress the transcendentalization of Jesus that had been going on in the Jewish Diaspora side-by-side with the initial tradition of Jesus the Jewish Messiah and his Glorious Return as Bringer of the Kingdom of God; the other concern, desperately urgent because of the bitterness surrounding the war, was to free the Jesist congregations in the Roman Empire from the stigma of the Zealots.

On the other hand, since there was no way of twisting the basic facts out of shape—i.e., the indictment and execution of Jesus as King of the Jews by a Roman official—it was necessary to create a narrative structure that, while accommodating the irrefragable fact of Jesus's execution, plausibly explained it away.

This was by no means due to hypocrisy; we have seen how Jesus the Messiah had been escalated into Lord of the Universe, Son of God, and Savior of Mankind in the Diaspora under the primary influence of Paul. Psychologically, indeed, the same impulse that divorced the real-life Jesus from his historical background paralleled the original impulse in the psyches of Diaspora Jews like Paul that made them transcendentalize all traditional Jewish national ideas while remaining convinced, like Paul, that that itself represented the realization of a Jewish idea.

The initial magnification of Jesus came about through an event that in the history of religion has been commonplace—a vision: Simon the Rock's vision on the Sea of Galilee very soon after the execution. This had an electrifying effect on Jesus's immediate entourage. Yet for that entourage, which moved to Jerusalem very quickly, the vision, while representing a unique event, was nevertheless held within the framework of Jewish ideas; the vision merely confirmed, so to speak, Jesus's status as Messiah; his messiahship was still in accordance with the basic conception of the Kingdom of God as a transformation of the real world brought about by God's decision. Hence the function of Jesus the Messiah was now merely to come again, this time bringing with him the Kingdom of God.

But another tendency, a schismatic, anti-Torah tendency, began to make itself felt in this coterie of Jews who believed in Jesus's special status, epitomized by the name of the first "Christian" martyr, Stephen. This tendency elevated Jesus far beyond the status of the Jewish Messiah to that of Lord of the Universe and Savior of Mankind. When Stephen was stoned to death as an apostate and his followers expelled from Jerusalem, they took their views to Antioch in Syria and no doubt many other Jewish centers in the Diaspora. It was just these views that were expanded, elaborated, and streamlined by Paul, and provided the doctrinal framework that served as superstructure for the Gospel-writers' apologetic aim in camouflaging the true history of Jesus's career. Yet while the Temple stood, the anchor and magnet of world Jewry, this deification of Jesus had no potential.

It was thus a natural development, around the time the Zealot movement was swinging the masses of Palestinian Jewry into the titanic war against Rome, for the authors of Mark not merely to suppress and distort the real-life meaning of the Kingdom of God—that is, its political element—but simultaneously to stress the transcendentalization of Jesus that had been going on in the Diaspora.

Thus there are two factors in the genesis of the first three Gospels:

The global transformation of perspective between the events of Jesus's own lifetime and the germination of a new belief founded on Simon the Rock's vision of Jesus resurrected was paralleled by a sociopolitical upheaval—the destruction of the Temple in Jerusalem, the consequent emancipation of the new belief from its institutional restraints, and the concomitant fact that for generations after the destruction of the Temple the new sect of believers in Jesus was opposed by the Jewish elite, the rabbis who had inherited the Pharisee tradition.

Hence the writers and editors of the Gospels, whose belief in the vision of the Risen Jesus necessarily distorted their view of events beforehand, found it natural to transpose their own contemporary disputes with the rabbis to the lifetime of Jesus, especially since by then the Jews were no longer regarded as targets for conversion and the leaders of the new sect were directing their propaganda at all mankind.

Thus the Gospels, written under the pressure of a specific situation, are biased in a systematic way. They have an air of timelessness, of motionlessness, in which Jesus expresses various ideas without the readers' being able to see their meaning against a historical background. It is hard to see from the text alone just what there was about the Kingdom of God or about Jesus's ideas in general that could have led to his crucifixion. Jesus's whole career as outlined in the first three Gospels could scarcely have lasted more than a few weeks. The Kingdom of God he proclaims at the outset of all three accounts seems peculiarly abstract and anodyne.

The homey, small-scale, intimate atmosphere that emanates from some parts of the Gospels does not make them histories.

They are in fact full of disguised polemics whose fossilization makes them inaccessible to a naive reading.

The key element in this obscuration of real life is the comprehensive elimination of the Romans.

The Gospels and the church tradition founded on them indicate no friction at all between Romans and Jews in Palestine. Everything that happens to Jesus takes place in a Jewish milieu; even his trial before the Roman procurator is explained as a Jewish plot. The stateliness of the seemingly simple anecdotes, shot through with camouflaged theological motifs, casts an atmosphere of frozen pageantry over what we know was a most turbulent era.

The Gospels suppress *any* criticism of the Romans. The word *Roman* itself, indeed, occurs only once (John 11:48), and the Romans are assigned a role only twice: Pilate himself and the Roman centurion who on seeing Jesus on the cross calls him "Son of God" (Mark 15:39).

Thus the Romans, who crucified countless thousands of Jews, so that the cross became the conventional symbol of Jewish resistance to Roman power, go completely unnoticed by the writers and editors of the Gospels. Contrariwise, the Pharisees, equated with the rabbis, the chief opponents of the nascent sect by the time the Gospels were composed, are more or less constantly reviled (though here too numerous indications of the opposite peep through the web of apologetics).

The Acts of the Apostles (the sole Christian source for this period), also says nothing of the violence endemic in Judea in the first century. The Romans are scarcely mentioned. The Jewish authorities are treated ambiguously—the followers of Jesus are described as eminently pious, the hostility of the religious leaders remains unexplained. All is seen through the prism of much later theological propaganda whose purpose is to harmonize everything. The vast movement of religious-political disaffection that churned up the country is never referred to.

It was the global transformation of perspective inherent in the germination of a new belief inspired by Simon the Rock's Vision of the Risen Jesus, reinforced by the reaction of the new sect to the Jewish debacle of A.D. 70, that distorted the Gospels systematically. All the basic ideas that had a living context in the life of Jewry beforehand—Kingdom of God, the Messiah, Son of David, salvation—were wrenched out of their true context, national insurrection.

In Jesus's lifetime not a single day could have passed without some inflammatory incident; the mere presence of the Romans constituted a constant provocation. All of this is glosssed over in the Gospels.

Nevertheless, it is obvious that the mere fact that what Jesus was announcing was the Kingdom of God—that is, a world transformation in which the pagan powers, preeminently Rome, were to be destroyed—together with his execution by the Romans for sedition, irresistibly brings to mind the Kingdom of God agitation that had dominated life in Palestine from the installation of direct Roman administration in A.D. 6 until it brought about the Roman-Jewish War in A.D. 66 and even later flared up in the abortive Bar Kochba revolt in A.D. 132–135.

It is evident, in short, that any discussion of Jesus's career, even if limited to the Gospels alone, will bring us face to face with the Zealots. These diehards, capable of swinging the bulk of the Jewish population of Palestine into desperate rebellion against Rome, represented the culmination of a mood that had been intensifying for a long time.

And we know that with certainty through the histories of Flavius Josephus, our only real source for the study of the long-drawn-out turmoil leading up to the Roman-Jewish War. His histories are indispensable not only for an account of Jewish politics for the generations preceding the war, but because they fill in the background obliterated very nearly in toto by the Gospels.

An aristocratic priest, Josephus was a commander in the war. After defecting to the Romans in the course of the war he became an outstanding propagandist of the Flavian dynasty that came out of it victorious. The Church Fathers took over the texts of Josephus's works very early on (he died at the end of the first century) because it was the *only* account covering this densely packed epoch and because it served as vehicle for a very early forgery designed to make Josephus a "witness" to the supernatural status of Jesus, a forgery whose blatancy, while obvious in any dispassionate examination, was not appreciated until the sixteenth century.

Yet Josephus has become a special subject. Specialists concentrate on fine points called for by each one's specialty. Thus, by segregating Josephus's chronicles within a special area of biased, though recondite, scholarship and by projecting its own version of events as exclusively authoritative, Church tradition insulated the whole era against empirical enquiries. At the same time Josephus's writings were spurned by "official" Jewish tradition, even though that had long since turned against the "Forcers of the End" as Josephus himself had. His renegacy overshadowed his acceptably negative view of the Zealots.

Josephus's account is packed with action and personalities. It conveys unmistakably the throb of life in Palestine for the generations preceding the outbreak of the Roman-Jewish War. It is steeped in blood: murders, revolts, cruelty, rapacity, cataclysms of all kinds are intertwined. Grinding oppression on the part of the Romans, desperate uprisings on the part of the Jewish Kingdom of God activists against a background of well-nigh total corruption, ferocity, and deceit are routine. His descriptions provide a blanket contrast with the eerie calm of the Gospels.

Josephus's account, dense with real-life detail and vivid characterizations that articulate a long-drawn-out process of alienation leading to a last-ditch insurrection, fills in the background of the Zealot agitation.

He has, to be sure, a bias of his own. He comprehensively vilifies the Zealot movement in all its variations, partly in the conviction, no doubt sincere, that the Kingdom of God activists were destroying Jewry and that God himself had favored the Romans by giving them victory, and partly, of course, because he was making propaganda on behalf of his Roman patrons.

Even more serious, he plainly minifies their importance. It is evident, from the balance and thrust of his narrative, that the agitation capable of launching the masses of the population against the Roman Empire must have involved huge numbers of people; yet Josephus, while vilifying and denigrating them, says as little about them as possible. He emphasizes, in contrast, the behavior of the Roman procurators, personal intrigues, acts of individual heroism, and so forth.

Nevertheless, the texture of his chronicles is so close-knit that the broad outlines of the Zealot movement, beginning with Judah the Galilean's agitation in 6 A.D., are unmistakable. It is easy to allow, so to speak, for Josephus's bias; when he describes people he calls "thieves" and "brigands" as being tortured to death for refusing to call Caesar "Lord," we are bound to conclude that they could not, after all, have been mere thieves and brigands.

On the other hand, Josephus says nothing whatever about Jesus (aside from the forged paragraph mentioned above, it is also quite conceivable, of course, that references to Jesus might have been eliminated from his early [non-existent] manuscripts for reasons of bias). He does mention John the Baptist, innocuously, and also Upright Jacob, in a brief and equally innocuous passage. But in addition to the fleshing out of the realities of life in Palestine around this time he is priceless for the study of the earliest phase of the belief in Jesus. His chronicle creates an infinitely broader, deeper, and more ramified framework for judging the historical material in Paul's letters, the Gospels, and the Acts of the Apostles.

If we compare Josephus's treatment of the Zealot movement with the treatment given by the Gospels, especially Mark, to the complex of ideas, personalities, and events involved in the Kingdom of God movement, we see a striking parallel. Both, for substantially the same reasons, ignore the true content of the whole movement. Josephus describes the Kingdom of God activists in such a way as to downgrade their ideological, idealistic concerns; the Gospels wholly disregard their political aims, too.

Most illustrative of this negative attitude of the Gospels is no doubt Jesus's complete silence about the Zealots. The Gospel writers, intent on whitewashing the Romans and dissociating the nascent sect from any connection with the Kingdom of God activists who after harassing the Romans for so many decades had brought about the ferocious war of A.D. 66–70, would surely have found it very convenient to set down Jesus's denunciation of the architects of the catastrophe, if he had ever made one. In Rome, especially (where Mark was probably written during or shortly after the war), some negative remarks attributed to Jesus would have eased the embarrassment of his followers. But since the author, or authors, of Mark did not forge anything, they were obliged to disregard the subject altogether; this is all the more striking since they did find, in the reminiscences they had at hand, echoes of Jesus's opinions about real people (Pharisees, "Herodians," even, occasionally, Sadducees).

Taken together, however, both Josephus and the Gospels enable us to divine the presence of a grandiose, turbulent movement capacious enough to bring the Jewry of Palestine to destruction during the Roman Jewish War. Both accounts, accordingly, radically contrasting with each other in all respects, confirm, through this same negative attitude, the existence of a vanished movement that in the desert of our documentation can be pieced together only through deduction.

Thus the basic problem in assessing the "official" tradition arising out of the Gospels is not merely the scantiness of the historical material: the tradition, indeed, merely replaces the missing evidence.

The Gospels are, accordingly, tendentious: much has been disregarded, or distorted, not through a desire to falsify, but because the faith in the Incarnation had become the perspective in which the past was recalled. And this shift in perspective naturally produced a corresponding forgetfulness.

Efforts were evidently made, as those who had been in contact with Jesus's milieu began to die off, to set down reminiscences, not for the sake of the information itself but as a way of fleshing out the earthly background of the glorified Risen One. From the skimpiness of these scraps we can see both how meagre the information was and how a different reality peeps out from between the disharmonious fragments that were later harmonized.

Because these reminiscences were focused through a much later point of view, and at the same time were handled with reverence, many fragments were dislocated, becoming more or less unintelligible in a naive reading. Some parables, for instance, referred more or less clearly to an early view of the Kingdom of God. Other material had evidently lost its anchorage in real life so that some parables remain enigmatic. (Since a parable is devised to clarify something obscure, a parable that is itself obscure must be explained as a displacement of one kind or another.)

In the nature of things, revered relics could not be tampered with. What happened was that a framework that arose organically out of the new perspective of Jesus as Son of God and the Savior of the World integrated, up to a point, the mass of fragments and gave them meaning—the meaning of just that new perspective.

If the Gospels had been fabricated, after all, there would be no way of knowing anything whatever about the career of Jesus the man. If we recall the sweeping powers assumed by the Church when Christianity became a state institution under Constantine in the first quarter of the fourth century, and if we recall the severity of the censorship he authorized, which after him, from the fifth century on, was applied with energy, the survival of the few scraps of information we have is remarkable. We owe such scraps to an indifference to mundane history and to the reverence for texts that piety forbade tampering with.

Some principle for distinguishing between grades of evidence is indispensable. It seems sensible to me to take as a starting point the global transformation of perspective I have mentioned, that is, the germination of the belief in the Vision of the Risen Jesus, which intervened between the events and their chroniclers.

In *The Death of Jesus* I proposed a "Cardinal Criterion": *Anything that conflicts with that global transformation of perspective is likely to be true.*

If a document records something countering the prevailing tendency in the Gospels to exalt Jesus, to preach his universality, and to emphasize his originality, it should be regarded, other things being equal, as being ipso facto likely.

We have already seen that very soon after the execution of

Jesus and until the Roman-Jewish War, the predominant attitude among the believers in the Vision was that of the Jerusalem coterie. There was also at the same time a contrary tendency—against the Torah and toward the escalation of Jesus as Lord of the Universe—which had already made itself felt even in Jerusalem when the so-called "Hellenists," epitomized by the name of Stephen, were expelled. Paul, after attacking the new sect, as he himself says, was then converted and began to express a point of view he shared with some unknown predecessors. Indeed, Paul's own hostility toward the Jesists is doubtless to be explained as due to the anti-Torah views of such Hellenists, since before his conversion Paul had devoted his passion to the defense of the Torah and only afterwards went to the opposite extreme.

At the same time it is evident that Paul's views were not predominant among the Jesists in general; when they were made known in Jerusalem they put him in a predicament that undid him.

It is evident, moreover, not only that Paul fell foul of the Jesists in Jerusalem led by Jesus's brother Upright Jacob, but that throughout his own lifetime he had no serious influence. A moment's reflection on the conflicted background, totally divergent from the sugary, harmonious version of Paul's relations with the Jesists in Jerusalem as recorded in Acts, will restore the historical balance.

While the Temple—the most celebrated edifice of antiquity, the citadel of all Jewry—was at the peak of its majesty, Paul was necessarily overshadowed.

It is plain from Paul's letters themselves that he must have written far more than have come down to us. He was intensely active, apparently, for some two decades, from about A.D. 35 to about A.D. 55. It is hard to believe that all he wrote is summed up by the small number of letters that now form the backbone of the New Testament.

The condition of the letters itself indicates as much; they are plainly random selections, often fragmentary to boot. One of the major ones, 2 Corinthians, is practically incomprehensible;

it is best understood as a mosaic of scraps of other, leftover letters gathered together after the emergence of "Paulinism."

Moreover, it is evident from the content of the letters we have that a dominant theme in all his major letters—the theme that often makes them sound hysterically demanding—is his conflict with others. He is plainly describing a situation in which he is promoting his own ideas against rivals. And the rivals are, equally plainly, precisely the leaders of the community of Jesists in Jerusalem.

It is obvious that during Paul's lifetime his letters were disregarded. It was only later, with the debacle of the Jewish State and Temple in A.D. 70 and the consequent disappearance of any institutional brake on the spread of the new faith among the Jews, that Paul's ideas, originally conceived as an explanation of what was for Paul a current historical crisis, became, through a systematic misunderstanding of the key phrase "the Kingdom of God," the foundation of something he could never have dreamed of—a timeless theology.

The Jewishness of the first Jesist coteries, under the leadership of Jerusalem, can scarcely be exaggerated. This also applies to the coteries Paul himself was connected with: for despite the development of his own views, it is plain that in developing those very views Paul takes for granted the overwhelming authority of the Scriptures as, quite simply, unchallengeable. Not only does he use scriptural texts in a rabbinical manner (which might of course have been a mere personal mannerism taken from his training), but he expects his readers to be familiar with Jewish ideas: that the Messiah had come, died, and been raised again "according to the Scriptures" (Rom. 1:2; 1 Cor. 15:3). He assumes they will get the point of the examples he gives of Abraham and Isaac (Rom. 4:2, 3; Gal. 4:28), Sarah and Hagar (Gal. 4:21–31) and, even more striking, Moses's tablets of stone (1 Cor. 3:2, 3), the covenant (2 Cor. 3:6), Adam's sin (Rom. 5:14), and the Stumbling Stone (Rom. 9:32, 33). He makes flat statements based on the unquestionable acceptance among his readers of the Hebrew Scriptures: "By the encouragement of the Scriptures we might have hope" (Rom. 15:4).

This makes it obvious that, whatever might have been the background of the pagans whose lives had become linked to the Synagogue, once they had become involved either as God-fearers or something similar, their locus of authority automatically became the Hebrew Scriptures; this in and of itself entailed the giving of respect to the Jewish authorities in Jerusalem, in this case, of course, the Jesists.

The original centrality of the Jerusalem Jesists is evident from all the earliest documents on: even Acts, which takes pains to harmonize the disputes that separated Paul from the Jerusalem Jesists, concurs with Paul in accepting the centrality of the Jesists in Jerusalem.

It does this at the cost of unconsciously creating enigmatic situations, as when, in praising Apollos of Alexandria, it refers to him as being "well versed in the Scriptures" (Acts 18:24). At the same time Acts indicates that Apollos was entirely unaware of any of Paul's ideas, since despite his being "instructed in the way of the Lord" (v. 25) he knew no more about it than the baptism of John the Baptist, so that two of Paul's friends had to "expound to him the way of God more accurately" (Acts 18:26). This is surely evidence that Apollos had come into the Jesist coterie in Alexandria, where people looked at things quite differently from Paul, the hero of Acts.

In their own way the Gospels disclose a profoundly Jewish substratum. It peeps unmistakably out of texts that include additions or changes designed to camouflage that substratum or focus it differently. Though the Gospels were written and compiled to serve an apologetic purpose, the many elements they contain, if detached from the *tendency* of the editors, can point to some historical realities, in accordance with the Cardinal Criterion I have mentioned.

The firmness of the Chosen People idea taken for granted by Jesus's immediate followers is graphically illustrated in the story of Jesus and the pagan woman: it surely goes back to the first community. Here Jesus rejects the pagan woman's appeal for help by saying: "Let the children first be fed, for it is not right to take the children's bread and throw it to the dogs" (Mark 7:27). Whether this was said by Jesus himself is uncertain, but it must surely imply its being embedded in documents too revered to be disregarded. It means, plainly and simply, that the Jews come first, that is, that the pagans—"dogs"—are outside the Torah. Jesus relents, to be sure, in the story, but only after the woman modestly asks no more for herself and her daughter than a few of the "children's crumbs" (Mark 7:28).

This theme is repeated a number of times in the Gospels; for example, where Jesus is seen sending out his twelve "apostles" to go through Palestine, but to "go nowhere among the Gentiles [pagans] and enter no town of the Samaritans, but go rather to the lost sheep of the House of Israel" (Matt. 10:5–6).

There are many other remarks, recalled, no doubt, from Jesus's actual life, that indicate the same thing.

Jesus is asked a fundamental question: "Which commandment is first of all?" He answers:

> "You shall love the Lord our God with all your heart, and with all your soul, and with all your mind. This is the first and great commandment. And a second is like it, You shall love your neighbor as yourself." (Matt. 22:36–39)

The first statement is the key affirmation of Judaism; the second sums up its ethics.

> "Think not that I have come to abolish the law [Torah] and the prophets; I have come not to abolish them but to fulfil them." (Matt. 5:17)
>
> And day by day, attending the temple together . . . they partook of food . . . praising God and having favor with all the people. (Acts 2:46–47)
>
> Now many signs and wonders were done by the . . . apostles. And they were all together in Solomon's portico. (Acts 5:12) God exalted [Jesus] . . . to give repentance to Israel. (Acts 5:31)
>
> [The pilgrims en route to Emmaus] "We had hoped that [Jesus] was the one to redeem Israel." (Luke 24:21)

Homely details, such as the names of his associates, give an impression of "folk" activity; Jesus's group was large enough to make it necessary to distinguish between individuals by nicknames. Names traditionally accepted as normal—Thomas, Peter—really meant something. Peter meant the "Rock"; Thomas meant "Twin." Thus the scrappy reminiscences that survived into the later chronicles would, if restored, make the atmosphere of Jesus's movement down-to-earth: Little Jacob, Stormy John, Judah Twin, Simon the Rock.

The locale of the very first expression of the new belief must have been Palestine, of course, since the handful of words retained even in the Greek texts of our oldest documents are in Aramaic—*Maranatha, Talitha Kumi, Abba, Amen,* etc.—though their translation into formulae took place later on Greek-speaking terrain.

It seems likely, in accordance with our Cardinal Criterion, that Jesus, despite his constant arguments with the Pharisees, was in fact a sort of Pharisee himself (like the Zealots in general). He says *only* Pharisees can interpret the Torah (Matt. 23:1–3).

In Chapter 2, I gave a matter-of-fact account of Jesus's attack on the Temple; though by and large details are missing in all Gospel accounts, it is impossible to escape the implications of the enterprise, whatever its specific shape. It is indissolubly linked to the primary fact of the tradition—the most solid, unchallengeable fact of all—that Jesus was executed by the Romans as King of the Jews.

If we start from this fact, and consider the skimpy details embedded in the Gospels—Jesus "preached" in the Temple for three days, "overturned the tables of the money-changers" and "drove them out with a whip of cords"—we see that the whole incident, presented in the Gospels as though it were symbolical, or in any case nonviolent, becomes portentous: *Jesus held the Temple.*

Now, how could he seize the Temple, and hold it for any length of time? The Temple was a vast edifice, guarded by a Roman cohort of 500–600 as well as by a Temple force of 20,000. How could Jesus have scattered the money changers and overturned their tables in the face of the armed police? (To say nothing of the money changers themselves!)

The group led by Jesus must have been armed themselves. This simple fact makes understandable the many references to arms that have withstood the harmonization of the present text:

> One of the party drew his sword, and struck at the High Priest's servant, cutting off his ear. (Mark 14:47, NEB)

> 'Look, Lord, . . . we have two swords here.' (Luke 22:38, NEB)

> 'Lord, shall we use our swords?' (Luke 22:49, NEB)

Jesus could seize the Temple only by armed force; his execution by the Romans as "King of the Jews" was directly linked to his seizure of the Temple. Behind the skimpy, distorted, and obscure Gospel references to the events preceding his arrest there was a real-life, stark event—an abortive insurrection.

This was the general background that the author of the first draft of Mark had to camouflage (later his draft was given, as was normal, accretions, emendations, glosses, and so forth, in the lengthy course of being edited into the text we know).

If we recall that the Temple had been standing in Mark's own lifetime, that the insurrection he was camouflaging had taken place only the generation before, and that the reminiscences he himself was making pious use of must have had at least partially a circumstantial element, we can see that Mark had to contrive an overarching aesthetic framework to achieve plausibility. Some oversights, perhaps inevitable, were to survive.

The echo of the Zealots, for instance (see page 37), is arresting. One Simon the "Kananean" (in the list of the Twelve appointed by Jesus) is mentioned (Mark 3:18). The two sons of Zavdai (John and Jacob) are called "sons of rage," echoing the violence associated with the Kingdom of God activists. Also, Simon the Rock is called "Baryon," as though it meant "Bar Yonah," or son of Yonah; but "Baryon" meant "rebel, outlaw," a political or social outcast living "on the outside," away from the settled areas controlled by the state.

Also, two Kingdom of God activists called "bandits" and "thieves" were crucified alongside Jesus. These were simply pejorative expressions for such rebels used by Flavius Josephus, as well as by the Romans, for tendentious reasons. Barabbas too, "arrested in the insurrection" (Mark 15:7), was also, evidently, a Kingdom of God activist.

Simon the "Kananean" is revealing. "Kananean," a word incomprehensible in the Greek text, is evidently a transliteration of a Hebrew-Aramaic word ("Qanna'i") for "Zealot." It was Mark's habit to explain such words. Just before this, the epithet "Boanerges" ("sons of rage") for the sons of Zavdai, has been explained by the narrator. Hence it is obvious that a real translation of the meaningless "Kananean" would have been embarrassing in the atmosphere of Rome at the time. Later, to be sure, it lost its odium. Thus, a half generation or more after the destruction of the Jewish State it was possible for Luke to translate it, for a different readership, quite straightforwardly as "Zealot" by using the Greek word "Zealot" instead of a transliteration of the Hebrew-Aramaic (Matthew 10:4 NEB).

It is evident that these nuggets of history have been tucked into a framework contrived to accommodate a much later situation. And the historical rationale for this is obvious: On the face of it, it must have been a source of acute embarrassment for believers living in Rome during the years just preceding the Zealot war against Rome that their own leader, Jesus of Nazareth, had himself been executed only a few decades earlier for just the same reason: sedition. It was vital for them to dissociate themselves somehow from the opprobrium naturally clinging to followers of an enemy of Rome at a time when Rome was engaged in a ferocious struggle against Kingdom of God activists. It was just this crisis in the Roman Jesist community, indeed, that led to the composition of our Mark.

Whoever wrote Mark solved the problem more than adequately; he created a model, in fact, that still enthralls the hundreds of millions of people indoctrinated by the Gospels and by the vast cultural heritage they underlie.

We have already seen (page 34) that in the Palestine of Jesus's day the statement, "Pay Caesar what is due to Caesar, and God what is due to God" (Mark 12:13–17), would be taken by any Kingdom of God agitator in a real-life situation as self-evidently insurrectionist; to such an agitator it went without saying that the Holy Land was God's alone and no pagans could profit from it, and in particular that the taxation imposed in 6 A.D. was an outrage; but Mark places it in a context in which it sounds unmistakably as though Jesus were endorsing the tribute to Rome. He uses the phrase as Jesus's *response* to a trap set for him by the Pharisees and the Herodians. It was natural for the Romans to expect a subject people to pay tribute, just as it was natural for a Kingdom of God agitator to refuse to pay tribute; by transposing the context of the question, accordingly, the architect of the Markan theme extracted its political taint, and soothed his readers among the Jesists in Rome as the Zealot war erupted.

In general, Mark depicts the Jewish authorities as hostile to Jesus from the outset. "Pharisees" plot with "Herodians" (the pro-Roman Jews headed by sons of Herod the Great and ruling Galilee at the time) against Jesus, even though it is the high priests who finally engineer the crucifixion (Mark 15:10–11).

By the time the Gospels were established, the high priests had vanished with the Temple cult, while the Pharisee tradition was sustained by the rabbis who were now the chief opposition to the new sect. Thus, for the Gospel writers, the word "Pharisees" stood for the Jewish authorities in a comprehensive, absolute sense.

Jesus in turn vilifies all Jewish authorities as cultically, legally, and spiritually sterile, even evil. The hostility attributed to the Jewish authorities is extended to the Jewish people as a whole, who fail to perceive that someone they are familiar with since childhood is meritorious. Hence Jesus's comment that a prophet is without honor in his own country, and among his own people, and in his own house (Mark 6:1–6). The Jewish people as such are condemned for ritualism (7:6–8). To cap the process the Jewish mob actually calls for his death and derides him (15:11f., 29–30).

Moreover, Jesus is described as cutting himself off from his kinship not only with his people but with his own family:

And his mother and his brothers came; and standing outside they sent to him. . . . Jesus replied: "Who are my mother and my brothers?" "Whoever does the will of God is my brother, and sister, and mother." (Mark 3:31–35)

Mark tells us, in short, that mere biology is meaningless: the Roman Jesists can be as close to Jesus as his own family. If we recall the importance of the dynastic factor in the emergence of Upright Jacob in the Jerusalem coterie before the Roman-Jewish War, we discern a polemical thrust at Jesus's family *at the time the Gospel was set down.*

Hence, when the preeminence of Jesus's family in the Jerusalem coterie was made obsolete by its extinction together with the Temple, it was possible to defy the vanished authority and virtuously separate the Roman Jesists from it.

Thus, the family of Jesus is presented as having thought him out of his mind, to begin with, and as explicitly repudiated by Jesus.

This is complemented by the contemptuous description of the Apostles, who also constituted, together with Upright Jacob, the core of the Jesist coterie in Jerusalem. They are constantly described as bickering over precedence and rewards (Mark 9:34, 10:35–45) and as devoid of Jesus's own remarkable powers (9:6, 10, 18). One betrays him (14:10–11, 20–21, 43–45); on his arrest they all abandon him and flee (14:50). For that matter the leading apostle, Simon the Rock, though acknowledged as the first to see in Jesus the Messiah, is said to rebuke Jesus for speaking of his resurrection and because of that, indeed, is called by Jesus "Satan" (31–33). On top of that there is an account of Simon the Rock's unappetizing denial of any acquaintance with Jesus. Not only is it excessively long in such a short document, but it is negative through and through.

The counterposition of these two attitudes—that Simon the Rock recognized Jesus as Messiah but denied the salvational function of the resurrection—is no more than a way of indicating that the Jerusalem group headed by Upright Jacob did not believe in Jesus except as the Jewish Messiah. His role as Lord of the Universe, of Divine Savior of Mankind, meant nothing to them. In short, the viewpoint of Paul is put forth in Mark in such a way as to take advantage of the Jewish debacle.

The ground plan of Mark goes far beyond details; it has a profound apologetic aim.

While bound to accept the historical fact that the Roman indictment was followed by a Roman execution, Mark tells us that Pilate was forced by the Jews to do what they wanted. In the narration this has already been built up—"planted," in literary parlance—by clear-cut suggestions of a Jewish conspiracy to destroy Jesus.

The assignment of an executive role to the Jewish authorities in explaining away the Roman indictment and execution of Jesus in and of itself expresses the anti-Jewish tendency of Mark's ground plan.

It is more than likely, of course, that the Kingdom of God agitation engaged in by Jesus would have set him against the Jewish aristocracy as well as the Romans, but there was no need at all for them to be involved in an actual trial. In view of the public nature of the agitation, indeed, it is hard to see why the Romans had any need for a trial either; a perfunctory hearing would seem to have been sufficient.

In any case, any number of Kingdom of God agitators, would-be Messiahs, and pretenders of all kinds were routinely exterminated by the Romans. There was no need for the Jewish authorities to intervene at all.

Moreover, since the tendency in Mark is to highlight the evil intentions of the Jews, had there been any Jewish intervention to undo Jesus it would have been both natural and easy to stress that theme and omit the Roman role altogether.

The fact that the original writer of the ground plan for Mark was obliged, despite his reluctance, to record an important role for the Romans confirms the matter-of-fact historicity of the Roman charge on the cross itself—"King of the Jews"—and demonstrates the tendentious artificiality of Mark's emphasis on the role of the Jews.

The theme was vital for Mark. To amplify it he enlarges on how Jesus, though of course a Jew, was not appreciated by Jews and how he expressly denied the importance of any kinship.

From the outset, the reader is informed that Jesus did not follow the tradition represented by the "scribes." He, in contrast, "has authority" (Mark 1:22). Jesus, by absolving the sins of a paralytic he has just healed, forces the scribes to charge him with blasphemy (2:6–7); then he attacks the "scribes of the Pharisees" for their objections to his eating with "tax collectors and sinners." In explaining that his disciples do not fast like "John [the Baptist's] disciples and the disciples of the Pharisees," Jesus uses a metaphor (the futility of using new cloth to repair an old garment or of putting new wine into old wineskins), evidently intended to drive home the point of Judaism's obsolescence.

This metaphor would have had compelling force precisely in the wake of the destruction of the Temple, *and not before;* it gives lapidary cogency to what has now become a historic fact—that the Roman Jesists, with a large admixture of converts and semi-converts, have found the solution to a problem that, as we know from the evolution of Paul's ideas, must have begun to weigh on them beforehand, i.e., the authority of the Torah and of Jewish traditions in general.

This has little to do with the much later doctrine of the church. In that generation, when faith in the transcendental Kingdom of God was still ardent, the object of worship of that faith was Jesus as God Incarnate, not Jesus as the architect of a new religion.

Of course, since the reverence accorded to Jesus, Son of God, was boundless, it was quite natural for some actual statements of Jesus to be tucked into the evolving cult. In Judaism Jesus seems to have belonged to the lenient, non-literal school of Hillel, as against the more rigorous school of Shammai. His indulgent view of adultery—"let him who is without sin cast the first stone"—certainly nullifies a whole area of Jewish Law, reinforcing his attribution to himself of special "authority," unlike the "scribes" (Mark 1:12). In some respects, he was far more narrow minded, as in his prohibition of divorce (a prohibition Paul naturally considered binding).

Generally speaking, however, no record was left of any other eccentric views; Paul, in his dispute with Jesus's immediate entourage in Jerusalem, finds nothing else in the infant tradition that he can quote. More particularly, there is no record of any creed formulated by Jesus. It is obvious that the basic documents of the New Testament were compiled much later into a vehicle for a systematic body of beliefs. In the era of the Gospel writers and editors that still lay in the future.

The fundamental theme of Mark can be tersely summed up: the Jews, both leaders and masses, are responsible for Jesus's death; his immediate family thought him crazy; his Apostles, having misunderstood him, also abandoned him.

Jesus himself provides the counterpoint to this series of negatives; he rejects those who reject him, emphasizes the importance of worshiping God through him in contrast with blood-relationships, and denounces the chauvinistic limitations of Simon the Rock, his pre-eminent follower.

In short, Mark, while depicting Jesus in a Jewish environment, has extracted him from it and glorified him far beyond it.

There may be a further complication in Mark's treatment of Jesus's Jewish background:

If, as seems likely, the agitation linked to Jesus, which must be deduced from the apologetic harmonization of the texts, was the true beginning of the upheaval foreshadowed by Judah the Galilean's more restricted rebellion, and if it was Jesus's movement that triggered the rapid, explosive concentration of insurrectionary forces in Palestine from Pontius Pilate on, the possibility of Jesus's royal status, and more particularly of his importance in the politics of the era, cannot be dismissed.

If we recall Paul's downright casual statement, in a context of no spiritual or intellectual significance for him, that Jesus was a descendant of King David, and the fact that Jesus was crucified as King of the Jews—there is no evidence that any of the countless thousands of Kingdom of God activists crucified by the Romans were attributed a similar status—it seems reasonable to suppose that the rebellion he led was exceptionally important.

It is certainly a monumental fact that an imperial edict condemning all "Davidides" to death on sight was still current two generations after Jesus's insurrection. Jesus's action must have been considered particularly important if the members of his immediate family, specifically, were still being hunted by the Roman police in the reign of Domitian (see pages 122–23).

Nor should still another element be forgotten: There are indications in the Gospels (Mt. 19:23–4) that Jesus might have thought the rich were disadvantaged vis-à-vis the Kingdom of God.

We know, from Josephus, that some of the Zealots were levellers (the reason for burning the ledgers containing debtors' receipts). We also know that of the two main leaders of the Jewish revolt of 66–70 one, Simeon Bar-Giora, was a leveller, while the other, John of Gush Halav (John Gischala), had conventional views on property, etc. Bar-Giora was executed, John of Gush Halav merely imprisoned for a time. This, if it is relevant to Jesus's seeming prejudice against the rich, might be a further reason for the Romans to look on his enterprise with particular hostility.

Mark, too, in its determination to slight the element of Jesus's lineage as part of its downgrading of the whole of Jesus's Jewish background, disregarded the down-to-earth, political sense natural to the times. Only the emblematic, honorific element survived.

In any event, Mark's detachment of Jesus from his Jewish roots is driven home explicitly in what is, thematically, the crux of the Gospel: after demonstrating how the Jews had failed to understand the divine nature of Jesus, the narrator puts a key phrase—"verily, this man was the Son of God"—into the mouth of the Roman centurion directing the Crucifixion. (The fact that Mark uses a Latin word ("centurion"), where Matthew and Luke use a Greek one, reinforces the impression that Mark was indeed composed in Rome.)

Thus the basic idea, perceived beforehand in Mark only by demons (responsible in antiquity for the supernatural knowledge ascribed to madmen), is expressed by a normal human being, that is, a pagan, like perhaps the bulk of the Jesists in Rome.

The preliminary stage for the deification of Jesus has reached its climax: Jesus has been crucified, the pagans have seen the Light; Judaism has been superseded.

The original author of Mark has solved the problem set for him by the historical circumstances of Jesus's arrest, indictment, and execution by the Roman authorities. He has demonstrated that it was a machination of the Jews, who had either misunderstood or opposed him, hence that Jesus had not been executed as a freedom fighter in a nationalist movement against the Romans at all, but was, in fact, a divine figure whose fate was the key to a cosmic plan.

By elevating the drama to this supraterrestrial terrain, Mark has wrenched Jesus out of his historical framework. He gives the remark about paying tribute to Caesar, which in a historical context would have been understood as an insurrectionist slogan, a seemingly natural background in which its meaning is reversed, and Jesus, in his only comment on politics, seems to be endorsing tribute to Caesar. Mark blandly slides past the Zealots in Jesus's entourage by misrepresenting Simon the Zealot through an unintelligible transliteration.

Mark's extracting of Jesus from his folk heritage bridges the main chasm between Judaism and the world outside by making it entirely unnecessary for pagans to become Jews for any reason whatever, and facilitates their conversion by showing that belief has nothing to do with communal or biological bonds. Thus, though Mark did not specifically strip the traditional Messiah of a martial function, by transcendentalizing Jesus out of his political background he promoted a grander conception that also transcended the provincial background of politics in Palestine and thus laid the underpinnings for a cosmic role to be played by an eternal, divine Christ.

There is no reason to assume that Paul's writings, which as we have seen were not paid much attention to in his lifetime, necessarily served as matrix for this idea. As we have seen, an anti-Torah, transcendent view of Jesus was adumbrated, if not elaborated, only a few years after the crucifixion. There is no reason it should not have been represented in Rome as well as in Antioch, or indeed in any Jesist coterie anywhere at all. It surfaced very naturally, just as Paul's ideas in general were recovered after the destruction of the Temple and came to embody the official view of an evolving religious fellowship.

Once a sharp contrast was drawn between Jesus the Jewish Messiah and Jesus, Lord of the Universe, the contrast itself became the pivot on which all subsequent speculation turned; and once the contrast was grasped by the believer and internalized, it became in and of itself a natural matrix for still further speculation.

Thus Mark solved the primary problem involved in the transformation of a cluster of Jewish beliefs into a universal, transcendent religion expanded far beyond the horizons of Judaism. His solution, simply by explaining away the real cause of Jesus's execution as being the indictment of sedition, by shifting it to a theological plane involving a radical and unbridgeable difference with Jewry, served simultaneously as the model for the dehistoricizing and theologization of the new religion.

Just as Paul's ideas were to create a universe of ideas for the new sect, so the ground plan of Mark created an original historical basis for it. By camouflaging a simple fact—that Jesus was executed not as a reformer of Judaism but as a rebel against Rome—Mark provided a historical foundation from which Paul's ideas could soar aloft.

But before that something else had to happen; the idea that the World's End was imminent had to be given up.

We have already seen a number of postponements of the advent of the Kingdom of God recorded in the Gospels, from the "at hand" of the very first fervor, to the few weeks implied by the disciples going through the towns of Israel, to the end of the lives of the listeners to one of Jesus' speeches.

Doubtless the very first believers repeated the phrase I have referred to before: "This generation will not pass away before all these things take place" (Mark 13:30). (See pages 38–9)

The first believers might also have consoled themselves with the reflection that calculations were in their nature pointless, since the "day and the hour" were bound to remain a secret of God (Mark 13:32): "It is not for you to know about times . . . the Father has fixed by his own authority" (Acts 1:7).

Still, it may well be that even by the time the first draft of Mark was fixed, the imminence of the World's End was no longer felt to be certain. By the time John was composed, around the turn of the second century, the notion of the World's End had been totally dislocated from the author's cosmology. For him there is to be no Glorious Return at all; the Lord has *already* come. On the other hand, some scraps in the New Testament, such as 1 and 2 Peter and Revelation as well as small fragments of the Gospel of John itself, seem to return to the perspective of an imminent Final Judgment (John 5:27–29; 6:39ff.).

Though it took varying lengths of time before the World's End idea was wholly extinct, it is plain that by the time Luke was written, some decades after the destruction of the Temple, the idea had become at least quiescent. It was no longer held seriously. Most important, it was not *felt*.

Thus the general feeling has moved definitively away from Paul's state of mind. He wrote because he felt the World's End was imminent *despite* delay: but by the time this had evolved into the conviction that the delay was no longer a delay but a condition of nature, it was possible, indeed indispensable, for something to be put down on paper.

Thus some decades after Mark, Luke plus Acts was drafted (parts of both of which were the work of the same hand).

Acts is, indeed, our sole source for the earliest period of the new sects. It carries the process of sociopolitical accommodation begun by Mark still further.

The sources embodied in Acts are so fragmentary that no coherent account is possible; still less does it say anything about any individual except Paul himself. There is almost literally no information about anyone mentioned. The individuals are given names, to be sure, and an occasional sentence or two purports to flesh out an inchoate narrative; but there is no way of apprehending motive, character, or activity.

The writings set down in this very early period had the function of defining, that is, establishing, the leadership of the new sect. They were a major attempt at organization. And to do so, decades after the destruction of the Temple and two generations after the death of Jesus, it was vital for the leaders to claim a living link between Jesus and themselves.

Accordingly, the newly evolving Church was defined by the Twelve Apostles, or rather, more accurately, by apostles in the plural. This claim, wedded to the claim, implicit and explicit, that the founding Apostles' authority was binding, became the theological principle underpinning the Church.

This principle in and of itself was never to be challenged by the great divisions of the later Church: Catholics, both Roman and Greek Orthodox, and Protestants. The only dispute was to be the manner in which the authority attributed to the Apostles was, in fact, binding (the Protestants, of course, accepted the Scriptures alone as binding; the Catholics considered "Church tradition" an indispensable complement).

But in fact the Apostles were simply part of a theory. In the very beginning there was no such institution as "The Twelve." The figure itself, reflecting the World's End expectations of the Kingdom of God activists, merely stood for the Twelve Tribes of Israel. Historically, however, The Twelve never played a role of any kind. After their first mention (in late sources) they are never, except for Simon the Rock, mentioned again, even though a major associate of Jesus, Jacob ben-Zavdai, lived for a decade after Jesus's crucifixion and must have been both eminent and active, since he was executed in A.D. 43 by Agrippa I.

Most striking of all, in discussing his trips to Jerusalem Paul makes no mention of The Twelve whatever. He talks only of the three "pillars," the only ones he confers with; they are obviously the leaders of the Jerusalem coterie. That is, even if there was such a group as The Twelve, it was no longer in existence in the middle or perhaps end of the Forties (A.D. 44 or A.D. 48). Later on only Upright Jacob, Jesus's brother, is mentioned as leader of the Jerusalem coterie (Acts 21:18).

It is obvious that the statement that there were apostles is part of the early Church tradition itself; it is the way the tradition substantiates itself.

Though the Church "theory" is very old, it goes back only to the time when there was already a huge gap between the real-life background and an awareness of that gap. About A.D. 100, when the Jewish Temple had been extinct for a whole generation and when the Jesists themselves were swiftly being transformed into the first stage of what could now be called "Christians," or perhaps only "proto-Christians," even though Paul was now accepted and the foundations of the religion accordingly laid, the organization of the Church itself was still rudimentary and uncertain. A dogma that was to be indispensable, the Trinity, had not yet been thought of, let alone worked out.

But the generation of A.D. 100, aware that they were different in essence from the historical Jesus, Simon the Rock, Upright Jacob, and Jacob and John ben-Zavdai, and aware of the gap between them, conceived of themselves as being not the second link in the chain of generations (the gap made that impossible) but the third. They had to create a link between themselves and the first generation. This was what the concept of the Apostles fixed and amplified. It became the "apostolic tradition," as though it were a tradition about an historical situation.

Thus the traditional definition of the "Apostolic Age" as ending with the deaths of Simon the Rock (Peter), Paul, and probably Upright Jacob rests on the claim that until a few years before A.D. 66 reminiscences directly derived from Jesus were still alive. Nevertheless, this "living tradition" about Jesus itself consists of assertions made about it by—the tradition.

Hence the Gospels and Acts, while containing particles of historical fact or probability, no longer reflect the circumstances of Jesus's real life, but the pseudo-tradition about them embodied in revered documents. The handful of what might have been historical reminiscences committed to writing as the real-life first generation began to die off survive merely as fragments embedded in theologically tinctured and slanted texts that began to be assembled as a "canon" around the middle of the second century.

Even the earliest current of belief in Jesus was already expressed in two different styles. One had to do with the homely tradition of Jesus the Jewish Messiah who had lived in Palestine, been crucified and resurrected at the right hand of God; the second was the visionary Jesus stripped completely of all earthly attributes and embodying a simple principle, to wit, that he had died and been raised again in glory.

Yet, basically the two traditions were to become one, since the tradition about the earthly Jesus, though it underlies what seem to be the facts in the Gospels—sayings, miracles, snippets of statements—has been twisted around as a form of adaptation to the disembodied, spiritual, abstract, principled framework of the confessional formula inherited by Paul from his own predecessors very early on, so that the significance of the seemingly historical framework of the Gospels is found only within the capsule of the confessional formula of the death and resurrection of Jesus Christ. That is, the seemingly factual framework of the Gospels was itself an adaptation of historical or semihistorical fragments about Jesus's life on earth only from the point of view of fleshing out the formula of the confession.

This had little to do with a lapse of time; it was a transformation of view that took place very rapidly. It was already given a sort of schematic representation by Paul. Whereas before his resurrection Jesus was the son of David, that is, the Jewish Messiah, afterwards he was the Son of God, Lord of the Universe (Rom. 1:3–4). Thus the process of transforming historical into theological materials that took place after the destruction of the Temple was the same, writ large, as the transformation already seen at work in Paul's letters, written before A.D. 55.

For Paul, too, a communal repast had already become sacramental. It can be summed up in a single sentence:

> When we bless "the cup of blessing", is it not a means of sharing in the blood of Christ? When we break the bread, is it not a means of sharing in the body of Christ? (1 Cor. 10:16, NEB)

The transition from the time in which the early Jesists interpreted the Lord's Supper as a Passover meal—a seder—to the time, much later, when Christ was himself called the Passover lamb, is evident.

Though the factual information in Paul's letters is peripheral as well as scanty (he was arguing a case, exhorting his audience, justifying his position), it is, to be sure, illuminating. It gives us an insight, for instance, into the authoritative position of Up-right Jacob and his possible role in Temple politics just before the Roman-Jewish War. Negatively too, his letters tell us some-thing: before the destruction of the Temple Paul was over-shadowed by the Jerusalem Jesists. We can also estimate the speed of expansion in the very earliest tradition. When Paul mentions the appearance of the Risen Jesus to more than "five hundred brethren" (1 Cor. 15:6), it is obvious, even if we accept the figure, that he is referring to a stage some time, though evidently fairly soon, after Simon the Rock's Vision.

The Jerusalem coterie, as we have seen, did not interfere with the new speculations that under Hellenistic influence began in the Jewish Diaspora after the Vision. No doubt they were shapeless, unsystematic. Perhaps such speculations came to the surface in only a few centers such as Antioch that were to become important after the extinction of the Jerusalem coterie in the debacle of A.D. 70. And it was just this fact that after the debacle was concealed by the instinctive creation of a legendary, mythological fabric to manifest the continuity claimed by all institutions.

The conventional view of theologians today would have it that the anti-Torah, transcendental conception of Jesus held by Paul and Stephen had already struck deep roots throughout the "Christian" community long before the destruction of the Tem-ple in A.D. 70. From that point of view, accordingly, the elim-ination of the "Mother Church" and all the more so of the Temple and the Jewish State meant nothing—a mere clearing away of the debris long since left behind by the evolving faith.

This conventional view is also the grand theme of Acts—indeed, its purpose. Yet it can hardly be historically valid. We have already seen the plain evidence of Paul's second-class sta-tus, as recorded in his letters, written many decades before the destruction of the Temple and long before the evolution of any theological "views" at all. We have seen his irritation about the contending "Gospels" he kept colliding with, the hostile at-titude of the Jerusalem "pillars," the atmosphere of contention and self-justification. The impression left by these striking motifs in Paul's letters is reinforced negatively, as we have seen, by their physical condition.

Paul does, to be sure, attack "the Jews" for persecuting the Jesists in Judea (1 Thess. 2:14–15), but this cannot have been so since there is no indication that after the expulsion of the Hellenists after Stephen's execution in the Forties the Jesist coterie was molested at all up to and during the Roman-Jewish War. This is all the more obvious since the background of Paul's trial under Upright Jacob during his last trip to Jerusalem takes for granted the entire acceptance of Upright Jacob and the Jesist coterie within the Temple milieu.

Paul died long before the triumph of his ideas. The destruction of the Temple cleared the way for the tendentious slanting of the Gospels, beginning with Mark, away from the real-life career of Jesus, executed by the Romans for sedition, into the Pacific Christ, Lord of the Universe and Savior of Mankind, whose salvational powers were to be mediated to believers via the magical apparatus of the Church.

In one respect, proto-Christianity carried on the tradition of Judaism. It was grounded in mundane history as well as in reflections on its meaning. Yet the difference was vital. The Incarnation, propped up on two great events—the crucifixion (and its meaning) and the Vision of the Risen Jesus (and its meaning)—was the very core of the new faith.

For this reason the combination into a canon of the pseudo-historical Gospels and Acts of the Apostles and the theological framework provided for them by the surviving letters of Paul is fundamental for grasping the significance of the factual material so painstakingly camouflaged.

With the destruction of the Temple in A.D. 70 Paul's ideas could flower fully. And since, at the same time, the new sect of believers in Jesus was opposed by the Jewish elite—the rabbis who had inherited the Pharisee tradition—the Gospel writers and editors, whose transcendentalizing tendency dominated their view of history, found it natural to develop limitlessly their hostility to the rabbis and the Jews they represented.

This was all the more tempting since after the destruction of the Temple and the state the Jews were no longer worthwhile targets for conversion. The target was now all mankind.

Paul's views, sincerely conceived of by him as a response to a Jewish problem—how could God delay the installation of his Kingdom once he had begun it?—themselves naturally shunted attention away from the down-to-earth background of the agitation against Rome. His views, further misunderstood as the Kingdom of God idea shriveled rapidly after the debacle of A.D. 70, became a mere "spiritual" metaphor by the middle of the next century, after the conclusive debacle of the Bar Kochba revolt in A.D. 132–135.

This whole process, coinciding with the gap in Jewish historiography, created a fundamental hiatus in Jewish history, and this hiatus was itself bridged over on the level of secular as well as religious history by a vast edifice—the edifice of Christian mythology.

Jewish historians, accordingly, like historians in general, hamstrung by a dearth of documentation and prejudiced by the radical distaste for the Kingdom of God activists (if only because their failure demonstrated the loss of God's favor) have perforce slid by the real import of the Kingdom of God movement.

This constitutes, of course, a remarkable irony; Jewish historiography has lost the century that saw the transformation of the Jews into a Diaspora people, i.e., Jewish self-consciousness lacks a real-life anchor for its own condition.

Although the Jewish debacle of A.D. 70 did not eliminate the Jewish population of Palestine, the bloodletting was vast; also, huge numbers were sold off into slavery abroad. And with the destruction of the Temple the scattered Diasporas, long a feature of Jewish life, no longer had a center. The abortive Bar Kochba revolt two generations later, by putting the seal on the territorial phase of Jewish history, established the Jews as the people they have since remained.

Just as Christian mythology obliterated its own real-life background, so in Jewish consciousness, during the long-drawn-out Diaspora, the debacle of A.D. 70 led organically to a stressing of religion, the leitmotif of the very genesis of the Jews as a people.

Thus the catastrophe of A.D. 70 was fitted into just that strand of Jewish historiography anchored in the contemplation of God's will in history.

Because of this the secular components of the catastrophe of A.D. 70 have been perceived through a religious prism. In the religious consciousness of Jews, the destruction of the Temple wholly overshadows the destruction of the state, or rather, the dual destruction is conflated to constitute the identical religious disaster.

This surely accounts for the fact that conventional Jewish historiography does not make much of what was, on the face of it, a remarkable gap in national evolution—from a "normal" people with a center, at least, rooted in a land of its own, to the special case of a people with no territorial anchor surviving through portable documents.

It is true that the antiquity of the Jews makes it easy to tuck the debacle of A.D. 70 into the endless succession of triumphs and calamities stretching from the captivity in Egypt through the glory of the monarchies into the complexities generated by the triumph of Hellenism in the ancient world, when the Jews, after a brilliant but brief resumption of sovereignty under the Maccabees, began to collide with the Roman Empire in the chain of setbacks leading from Pompey's conquest of Jerusalem in 63 B.C. down to the penultimate but decisive defeat by the Romans a century later.

Nevertheless, the extinction of the Jewish center in A.D. 70 was unique. It was qualitatively different from the Babylonian captivity six centuries before, which merely relocated the upper classes for a short time. It would be reasonable to expect Jewish historians to highlight the radical turning point in Jewish history constituted by the obliteration of the territorial foundation of Jewish life and its replacement through institutions shaped and implemented by abstract ideas.

The powerful tradition of explaining the debacle of A.D. 70, like all debacles, as a divine punishment, meant that Jewish historians were trapped, so to speak, by the amputation of the secular background of the Exile, into accepting the mythology encasing the New Testament.

The failure to appreciate the qualitative uniqueness of this caesura in Jewish history, the radical turning point that made the Diaspora co-extensive with Jewish national existence for almost two millennia, is surely due to the fact that Jewish historians, too, have accepted the Christian view of the origins of Christianity.

To sum up: The Kingdom of God activists, of whom Jesus was one, kept Palestine churned up for two generations; their agitation culminated in the massive insurrection that destroyed the Temple and Jerusalem in A.D. 70. Christianity at its inception was a spin-off of messianist ardor: the destruction of the Temple and the state removed the barrier to the spread of a new faith elaborated by Hellenistic ideas from a messianist germ.

In short, the grand arch of Christian doctrine spans two deficits: the misunderstanding through apologetics of the Kingdom of God in its first phase—Jesus's expectation of an immediate world-transformation—and Paul's conviction of a somewhat longer delay *guaranteed* by the resurrection of Jesus.

The emotional need for the Kingdom of God, transposed to a Hellenistic milieu, was absorbed, simplified, magnified, and elevated in the deification of the man who had announced the Kingdom. With the deification of Jesus, the Kingdom of God could be dropped altogether.

It seems fair to say that until very recently all scholarship dealing with Christian origins has been confined to tendentious documents; since it reaches conclusions implied in its premises, it constitutes no more than a vast circular argument, a begging of the question.

The documents that have come down to us were organized through the convergence of two tendencies: the need for the nascent movement of faith in Jesus to gloss over the real-life reasons for his crucifixion as a rebel against Rome, and the parallel rejection, though for different reasons, by authoritive Jewish opinion of the Kingdom of God as a formula for political action.

The warping of perspective inherent in our sources can scarcely be exaggerated. Because of the very fact that Christian tradition was itself fabricated by biased documents, the conventional view today accepts without question a transcendental interpretation of Christian origins, an interpretation that, overshadowed at first by the historical expectations of the first Jesist coterie, swept the field after the Jewish debacle in A.D. 70 and was later amplified, magnified, ramified and consolidated precisely as the institutional expression of the triumphant tendency. This vacuum in the vast bulk of the literature on Christian origins is all the more disturbing since the key to a realistic treatment of the Gospels was indicated some two centuries ago at the very inception of the Higher Criticism in Germany.

Hermann Reimarus, the first scholar to scrutinize the Gospels realistically, thought it obvious that Jesus was, quite simply, executed by the Romans for sedition.

But for generations after Reimarus this simple, commonsense explanation of Jesus's death was ignored; the countless biographies of Jesus that proliferated through the 19th and 20th centuries reverted to the apologetic claim that while Jesus was indeed executed as a rebel the execution was based on a mere misunderstanding.

Nevertheless the simple explanation of Jesus's execution is also the correct one; it is, indeed, the very obviousness of this fact, as we have seen, that explains why the Gospels were composed to begin with. The political and emotional need to detach Jesus from his immediate roots led to the obliteration of the Kingdom of God movement and accordingly, to the genesis of Christian mythology. That obliteration, which radically warped the framework of the scanty documents that have survived in the New Testament, has imposed itself even on secular historians who might have been expected to pierce the veil created by the combination of bias in the compilers and flimsiness in the documents.

It has led to a permanent crippling of scholarship; it is more or less taken for granted that the origin of Christianity and the Jewish debacle in the revolt against Rome, despite their intimate symbiosis in the Kingdom of God agitation of the first century, are unrelated. This scholarly bias was reinforced, negatively, by the curious absence of any Jewish historiography for several centuries—from the last book of the Hebrew Scriptures (Daniel, around 165 B.C.) to the fixing of the Talmud centuries later. And, since the Roman writers themselves said practically nothing about the beginnings of Christianity, there was nothing from any other source to fill the vacuum left by the neglect of the real-life circumstances of the earliest agitation.

The result has been that the secular history of the first century, the fundamental era in the establishment of the modern world, has been veiled for almost 2,000 years. The reluctance to grasp the true dynamics of the history underlying the present skimpiness and confusion of our traditional documents is surely the reason for the radical failure of the Higher Criticism of the New Testament. Scholarship, confined to documents inherently and unconsciously tendentious, necessarily arrived at the unhistorical conclusions entailed by the unhistorical premises. The historical puzzles created by the apologetics, both theological and practical, that generated the New Testament as a whole, and in particular the Gospels and the Acts of the Apostles, cannot be solved without incisive analysis.

Because of this the most industrious probing of the only texts expressly relevant to Jesus—the Gospels, the Acts, Paul's letters give us no real information about Jesus the man. The sum total of the Higher Criticism has boiled down to practically zero.

After almost two centuries of the most painstaking, intense study by scores of thousands of able, conscientious scholars, the amount of information refined out of the sources can be contained in a few lines.

There is no assurance of the most primitive facts about Jesus the man: the significance of the word "Nazarene," the date and place of his birth, his parents, his family, his milieu. All such information is summed up in a disconcertingly barren statement: in the words of Charles Guignebert, Jesus was "born somewhere in Galilee in the time of Emperor Augustus, in a modest family that aside from him numbered a good half-dozen children."[1]

Moreover, the paucity of information about the background

and personality of Jesus the man is reinforced by the utter absence of any indication of original teaching; whatever Jesus thought about religion, and in particular about Judaism, his own ideas failed to survive his death. He could neither have foreseen nor desired the state of affairs that replaced the Kingdom of God he was promoting, and even though the genetic relationship between himself and Christianity is evident, it can only be in the narrow sense that the new religion coagulated through speculations around the meaning of his death.

This gap between the historical circumstances of Jesus's life and the later faith in his resurrection and what it meant entailed the incapacity of documentation to bridge that gap. The evolution of faith made it impossible for the faithful even to conceive of a historical situation that would contradict their faith. Even the primordial fact of the Crucifixion required the transformation into metaphor of the "deep meaning" that constituted the faith. The crucifixion—summed up in Paul's celebrated aphorism "[I] preach Christ crucified, a stumbling block to Jews and folly to Gentiles [pagans]" (1 Cor. 1:23)—is, indeed, the model for all such transformations.

But what was understandable for the believers of the first and second centuries is bewildering in scholars of the nineteenth and twentieth. Generations of higher critics have stubbornly disregarded the titanic fact staring at them from out of the desert of the documentation—the causal connection between Jesus's initial emergence as a herald of the Kingdom of God and his execution by the Romans as an insurrectionist—and have accepted as plausible what was a mere apologia on the part of the believers of the first phase of the evolving faith.

Scholars have in fact failed to see the cardinal element in the history of the germination of Christianity—that it was the history of a transformation. The faith, having germinated, was then shaped, absorbing in the process the cardinal events and the various views and ideas felt to be important by the earliest founders of what became the Church.

Thus the Higher Criticism, which has generated hundreds of thousands of books analyzing the texts of the Gospels and the New Testament generally, their parallels, echoes, repetitions,

ism: If Jesus was not resurrected the faith was in vain. Thus, in

sa

nuances, duplications, contradictions, doublets, enveloping the sparse account of Jesus's life and Paul's ideas, has inevitably bypassed the prime factor in the origin of the new sect—the Kingdom of God agitation that alone can explain it.

But once it is accepted that the thought of founding a new religion never even crossed Jesus's mind, it becomes obvious that Christianity derives not from anything Jesus did but from what happened after his death. Thus it was after his death that the germination and efflorescence of a new religion took place, rooted in the primordial vision of Jesus resurrected and glorified.

This in itself is simply another way of repeating Paul's aphorism: If Jesus was not resurrected the faith was in vain. Thus, in the most literal sense, it was the vision of Jesus resurrected that launched the process culminating in Christianity.

But if this is so, it means that the entire vast library of literature on Christian origins, to the extent that it struggled to fling a bridge from the religion itself to the figure of its putative founder, was condemned to sterility.

And the labor underlying that literature! The hundreds of thousands of books, all dissecting the Gospels, the Acts, Paul's letters, sentence by sentence; crystallizing out of this meager source—material layers, sublayers, parentheses, quotations; minutely scrutinizing the texts, all on the theory that if you could grasp the genesis of the texts you would somehow know more about Jesus.

This was so even for critics who at the same time accepted the fact that Jesus had originated nothing in the religion that sprang up over his dead body.

Yet the lesson to be drawn from this divorce between the living Jesus and the later religion is clear. Although it was Jesus who was taken as the object of the evolving religion from its earliest phase on, his own emergence as a figure in Israel must be explained against a previous background, the background of the Kingdom of God agitation whose echo, faint and distorted, has survived in the documents incorporated into the new religion's early phase.

Jesus, accordingly, may be inserted into the series of Kingdom of God agitators spanning the period between A.D. 6 and the outbreak of the anti-Roman insurrection of A.D. 66–70. Once that is understood and the aims of the Kingdom of God agitators are known, we shall be in a position to understand how it was that a Kingdom of God visionary, whose followers loved him after death, could be plucked from the oblivion normally the lot of failures in this world and transformed, over the space of a generation or two, into the object of an entirely unforeseen cult.

The ideas kindled by the vision of a Risen Jesus served as a pivot for switching one Kingdom of God agitator out of the fate that befell all other such agitators and transforming his memory, seen now in celestial perspective, into an element of a new religion for which it was, while historically irrelevant, metaphysically indispensable for the purpose of anchoring in the real world the staggering uniqueness of the Incarnation.

If the rationale of the church is summed up in the phrase ascribed to the Risen Jesus—"I am with you always, until the World's End"—and if its institutional continuity is guaranteed by the passage aimed at Doubting Thomas—"Blessed are those who have not seen [the Risen Jesus's] wounds and yet believe" (John 20:29)—we see how essential it was for Christian theology from the very beginning to wrench both Jesus and the Kingdom of God out of their historical matrix. It was thus the course of history itself that created Christian theology—conditioned, of course, by the longings of multitudes.

Yet historicized theology is imaginary history; the web of myth has suffocated the history of real people.

What is, perhaps, astonishing is the durability of that imaginary history. Christianity is the only major religion whose essence is substantiated by supernatural claims made on behalf of an historical individual—claims, moreover, expressed in actual documents. One might have thought, once the documents were closely scrutinized, that the real-life background of the supernatural claims would eventually edge aside or at least modify the claims themselves. Yet to this day the tradition has survived all the assaults of common sense; it has withstood the counterweight of probability, of rank impossibility, of pervasive discrepancies, of manifest contradictions, of outright nonsensicality.

The hundreds of millions of Protestants—recently joined by Catholics, now also allowed to read the Bible freely—who even in childhood read and study the New Testament, including the Gospels, which despite their ethereal atmosphere constantly hint at factual situations, look—and see nothing. Huge motion pictures have been made depicting, in a naturalistic setting, the supposed events of Jesus's life in Roman Palestine. These motion pictures, conscientiously made with the guidance of sincere experts, are so foolish when held up against their real-life background in the vividness called for by naturalism, that one might well think the insulating walls of traditional perception would surely be pierced.

They seem to elicit no reflection. Audiences are so conditioned by the theological interpretation of the historical setting that the setting itself is apprehended dimly or not at all. The mythology is potent enough to plaster over all the fissures between itself and real-life plausibility.

Accounts of Christian origins that diverge from the tradition are often called hypothetical even by skeptics, as though the tradition itself were true to life.

This attitude on the part of believers and nonbelievers alike seems to me due to a sort of shyness, a reluctance to accept conclusions arising out of the logic of analysis.

Some find it difficult to accept the contradictory nature of the sources, as when, for instance, the pacific passages attributed to Jesus contradict the martial passages, the references to arms and so on. Others, accepting one part of a Gospel but not another, will doubt the likelihood of the Romans having allowed Jesus to survive as long as he did, instead of arresting him, say, on the spot. At bottom many are put off by the notion that the historic Jesus could possibly have been so utterly different from the Jesus conceived of by Paul; they require a palpable demonstration, however tenuous, of a link between the two irreconcilable portraits.

The Higher Critics, after two centuries of analysis, have

become, in effect, a vast bureaucracy processing its own materials. Even those critics who have smashed the traditional account of Christian origins to smithereens have failed to fill in the empirical void left behind. No doubt this, too, is due to a reluctance to venture into conjecture, to abandon the safe haven of documentation even when the documentation can be shown to be self-annihilating. Thus the Higher Criticism, in Albert Schweitzer's words the "masterwork of German theology," has wound up in a dead-end.

It is not easy to see a way out. Though the connections between Judah the Galilean, John the Baptist, Jesus and the Zealots who launched the war against Rome are unmistakable, they cannot, after all, be fleshed out as a real chronicle. The historiography that would have covered the two centuries between two Jewish insurrections—the successful Maccabi insurrection and the abortive Bar Kochba insurrection—was, except for Josephus, simply never written. And despite his copious detail even Josephus, who in any case finishes up with the destruction of Jerusalem in 70 and its coda, Masada in 73, is warped by his hostility to the Kingdom of God militants and by the absence in his extant texts of the background to Christianity.

Nevertheless, the three paramount facts that survive all analysis—the Jesus who preached the "Kingdom of God," his execution as King of the Jews, and the Jewish character of everything expressly attributed to him—can enable us to extrapolate, against the background of the Kingdom of God agitation, a real-life, though, to be sure, skimpy account—a tripod sturdy enough to sustain a real-life explanation of Christian origins.

That account will situate Jesus and Paul in time and space, and describe how real-life events came to be transformed—again, in time and space—into a great Church with mythological, mystical and magical underpinnings, embodying the theology that after Jesus's death was layered around the concept of the Son of God, Lord of the Universe and Savior of the World.

Such an account will provide the Church with a foothold in factual history after all. And that foothold, the Kingdom of God movement against Rome in the first century, will be seen to be the true seminal factor of world history.

Obliterated by the cosmic surge of its offshoot, the Kingdom of God agitation against Rome is a sort of Lost Continent. Yet some skeletal vestiges can be descried—a few peaks, some ravines, a plateau or two, some alluring vistas. To those for whom real-life history holds out some interest, a few bones laid bare may seem better than nothing.

NOTES

CHAPTER I

1. Josephus *The Jewish War* 7.327.
2. Ibid.
3. In the Apocrypha, the Pseudepigrapha, and still later in rabbinic discourses.
4. Silver, Messianic . . . ; Josephus, Ant. XVII 2,4.

CHAPTER II

1. Philo of Alexandria *Leg. ad Gaius* (ed. E. M. Smallwood, 128); Brandon, *Jesus* . . . 68.
2. Josephus, *Antiquities* xviii.55ff. Joseph does not explain how such a radical enterprise could have been feasible. Presumably it was conceived of at the instigation of Pilate's superiors. See also Brandon, *Jesus*, . . . 69.
3. Josephus *War* 7.389–390.
4. Josephus *Ant.* xviii.61–62; see also *War* II.175–177.
5. Josephus *War* vii.416–419 (trans. Thackeray III.621.623).
6. Ibid., ii.427.

CHAPTER III

1. Herbert Danby, *The Mishnah* (Oxford: University Press, London, 1933), 391.

CHAPTER IV

1. Klausner, 398–399, also Note 6.
   399, also Note 6.
2. For a fuller discussion see my *St. Paul and the World's End*.
3. Franz Cumont, *Religions orientales dans l'Empire romain* (Paris, 1929), 104.
4. Albert Schweitzer, *The Mysticism of Paul the Apostle* (London, 1931; paperback, 1968), 110.

CHAPTER V

1. Josephus *Ant.* xviii.85–89; see also Brandon, *Jesus* . . . 80.
2. Suetonius *Claudius* 25.4; cf. Acts 18:1–2.
3. A. S. Hunt and C. C. Edgar, eds., *Select Papyri* II.86, 11.96–100; quoted in Brandon, *The Fall* . . . 22.
4. Josephus *Ant.* xx.6–15; *War* xx.220.
5. Josephus *Ant.* xx.97–99; cf. Acts 5:36.
6. Josephus *Ant.* xx.102–103.
7. Josephus, *War,* ii.13.2.
8. Josephus, *Ant.* xx.8.6.
9. Josephus *Ant.* xx.168; *War* II.259–260.
10. Josephus *Ant.* xx.169–172; *War* II.261–263.
11. Josephus *Ant.* xx.180–181.
12. Ibid., 185–186.
13. Ibid., 188.
14. Acts 6:7, 15:5.
15. Josephus *Ant.* xx.197–203.
16. Josephus *War* II.410.
17. Eusebius *Hist. Eccl.* II.xxiii.18.
18. Ibid., 5–6.
19. Epiphanius *Patrologia Graeca* Haer. xxix.3–4 (ed. J. Migne).
20. Eusebius, *Hist. Eccl.* II.xxiii.13–14.
21. Strabo, quoted in Josephus *Ant.* XIV.7.2.
22. Josephus *Ant.* XX.8.11 (195).
23. Josephus *War* VII.3.3 (45).
24. Josephus *Ant.* XX.2.3 (34).
25. Josephus *War* II.19.2 (520); VI.6.4 (356).
26. Rostovtzeff, 179.
27. Josephus *War* II.17.6 (427).
28. Ibid., IV.9.3 (508).
29. Josephus *Ant.* XIX.6.3 (299).
30. Matt. 9:10–11; Mark 2:11, 17; Luke 5:30.
31. Josephus *Ant.* XX.i.4 (214).
32. Ibid., 11.1 (255).

33. Tacitus *Hist.* V.10.
34. Josephus *Ant.* xxi–5 (204–215).
35. Josephus *War* II.9.10 (560f.).
36. Ibid., IV.9.10 (560f.).
37. Ibid., V.10.2.4 (424; 440–441).
38. Ibid., III.7.32 (307ff.).
39. Ibid., III.1.2 (3).
40. Ibid., II.16.4 (346).
41. Aberbach, 31, quoting *Git.* 56a; *Lam. R.* I.5.31.
42. Josephus *War* II.7.2. (409).
43. Ibid., ii.18.2–5.7–8; 20.2 (461–468, 487–498, 559–61).
44. Ibid., ii.19.7–9 (540–555).
45. Ibid., iii.4.2. (64–69).
46. Ibid., II.434.
47. Ibid., v.3.1; vi.9.3 ;(99–102, 421).
48. Ibid., vi.6.2–3; 7.1–3; 8.1–5 (323–355, 358–373, 374–408).
49. Ibid., 7.1.1 (1–4).

CHAPTER VI

1. Eusebius, *Hist. Eccl.* III.18.4–20.7, quoting Hegesippus, about 180.
2. Josephus *War* 6.312ff.
3. Ibid., III.xi.
4. Ibid., IV.v.1–4.
5. Lietzmann, 4:113.
6. Ibid., 114.

CHAPTER VII

1. This Scripture passage, traditionally attributed to Paul, was no doubt written long after him, around A.D. 100, by one of his "school."
2. Conzelmann, Appendix II.
3. Suetonius *Nero* 16.
4. Tacitus *Hist.* 5.5.
5. Hans Lietzmann, *Cambridge Ancient History,* Vol. 12 (Cambridge University Press), 516–517.
6. Conzelmann, 129.
7. Ibid., 131.

CRITICAL APPENDIX

1. Guignebert, *Jésus* 148.

BIBLIOGRAPHY

Aberbach, Moses. *The Roman-Jewish War.* London, 1966.

Bammel, Ernst & C. F D. Moule (Eds.) *Jesus and the Politics of His Day,* Cambridge University Press 1984 Jewish Quarterly, in association with R. Golub.

Baron, Salo. *Social and Religious History of the Jews.* Vol. 1 New York: Columbia University Press, 1937.

Brandon, S. L. F *The Fall of Jerusalem and the Christian Church.* New York and London: Scribners, 1957.

———. *Jesus and the Zealots.* New York and London: Scribners, 1967.

———. *The Trial of Jesus of Nazareth.* New York: Stein & Day, 1963.

Carmichael, Joel. *The Death of Jesus.* New York and London: Macmillan, 1962.

Cohn, Norman. *The Pursuit of the Millennium.* New York: Essential Books, 1957.

Conzelman, H. *History of the Primitive Church.* New York, 1973.

Cullmann, Oscar. *Jesus und die Revolutionäre seiner Zeit.* Tübingen, Mohr, 1970.

Cumont, Franz. *Religions orientales dans le paganisme romain.* (Rev. Ed.) Paris: P. Geuthner, 1929.

Danby, Herbert. *The Mishnah.* Oxford, 1933.

Eisler, Robert. *The Messiah Jesus and John the Baptist.* (Ed. A. H. Krappe). New York: L. Macveagh, 1931.

Goguel, Maurice. *Jean-Baptiste.* Paris: Payot, 1928.

———. *La Naissance du Christianisme.* Paris, 1946.

———. *Vie de Jésus.* Paris: Payot, 1950.

Guignebert, Charles. *Jésus.* Paris: La Renaissance du Livre, 1933.

———. *Le Christ.* Paris: Albin Michel, 1948.

———. *Le Christianisme antique.* Paris: Flammarion, 1921.

Hengel, Martin. *Die Zeloten.* Leiden: E. J. Brill, 1976.

Jackson, F J., and Kirsopp Lake, eds. *Beginnings of Christianity.* 5 vols. London, 1920–1933.

Jastrow, M. *Dictionary of the Targumim, Talmud Bavli and Yerushalmi, and the Midrashic Literature.* 2 vols. New York, 1950.

Josephus, Flavius. *The Jewish War.* London and New York. Loeb edition.

————. *Antiquities of the Jews.* London and New York. Loeb edition.

Kaufman, Yehezkiel. *The Religion of Israel.* New York, 1972. Abridged by Moshe Greenberg.

Klausner, Joseph. *From Jesus to Paul.* London: Allen & Unwin, 1944.

Lietzmann, Hans. *A History of the Early Church.* 1937.

Loisy, Alfred. *The Origins of the New Testament.* London, 1950.

Rostovtzeff, M. *Social and Economic History of the Roman Empire.* Oxford, 1921.

Schoeps, J. J. *Paul: The Theology of the Apostles in the Light of Jewish History.* Philadelphia, 1961.

Schürer, Emil. *A History of the Jewish People in the Time of Jesus.* New York, 1961.

Schweitzer, Albert. *Geschichte der Leben-Jesu Forschung.* Tübingen: J. C. B. Mohr, 1913.

————. *The Mysticism of Paul the Apostle.* London: A. & C. Black, 1931. Paperback, 1968.

Silver, Abba Hillel. *Messianic Speculation in Israel.* New York, 1927.

Weber, Wilhelm, *Josephus und Vespasian.* Stuttgart: W. Kohlhammer, 1921.

INDEX

Acts of the Apostles, 54, 174, 175, 178, 186, 199, 201, 203, 209
Adonis, 87, 89, 92
Agrippa I, 106, 107, 200
Agrippa II, 110, 114
Ananus, 110, 111, 112
Antiochus IV, 6, 19–20, 21, 22
Apostles, 192; and early Church, 200–201; and Jesus, 37–38, 49, 188, 189, 195; and Simon Peter's vision, 50–51; authority of, 200
Attis, 87, 89, 91–92
Augustine (Saint), 93, 138

Babylonian Exile, 2, 3, 23
baptism, and Kingdom of God, 83–84; and Spirit of God, 85; by immersion, 85; Ignatius on, 131; Jesists and, 82, 85; Jesus on, 32, 33; John the Baptist on, 30–31, 32, 82; Paul on, 93–94, 130, 133; rite of, 81–82, 93; role of, 83–84, 85–86
bar Giova, Simon, 114, 115, 116, 119, 120, 196
Bar Kochba Revolt, 103, 122, 123, 124, 125, 126, 138–139, 163, 179, 205–206, 214
Being-in-Christ, 94, 96, 97–98, 99, 100, 128, 130
ben-Zakkai, Yohanan, 116, 122
ben-Zavdai, Jacob, 106, 107, 189, 200, 201
ben-Zavdai, John, 37, 51, 106, 189, 201
Body of Christ, 75, 94, 96–97, 100, 131

Caligula, 19, 21; desecration of Temple, 105–106
Cardinal Criterion, 183, 186, 188
census, 9, 10, 13

Chosen People see Jews
Christianity, 101; acceptance of, by social classes, 146–147; and the Kingdom of God, 207; and Torah, 162, 169, 176; cultic, 60–62, 136; dogma of, 169–171; early, 136–140, 144; Hellenization of, 144–146, 148–149; interpretation of origins of, 207–215; Jesist evolution into, 56, 126, 140; mutations of, 142; organization of early, 152–155, 159, 161–163, 169–171; relation to Greek thought and Judaism, 136; relation to Judaism, 138, 140–141, 145, 149, 161, 163–164, 168–169, 204; relation to Mystery religions, 145–146, 148–149, 161; Roman treatment of, 164–167; uniqueness of, 212–213
Christians, and Hebrew Scriptures, 169; mythology, 205–206, 208; origin of the term, 60, 61; Roman treatment of, 164–167
Chrysostom, John, 141
Church, Apostles and the early, 200–201; misunderstanding of Paul, 130, 132–134; "Mother," 172, 203; offices, 153; organization of early, 152–155, 159, 161–162, 169–170; Proto-, 137–138, 149, 152–153; role of early, 153–154, 167–168; second-century, services, 162–163
Claudius (Emperor), 22, 106, 107, 164
crucifixion, 35; of Jesus, 45, 47, 49, 61, 64, 69, 71, 73–74, 87, 98, 106; redemptive, 146, 147, 153
Cybele, 89, 91, 92

Daggermen, 43–44, 55, 63, 109, 110, 115; and Roman-Jewish War, 116, 118

223

Daniel, 6, 22, 40, 76
David (King), 5, 9, 10, 36, 52; descendants of, 122–123
Davidides, 122–123, 195–196
Death of Jesus, The, 183
desert, symbolism of, 24
Diaspora Jews, 58–59, 60, 67, 106–107, 125, 176
Dionysius, 87, 91
disciples *see* Apostles
Domitian, 122, 123

Eleazar, 109, 116
Elect, 95–98, 99
election, 95–98
Epicureanism, 143
Essenes, 22
Eucharist, 81, 86–87, 93, 130, 131, 163; Paul on, 132, 133
evangelism, of Greek-speaking Jews, 58–61, 70; of Jesists, 54–55, 58–59, 62
Exodus, 14, 24

Felix, 109–109, 114
First Commandment, 10, 13, 30, 31, 33
Florus, Gessius, 114–115, 117
Four Gospels, 32, 33, 48, 156–157, 159–160, 174, 177, 182, 186, 209; distortion of facts in, 178–179, 182–183, 202; Higher Criticism of, 209–211; historicity of, 181–184, 189–190, 197, 201; Jesus in, 177–178; Kingdom of God in, 175, 183

Galileans *see* Zealots
Gallus, Cestius, 117, 118, 119, 124
Gnosticism, 145, 161
God *see* Yahweh
Gospel of John, 83, 131, 136, 140, 157, 199
Gospel of Luke, 9, 14, 157, 158–159, 199
Gospel of Mark, 80, 157, 174, 175, 177, 182; on Jesus, 177–178, 189–195, 196–197, 198–199; on Jesus's crucifixion, 193, 196–197
Gospel of Matthew, 157
Greek-speaking Jews, 58–61, 69, 70
Guignebert, Charles, 210

Hadrian, 123–124
Hasmoneans, 6–7, 18
Hebrew prophets, 2–3, 20

Hebrew Scriptures, 154–160, 169, 186; collection and canonization of, 156–162; Jesists and, 169; Marcion's canon, 158–159; role of, 162–164; *see also* Torah
Hellenization, 4; of Christianity, 144–146; of Paul, 126; of the Jews, 4–5, 6–7, 19
Herod the Great, 7, 9, 18, 22; death of, 21; rule over the Jews, 7–8, 17
Higher Criticism, New Testament, 209–211
Holy War, 23–24

Ignatius, 128, 129, 153; on baptism, 131; on resurrection, 129–130
imperial cult, 12–13, 22

Jehovah *see* Yahweh
Jerusalem, 3, 122, 124; fall of, 35, 118–120; Jesus's entry into, 38
Jerusalem Jesists, 58, 59, 70–71, 86, 107, 111, 123, 124, 125, 128, 186, 192, 203
Jesists, 51–63, 67, 68, 89, 138–139, 140, 152, 166, 168, 185, 192, 202, 208; and baptism, 82, 85, 93; and Hebrew Scriptures, 169; and Jews compared, 51–52, 140; and Kingdom of God activists compared, 52; and Paul, 67–73, 80, 184–185, 186, 203–204; and power of Jesus's name, 62; and role of Jerusalem, 124; and Roman-Jewish War, 117, 124, 125; and Simon Peter's vision, 51, 52, 53–54, 58; and the Kingdom of God, 52, 58–59, 62, 134, 139, 152, 208; and the Temple, 73; evangelism of the, 54–55, 58–59, 62; hatred of Pharisees, 122; Jerusalem, 58, 59, 70–71, 86, 107, 111, 123, 124, 125, 128, 186, 192, 203; movement development into Christianity, 56, 126, 140, 201; organization of, 152–153; political beliefs of, 52; prayers of, 62–63; resistance of, against Roman Empire, 108, 110–112; rift with Jews, 140, 168; rites of, 82, 85–86; split of, 60; synagogue practices of, 63; theology of, 51–53, 63, 125, 134, 137; use of Scripture, 63, 154; views of Jesus, 51–53
Jesus, 11, 15, 25, 28, 69, 158–159, 174, 175; and baptism, 32, 33, 82; and Kingdom of God, 1, 8, 15–16, 30, 34–39, 42, 43, 49, 50, 55, 56, 58; and Messianic Kingdom, 98; and the angels, 98; and the Maccabees, 32–33; and the "mes-

sianic secret," 44–45; and the pagan woman, 186–187; and the redemption of Israel, 49–50; Apostles of, 37–38, 49, 188, 189, 192, 195, 200; as Cosmic Savior, 91, 94, 183, 192; as herald of Kingdom of God, 50, 64, 65, 131, 171, 175, 179, 210; as incarnation of God, 64, 65, 76–78, 80, 136–137, 146, 147, 153, 161, 168–169, 171, 194; as Jewish Messiah, 69, 84, 107, 125, 134, 175, 176, 192, 198, 201, 202; as judge, 53; as King of the Jews, 36, 45; as Logos, 136; as Lord, 50, 76–77, 78, 192, 198, 202, 215; as Messiah, 40, 44–45, 47, 48–49, 50, 52, 58–59, 60, 67, 74–76, 77, 79–80, 111, 123, 129, 136, 154, 176, 192; as sin offering, 52; as Son of God, 77, 176, 178, 183, 194, 196, 202, 215; as Son of Man, 52, 76; as "stumbling block," 79, 81; authority of, 36; baptism in, 84, 93–94; Body of, 75, 94, 96–97, 100; "cleansing" the Temple, 40–41, 42–43, 45, 188–189; crucifixion of, 45, 47, 49, 61, 64, 69, 71, 73–74, 87, 98, 106, 166, 188–189, 190, 193, 195, 196–197, 208, 210, 214; early strategy of, 32–33; entry into Jerusalem, 38–39, 40–41, 43; Eucharist of, 81, 86–87, 93, 130, 131, 163; faith in, 81, 95, 201–202; historical, 84, 91; hostility toward Jewish aristocracy and priesthood, 43, 191; in Gospel of Mark, 177–178, 189–195, 196–197; in the Four Gospels, 45, 177–178; Jesists' views of, 51–53; Last Supper of, 45, 77, 86; lineage of, 36, 52, 58, 195, 202; magnification of, 48–49, 53, 58, 64, 79, 133–134, 176, 207; miracles of, 37, 62; mission of, 45–46, 47, 80–81; on adultery, 194; on Judaism, 194; on paying tribute to Caesar, 34, 36, 190–191; Paul's views on, 65–66, 69, 72, 73–83, 84–85, 87, 91–101, 155–156, 194–195, 203, 210, 211; postponements of the Kingdom of God, 39, 198; power of name of, 62, 76, 85; reasons for crucifixion of, 80–81, 87, 98, 166, 171, 188–189, 190, 193, 195, 196–197, 208; redemptive crucifixion of, 146, 147, 153; relationship of, with Yahweh, 78–79, 136; relationship to God, 48, 50, 53, 136–137; relationship with family, 191–192, 195; relatives of, 122–123, 124; resistance against Roman Empire, 42–43, 195; resurrection of, 48, 49, 50, 53–54, 60, 61, 74–75, 79, 94, 95, 97, 98, 99–100, 129–130, 168–169, 202; Risen, 57, 58, 61, 136, 212; salvation through, 93–94, 136; second advent of, 49, 52–53, 56, 58, 59, 62, 63, 64, 75, 77, 100, 111–112, 117, 128, 130, 139–140, 155, 199, 201; Simon's vision of resurrected, 48, 50, 51, 52, 53–54, 58, 66; the man, 209–215; view of John the Baptist, 32, 83

Jews, 1; activists, 10–26, 29, 30, 31; and Babylonian Exile, 2, 3–4, 206; and Herod the Great, 7–8; and Jesists compared, 51–52, 140; and Kingdom of God, 1–3, 5–7, 10–11, 20–21, 49, 67, 69, 73, 139; and Roman census, 9, 10, 13; and Roman-Jewish War, 23–24, 27, 41, 43, 45, 73, 103, 113, 115–120; Caligula and, 104–105; Diaspora, 58–59, 60, 67, 106–107, 125, 176, 205–206; division in aristocracy, 104–105, 114–115; economy and the Temple, 41–42; effect of Temple's destruction on, 204–207; election of, 96; Greek-speaking, 58–61, 69, 70; Hellenization of the, 4–5, 6–7, 19; -pagan fellowships, 80; Paul's concern for, 168–169; Pilate's treatment of, 28–30; proselytization of, 54, 58–59, 113; quietist, 11, 20, 30, 63, 111; relationship with Hebrew prophets, 2–3; resistance of, to Roman rule, 10–26, 69, 103–121, 178–180; rift with Jesists, 140; Roman rule over the, 7–26; status of, in Roman Empire, 151; taxation of, 16–17; *see also* Jesists; Pharisees; Sadducees

John of Gush Halav, 115, 116, 119, 120, 196

John the Baptist, 8, 11, 25, 28, 38, 43, 45, 82–83, 174, 175, 214; and Kingdom of God, 30–31, 38–39, 75; and the Torah, 30, 31, 32; execution of, 32, 33; Jesus's view of, 32, 83; meaning of baptism by, 30–31, 32, 82

Josephus, Flavius, writings of, 24, 120, 123, 179–181, 182, 189, 196, 214

Judah the Galilean, 30, 31, 32, 33, 34, 38, 103, 108, 123, 174, 195, 214; and the Roman census, 9, 10, 13, 25; resistance to Roman rule, 9–12, 13, 14, 18, 19–20, 24, 27

Judaism, 5, 49, 67, 107, 113, 122, 164, 168; conversion to, 113, 114; Hellenization of, 6; Jesus on, 194; laws of, 61, 83, 151–152; Paul's departure from, 75; relation to Christianity, 136, 138, 140–141, 145, 149, 161, 163–164, 168–169, 204; split between Jesists and, 63

Kingdom of God, 1, 3, 5–7, 10–11, 20–21, 26, 27–28, 31, 48, 51, 54, 63, 65–66, 81, 82, 103, 105, 106–107, 111, 116, 126–128; activists, 29, 30, 33, 35, 36–37; and Christianity, 207; and World's End, 15, 20–22, 30, 32, 33–35, 38, 40, 74–75, 106, 123, 126, 128, 135, 139–140, 199; baptism and, 83–84; in Four Gospels, 175; Jesists and the, 52, 58–59, 62, 134, 139, 152; Jesus and the, 1, 8, 15–16, 30, 34–39, 42, 43, 49, 50, 55, 56, 58, 62, 64, 74–75, 98, 106, 117, 134, 171, 176, 177, 193, 196, 210, 212, 214–215; Jesus as herald of, 50, 64, 131, 171, 175, 179, 210; Jesus's postponements of the, 39, 198; Jews and the, 1–3, 5–7, 10–11, 20–21, 49, 67, 69, 73, 139, 152, 208; John the Baptist and, 30–31; Judah the Galilean and the, 10–12, 20; levels of, 6, 8, 26; martyrdom for, 33; Messiah and, 5–6, 10; Paul and the, 65, 74, 94–95, 126–128, 135, 152, 158, 169, 205, 207; politics of, 7, 8; redemption and, 81–82; rule of Israel in, 14; Torah and, 16

Kingdom of God activists, 29, 30, 33, 35, 36–37, 38, 43, 44, 49, 52, 64, 104, 107–108, 112, 114, 166, 168, 173, 180, 181, 189–190, 200, 205, 207, 212, 214–215; and corruption of Roman Empire, 114–115; and Roman-Jewish War, 116–120, 124; martyrdom of, 35, 46, 108, 109, 189–190, 193, 195; miracles of, 37; postponement of, 126–128, 198

Last Judgment, 6, 14, 31, 51, 74, 95, 199
Last Supper, 45, 77, 86, 156, 202
laying on of hands, 85–86

Maccabees, 6–7, 8, 10, 18, 19, 20, 23, 32, 206; and Jesus, 32–33
Marcion, 158, 160; canon of, 158–159
Matithyahu, 18–19, 23, 24, 25, 32–33
Messiah, 5, 37; and the millenium, 16; expectation of, 15; in Old Testament, 5; Jesus as, 40, 44–45, 47, 48–49, 50, 52, 58–59, 60, 67, 74–76, 77, 79–80, 111, 123, 129, 136, 154, 176, 192; Jewish, 53, 54, 60, 69, 84, 107, 125, 134, 175, 176, 192, 198, 201, 202; lineage of, 5; "pangs of the, 21, 23, 33

Messianic Age, 98, 99
Messianic Kingdom, 21, 40, 74–75, 94–95; Jesus and, 98; Paul on, 94–97, 99, 128, 133, 135–136
miracles, of Jesus, 37; of Kingdom of God activists, 37; of Yahweh, 14; World's End, 37, 109
Mithra, 87, 89, 92
Mithraism, 91, 138
Mystery, Christian, 84, 94, 133, 138; religions, 88–94, 100, 138, 144–145, 148–149, 161, 168

Nero (Emperor), 109, 110, 164
New Testament, 64, 76, 155, 161, 169, 171, 207; Higher Criticism, 209–211
Noachide laws, 151–152

Old Testament, 2, 5, 155, 159, 161, 162, 169
Osiris, 87, 89, 92

pagan, 60–61, 64, 67, 98, 110; and Noachide laws, 151–152; baptism, 83–84, 85; conversion of, to Jesism, 71–72, 73, 152; conversion of, to Judaism, 54–55, 152, 197; -Jewish fellowships, 80, 84; mythology and religions, 87–94, 142–145, 148–149
Paul, 48, 54, 55, 107, 109, 114, 156–157, 174, 175, 201, 214; and conversion of pagans, 71–72, 73; and Jesists, 67–73, 80, 184–185, 186, 203–204; and primacy of Jerusalem Jesists, 70–71; and Simon Peter's vision, 67, 68, 69; and the Kingdom of God, 65, 74, 94–95, 126–128, 135, 152, 158, 169, 205, 207; and Upright Jacob, 71, 72, 204; background on, 66–67; concern for Jews, 168–169; conversion of, 67–68; Damascus vision of, 66, 74; departure from Judaism, 75; execution of, 72; gospel of, 67; Hellenization of, 126; letters of, 64, 65, 66–67, 76, 155–157, 160, 167, 174, 184–186, 197–198, 202, 204, 209; misinterpretations of, 130, 132–134; 140; on baptism, 93–94, 130, 133; on Being-in-Christ, 94, 96, 97–98, 99, 128, 130; on Body of Christ, 94, 96–97, 100, 131; on election, 95–98, 99; on Eucharist, 132, 133; on Messianic Kingdom, 94–97, 99, 128, 133, 135–136; on resurrection, 94–95, 99, 129, 133; on World's End, 65, 98, 99, 100, 127, 132, 133,

135, 167, 199; propagandizing of, 67, 68, 73; theology of, 73–83, 84–85, 87, 94–101, 126–130, 131–132, 135–137, 147–148, 158–167, 176, 185; views on Jesus, 65–66, 69–70, 72, 73–83, 84–85, 87, 94–101, 155–156, 194–195, 203, 210, 211; view on Scriptures, 154; views on Torah, 72–73, 127, 132, 203; violation of a Temple taboo, 72; vow of, 72

Pharisees, 10, 59, 63, 76, 110, 122, 178, 188, 191, 204

Philo, 19, 136–137, 142

Pilate, Pontius, 9, 28, 103, 104, 178, 193; characteristics of, 28, 104; desecration of the Temple, 28–29, 39; treatment of Jews, 28–30; treatment of Samaritans, 104

Pompey, 7, 21, 41, 206

priesthood, division among Jewish, 109, 110–112; hostility of, toward Jesus, 44; Jewish, 43

redemption, and Jesus's crucifixion, 87; and the Kingdom of God, 81–82

Reimarus, Hermann, 208

religion, during Roman Empire, 87–94, 142–145; of Roman Empire, 143–144; mystery, 88–94, 100, 138, 144–146, 148–149

resurrection, 3, 8–9; and Spirit of God, 129; Ignatius on, 129–130; myths, 88, 94; of Jesus, 48, 49, 50, 53–54, 60, 61, 74–75, 79, 94, 95, 97, 98, 99–100, 129–130, 168–169, 202; Paul on, 94–95, 129, 133

Roman Empire, 4; as enemy of God, 22, 167; as "Fourth Kingdom," 22; census, 9, 10, 13; conquest of Palestine, 7; corruption, 104, 106, 114–115; culture, 141–142; in Four Gospels, 178; Jesists resistance against, 108, 110; Jesus's resistance against, 42–43, 195; Jewish hatred of, and World's End, 21–23, 63, 104; Jewish resistance against, 10–26, 69, 103–121, 178–180; Judah the Galilean and the, 9–12, 13, 14, 18, 19–20, 24, 27, 30, 31, 32, 33, 34, 38; official religion, 143–144; protection of the Temple, 42; religions during, 87–94, 142–145; rulers during, 106–110; status of Jews in, 151; taxation of Jews, 16–18, 114; treatment of Christians, 164–167; treatment of Jews, 164

Roman-Jewish War, 9, 13, 23–24, 27, 41,

43, 45, 73, 103, 113, 115–120, 123, 174, 175, 179–180, 182; Josephus on, 179–180, 181

Sabina, Poppea (Empress), 110, 113

sacraments, 81–82

Sadducees, 10, 59, 111

salvation, 93–94, 136, 144–145, 169–170

Samaritans, 104, 115–116

Sanhedrin, 60, 110, 122

Sermon on the Mount, 55–56

Simon Peter, 37, 51, 54, 79, 106, 107, 189, 195, 201; denial of Jesus, 192; Paul and, 68, 69; vision of the resurrected Christ, 48, 50, 51, 52, 53–54, 58, 66, 67, 70, 73, 104, 106, 134, 176, 177, 178, 183, 203

Simon the Kananean, 189, 190

Simon Zealot, 37, 197

Son of God, 77, 176, 178, 183, 194, 196, 202, 215

Son of Man, 52; and World's End, 76, 80

Spirit of God, 20–21, 57; and baptism, 85; and resurrection, 129; Jesus as incarnation of, 64, 80; manifestations of the, 57

Stephen, 54, 69; stoning of, 54, 60, 69, 70, 73, 176, 204

Stoicism, 143–144

syncretism, 143, 145–146, 148

Tacitus, 114–115

Tammuz, 87, 89, 92

taurobolium, 91–92, 93

Temple, 15, 21, 41, 58, 73, 121, 184; A.D. 66 seizure of, 44; as national bank, 41–42; Caligula's desecration of, 105–106; desecration of, 33, 40; destruction of, 120, 125, 126, 152, 177, 204–207, 208; Jesus's "cleansing" of the, 40–41, 42–43, 45, 188–189; Jewish Jesists and the, 73, 104; Paul's violation of a, taboo, 72; Pilate's desecration of, 28–29, 39; security, 42; tax, 122

Theudas, 108, 109

Titus, 119, 120, 121

Torah, 3, 6, 9, 12, 16, 19, 43, 70, 122, 158; and Greek literature, 19; early Church's attitude toward, 162, 169, 176; Jesists and the, 52, 60, 125; John the Baptist and the, 30, 31, 32; Paul's views on, 72, 127, 132, 203; *see also* Hebrew Scriptures

Upright Jacob, 37, 51, 68, 110–112, 123, 174, 175, 192, 200, 201, 203; and Paul,

71, 72, 204; death of, 111–112, 124; vision of, 51

Vespasian, 118, 119, 122, 123, 124
Vitellius, 104–105

World's End, 3, 10, 13–14, 15, 18, 19, 24, 25, 56, 63, 129, 140, 155; and desecration of the Temple, 40; and Jewish hatred of Roman Empire, 21–23; and second advent of Jesus, 104; and the Kingdom of God, 15, 20–22, 30, 32, 33–35, 38, 40, 52, 74–75, 106, 123, 126, 128, 135, 139–140, 199; miracles of, 37, 109; Paul's view of, 65, 98, 99, 100, 127, 132, 133, 135, 167, 199; prophecy regarding, 21, 22–23; Son of Man and, 76, 80

Yahweh, 2, 5, 8, 51, 98, 158; and Holy War, 23; and Roman-Jewish War, 23; and the Messiah, 15; ascension of, 2, 5; as Creator, 2, 3, 98; covenant with the Jews, 2, 9; Day of, 2, 55; intervention of, in world history, 23, 45, 49; Jesus as incarnation of, 64, 65, 76–78, 80, 136–137, 146, 147, 153, 161, 168–169, 171, 174; Kingdom of, 1, 3, 5–7, 10–11; relationship of, with Jesus, 78–79, 136; relationship with the Jews, 2, 14, 23; resurrection of Jesus, 79; sovereignty of, 10–12, 13, 19, 31, 52, 89; will of, 8, 26

Zealots, 12, 14–15, 20, 22, 29, 37, 42, 43, 45, 52, 55, 63, 109, 110, 111, 113, 166, 173, 174, 180–181, 196, 197, 214; and Roman-Jewish War, 115, 116, 117, 119, 175, 177